on,

Happy Christmas Jonn.

* Here's to a successful Millenium.

Lots and lots of love Maureen x

THE CRICKETER'S
BEDSIDE BOOK

Also compiled by Julian Bedford
THE RACING MAN'S BEDSIDE BOOK

THE CRICKETER'S BEDSIDE BOOK

Compiled by

JULIAN BEDFORD

COLT BOOKS
Cambridge

Colt Books Ltd
9 Clarendon Road
Cambridge CB2 2BH
tel: (01223) 357047   fax: (01223) 365866

First published by Colt Books in 1999

Selection and linking passages copyright © Julian Bedford 1999
Illustrations: by Fougasse © the estate of the late Kenneth Bird 1999
by Bernard Hollowood © the estate of the late Bernard Hollowood 1999
Volume copyright © Colt Books Ltd 1999
The Acknowledgements on pages 240 and 241 constitute an extension of
this copyright page.

ISBN 0 905899 91 1
British Library Cataloguing-in-Publication Data
A catalogue record for this book is available from the British Library

Designed by Clare Byatt

Typeset by Ronset, Blackburn
Printed and bound in Great Britain
by Biddles Ltd, Guildford and Kings Lynn

CONTENTS

GRASS ROOTS

THE ASHES

THE GREATS

EARLY DAYS

ROUND THE WORLD

THE BEAUTY OF THE GAME

TO THE GRANNIES

FOREWORD

THE British cricket season has ended, an Ashes tour to Australia is about to begin and I am stranded in Sudan, halfway between the poles of the cricketing world. Nowhere could be further from the great stages of the modern game than Khartoum and yet, as I meander through the dusty streets, Salaam-ing the passing tarboushs, I do so in the knowledge that cricket was as surely played here as in every corner of the British empire. Cricket may have died out in Sudan, but elsewhere it put down roots strong enough to outlast the empire; the game that took shape on the downlands of southern England is still played on five of the six continents.

Several of the authors in this anthology examine how cricket took hold of, first the British, then the world's consciousness. It is an interesting line of inquiry but the glory of the sport is that it is played at all. A game which can require up to five days to reach no conclusion at all is a wonder. Even the one-day version, shunned by some as unclean is just that – one whole day. In an age of super-slow-motion replays, reverse angles and sound bites, that shows a healthy scepticism for technology and television schedules.

It may be true that the game is losing its hold on the public: this summer's cricket World Cup may not produce the frenzy of its football equivalent of last year. To accept that is not to wax nostalgic, nor is it to deplore changes made to adapt cricket to today's culture, but simply to take on board that times do change. Cricket's cousin, baseball, has been taking a similar pounding on the other side of the Atlantic, but considering cricket belongs to the era of radio and observation, it's not doing badly. And when five days of endeavour brings a thrilling final afternoon's sport, as happened on a couple of occasions this past, and every passing, summer, one understands why it is so precious to its devotees.

Then, there's the prose it produces. Save for boxing and horse racing, little of sports writing can touch that of cricket. Maybe it is the hours of the game that encourage the words, the long incubation producing a worthy child. Maybe it is the finality of the game, a day's sport ended prematurely by a jaffa of a ball leaves the batsman with an excessive tally of hours to man the scoreboard, study the afternoon's racing or meddle with words, oral or written. Whatever the reason, there is a rich stock from which to anthologise.

The compiler's quandary, therefore, is what to omit and how to use the selections he has chosen. There have been excellent cricket anthologies, especially those compiled by Alan Ross. But some of their selections have perhaps become overfamiliar and lost their edge, their ability to surprise us. Much that I admire, I have ignored; rather than Francis Thompson's 'At Lord's', with its refrain of glories past, or the Edwardian landscape of H. E. Bates, I have chosen the more recent recollections of Simon Hughes and Vikram Seth's Calcutta. I hope I have assembled a team with a bit of everything; the fiery pace of the West Indian C. L. R. James, the languid cover drives of Neville Cardus, and the surprising googlies of Ramachandra Guha.

I have had the luxury of choosing more than eleven to lead into the field. To narrow the selection down would be an invidious task, though those writers who are doubly or even triply represented would be the first down on the list: James and Cardus, supported by Arlott, Robertson-Glasgow and Ray Robinson. There are others I should have included, Matthew Engel especially. But such absences, I hope, are balanced by unexpected appearances; a wagging tale from Julian Barnes, cameos from Osbert Sitwell and Simon Wilde and a bristling spell from Mike Marqusee. As Jorrocks, a man who unfortunately had little time for cricket, might say, 'There is magic in the web of it.'

JULIAN BEDFORD
October, 1998

GRASS ROOTS

The First Match

T HE first match of the cricket season has been played. It
happened the other evening on a stretch of earth as virgin of
grass as the African veld. Behind the bowler's arm was a block of
tenement houses. Now and again from the doors of these houses a
Mrs Jones or a Mrs Carruthers would emerge, and after looking
closely into the heart of the conflict would shrilly inquire: 'Where's
our Willy? Come in, you young divil; yer farther wants yer.'
Thereupon some inglorious, but by no means mute, Hobbs discovered himself foiled in the hour of triumph. He might at this point be
wanting only a beggarly four past cover to complete his century, and
now out of the gaudy light of glory Fate was snatching him. He had
to surrender his militant bat, pass from the scene, go home and fetch
the coals up. 'Yer can't have yer innin's out when yer gets back,' was
the fiat that was sure to come to his ears as he put his coat on. 'Yer've
given yer bat up!' There's where the canker gnawed.

  This great game was not arranged by Lord's, and sometimes it
was conducted not so much under the rules of Lord's as under
Queensberry rules. A batsman while playing the ball would miss it,
and it would thud against a huge brick wall on which three wickets
were drawn in chalk. 'Out!' would howl the bowler, who if he were
big enough was also the umpire. And the field was invariably with
him to a man. 'Yer out! Give yer bat up!' Expostulation stared from
the batsman's face at this. 'Out be blowed! it didn't never 'it nowhere

1

near th' wickets!' If he chanced to be a small batsman the bowler showed no inclination to bandy words. Down the pitch he would move to administer justice by strength of his right arm. 'Give yer blinkin' bat up else yer'll cop it.' The batsman, name of Jenkins (*soi-disant* Hendren), had to go. Maybe he would depart not only from the crease but from the field altogether, announcing to the world as he went, and setting the tidings to a chant in the Lydian mode: 'Bill Brown's a cheater – can't bowl for nuthink.'

The wickets in this Olympian game were, as I have said, drawn in chalk on a wide wall. Whoever designed them, plainly was a bowler himself. In the olden times at Hambledon the bowlers used to get up early in the morning and mark out the pitch on the 'nobbliest' bit of land they could find. In this match between Union Street and Summer Place the bowler had exercised a privilege not unlike that of the Hambledon men. He gave his chalk freely to the erection of his wickets, which possessed immense height and width. Whenever the ball hit them it would be made white on one side. Batsmen who owned mother wit and the muscle to support it would parry the bowler's aggressive 'Out!' flung at them each time the ball beat the bat by demanding with implicit irony: 'Wher's the chork mark on the ball? Garn, that's not a noo mark. It 'it them wickets wot we was usin' for practice larst night. 'Ere's the noo wickit, my lad. Carry on. We've got yer licked this time. Play up, Union Street!'

The match passed through widely different moods. It began with every combatant armed to the teeth, so to say. The bowler, before going into action, swung his arm round furiously. 'Get ready, lads,' he declaimed. 'Goin' ter bowl fast ternight; chuckin' googlies fer good.' Meanwhile the batsman was seeking to get himself into an attitude he had once seen assumed by greatness at Kennington Oval. 'Andy Sandham,' he said, and then he made sundry wonderful curves through the air with his bat, playing an imaginary ball wherever it was his fancy to direct it. The fieldsmen drew a tight net round the bat – the nearest man to the wicket, it seemed, was the one most likely to get the bat, and in consequence an innings, at the fall of the first wicket. It so happened, though, that tonight Andy Sandham was in great form. He drove powerfully, and the match was stopped while Horace Wilkinson, the youngest combatant, climbed over Moggridge's wall and threw the ball back. There was a little further hot disputation here between bowler and batsman. 'Yer out. It's allus "out" over Moggridge's wall.' Apparently this ruling had been rendered necessary by experience, Mr Moggridge

2

in the past having retained every ball that had disturbed his reflections on Form and Weights as he sat in his retreat in the summer evening's sun. But Andy placed himself beyond the law tonight. 'It's my ball, and if I'm out yer can orl put yer coats on and 'op it.' And thus he persisted in his mastership at the crease. And as he did so a strange lethargy fell on the fieldsmen. Point and cover-point went in for wrestling, as a *divertissement*; long-field met Miss Auriol Tompkinson, and, after a few courtier-like addresses to the lady as she went by, he shouted after her, 'Cedar mop!' – which, one inferred, was an oblique reference to the way her mother had decreed she should wear her hair, in an ambitious moment, some months ago.

Once the batsman hit the ball far across the brickcroft, and the parson happened to be passing. 'Thank yer, sir,' howled the bowler. 'Leave it – leave it, sir,' howled the batsman, starting his fifth run. The parson hesitated, then threw it back to the bowling crease. 'Interferin' old –,' murmured Sandham. He was defeated at last, and the bat taken from him despite his assurances that he 'hadn't been ready.' The game woke up here. ''Ow many are yer?' inquired the captain of Summer Place. 'Thirty-eight,' responded Sandham, dropping the 't' in 'thirty.' 'Yer've been putting 'em on,' came the accusation from all over the field. Batsmen, it seems, are in Union Street League cricket trusted to keep their own scores. 'I mean twen'y-eight,' admitted Andy, feeling the weight of evidence dead against him.

As the light faded it was difficult to follow the contest to its crisis. Mrs Carruthers or Mrs Jones or Mrs M'Dermott did great damage now from their respective doorsteps. Even those spared to fight on got a little confused. 'Yer've 'ad your innin's onst. Get out of it!' This cry went up time and again into the darkening sky. Then suddenly over the field flashed rumours of the first importance to those that had no coals to fetch up. 'Chips and fried fish is ready at 'Uddleston's.' This indeed meant the end. (It was, at any rate, usually chips and fried fish that caused play to be abandoned for the day amongst boys of a score or so years ago; in our times perhaps the second house at the pictures serves the same purpose, but what a poor substitute! Memory still holds that whiff of vinegar, the squelching noise as one shook the bottle, and the hailstone rattle of the salt out of those capacious tin castors.)

Union Street and Summer Place now went their opposite ways, but as they did so the ancient feud broke out again, with derision the weapon, and continued till the strongest lungs could not penetrate

3

the distance and the houses between foe and foe. The more or less Parthian thrusts were: 'Call yerself Andy Sandham – wait till we get yer on our middin.' 'Our Willie, come and get the coal up!' (Very mocking this.) 'Summer Place? Garn! Ours is a nice 'ouse, ours is!'
NEVILLE CARDUS, *Days in the Sun*, 1923

Such are cricket's roots. Whether it be in Neville Cardus's Manchester backstreets or on the downs of southern England where the game took shape, cricket will be played on whatever strip is available, by enthusiasts spurred by hope if not talent. Nowhere on god's earth is cricket played harder than in Yorkshire as a visiting Scot, the vet James Herriot, discovered.

A Yorkshire Match

THE weather was still fine on Tuesday and, going round my visits, I found it difficult to assimilate the fact that for the first time in my life I was going to perform in a real genuine cricket match.

It was funny the way I felt about cricket. All my experience of the game was based on the long-range impressions I had gained during my Glasgow boyhood. Gleaned from newspapers, from boys' magazines, from occasional glimpses of Hobbs and Sutcliffe and Woolley on the cinema newsreels, they had built up a strangely glamorous picture in my mind. The whole thing, it seemed to me, was so deeply and completely English; the gentle clunk of bat on ball, the white-clad figures on the wide sweep of smooth turf; there was a softness, a graciousness about cricket which you found nowhere else; nobody ever got excited or upset at this leisurely pursuit. There was no doubt at all that I looked on cricket with a romanticism and nostalgia which would have been incomprehensible to people who had played the game all their lives.

Promptly at six Mr Blenkinsopp tooted the horn of his little car outside the surgery. Helen had advised me to dress ready for action and she had clearly been right because the curate, too, was resplendent in white flannels and blazer. The three young farmers crammed in the back were, however, wearing open-necked shirts with their ordinary clothes.

'Hello, James!' said Mr Blenkinsopp.

'Now then, Jim,' said two of the young men in the back. But 'Good afternoon, Mr Herriot' said the one in the middle.

He was Tom Willis, the captain of the Rainby team and in my opinion, one of nature's gentlemen. He was about my own age and he and his father ran the kind of impoverished small-holding which just about kept them alive. But there was a sensitivity and refinement about him and a courtesy which never varied. I never cared how people addressed me and a lot of the farmers used my first name, but to Tom and his father I was always Mr Herriot. They considered it was the correct way to address the vet and that was that.

Tom leaned from the back seat now, his lean face set in its usual serious expression.

'It's good of you to give up your time, Mr Herriot. I know you're a busy man but we're allus short o' players at Rainby.'

'I'm looking forward to it, Tom, but I'm no cricketer, I'll tell you now.'

He gazed at me with gentle disbelief and I had an uncomfortable feeling that everybody had the impression that because I had been to college I was bound to have a blue.

Hedwick was at the top end of Allerdale, a smaller offshoot of the main Dale, and as we drove up the deep ever-narrowing cleft in the moorland I wound down the window. It was the sort of country I saw every day but I wasn't used to being a passenger and there was no doubt you could see more this way. From the overlapping fringe of heather far above, the walls ran in spidery lines down the bare green flanks to the softness of the valley floor where grey farmhouses crouched; and the heavy scent of the new cut hay lying in golden swathes in the meadows drifted deliciously into the car. There were trees, too, down here, not the stunted dwarfs of the high country above us, but giants in the exultant foliage of high summer.

We stopped at Hedwick because we could go no further. This was the head of the Dale, a cluster of cottages, a farm and a pub. Where the road curved a few cars were drawn up by the side of a solid-looking wall on which leaned a long row of cloth-capped men, a few women and chattering groups of children.

'Ah,' said Mr Blenkinsopp. 'A good turn-out of spectators. Hedwick always support their team well. They must have come from all over the Dale.'

I looked around in surprise. 'Spectators?'

'Yes, of course. They've come to see the match.'

Again I gazed about me. 'But I can't see the pitch.'

'It's there,' Tom said. 'Just over t'wall.'

I leaned across the rough stones and stared in some bewilderment at a wildly undulating field almost knee deep in rough grass among which a cow, some sheep and a few hens wandered contentedly. 'Is this it?'

'Aye, that's it. If you stand on t'wall you can see the square.'

I did as he said and could just discern a five foot wide strip of bright green cut from the crowding herbage. The stumps stood expectantly at either end. A massive oak tree sprouted from somewhere around mid-on.

The strip stood on the only level part of the field, and that was a small part. Within twenty yards it swept up steeply to a thick wood which climbed over the lower slopes of the fell. On the other side it fell away to a sort of ravine where the rank grass ended only in a rocky stream. The wall bordering the near side ran up to a group of farm buildings.

There was no clubhouse but the visiting team were seated on a form on the grass while nearby, a little metal score board about four feet high stood near its pile of hooked number plates.

The rest of our team had arrived, too, and with a pang of alarm I noticed that there was not a single pair of white flannels among them. Only the curate and I were properly attired and the immediate and obvious snag was that he could play and I couldn't.

Tom and the home captain tossed a coin. Hedwick won and elected to bat. The umpires, two tousle-haired, sunburnt young fellows in grubby white coats strolled to the wicket, our team followed and the Hedwick batsmen appeared. Under their pads they both wore navy blue serge trousers (a popular colour among both teams) and one of them sported a bright yellow sweater.

Tom Willis with the air of authority and responsibility which was natural to him began to dispose the field. No doubt convinced that I was a lynx-eyed catcher he stationed me quite close to the bat on the off side then after a grave consultation with Mr Blenkinsopp he gave him the ball and the game was on.

And Mr Blenkinsopp was a revelation. In his university sweater, gleaming flannels and brightly coloured cap he really looked good. And indeed it was soon very clear that he was good. He handed his cap to the umpire, retreated about twenty yards into the under-growth, then turned and, ploughing his way back at ever-increasing speed, delivered the ball with remarkable velocity bang on the wicket. The chap in yellow met it respectfully with a dead bat and did the same with the next but then he uncoiled himself and belted the third one high over the fielders on to the slope beneath the wood. As one of our men galloped after it the row of heads above the wall broke into a babel of noise.

They cheered every hit, not with the decorous ripple of applause I had always imagined, but with raucous yells. And they had plenty to shout about. The Hedwick lads, obviously accustomed to the peculiarities of their pitch, wasted no time on classical strokes; they just gave a great hoick at the ball and when they connected it travelled immense distances. Occasionally they missed and Mr Blenkinsopp or one of our other bowlers shattered their stumps but the next man started cheerfully where they left off.

It was exhilarating stuff but I was unable to enjoy it. Everything I did, in fact my every movement, proclaimed my ignorance to the knowledgeable people around me. I threw the ball in to the wrong end, I left the ball when I should have chased it and sped after it when I should have stayed in my place. I couldn't understand half the jargon which was being bandied around. No, there was not a shadow of a doubt about it; here in this cricket mad corner of a cricket mad county I was a foreigner.

Five wickets had gone down when a very fat lad came out to bat. His appearance of almost perfect rotundity was accentuated by the Fair Isle sweater stretched tightly over his bulging abdomen and judging by the barrage of witticisms which came from the heads along the wall it seemed he was a local character. He made a violent cross-batted swish at the first delivery, missed, and the ball sank with a thud into his midriff. Howls of laughter arose from players, spectators and umpires alike as he collapsed slowly at the crease and massaged himself ruefully. He slashed at the next one and it flew off the edge of his bat like a bullet, struck my shinbone a fearful crack and dropped into the grass. Resisting the impulse to scream and hop around in my agony I gritted my teeth, grabbed the ball and threw it in.

'Oh well stopped, Mr Herriot,' Tom Willis called from his position at mid on. He clapped his hands a few times in encourage-ment. Despite his girth the fat lad smote lustily and was finally caught in the outfield for fifteen.

The next batsman seemed to be taking a long time to reach the wicket. He was shuffling, bent-kneed, through the clover like a very old man, trailing his bat wearily behind him, and when he finally arrived at the crease I saw that he was indeed fairly advanced in years. He wore only one pad, strapped over baggy grey trousers which came almost up to his armpits and were suspended by braces. A cloth cap surmounted a face shrunken like a sour apple. From one corner of the downturned mouth a cigarette dangled.

He took guard and looked at the umpire.

'Middle and leg,' he grunted.

'Aye, that's about it, Len,' the umpire replied.

Len pursed his little mouth.

'About it . . . about it . . . ? Well is it or bloody isn't it?' he enquired peevishly.

The young man in white grinned indulgently. 'Aye it is, Len, that's it.'

The old man removed his cigarette, flicked it on to the grass and took up his guard again. His appearance suggested that he might be out first ball or in fact that he had no right to be there at all, but as the delivery came down he stepped forward and with a scything sweep thumped the ball past the bowler and just a few inches above the rear end of the cow which had wandered into the line of fire. The animal looked round in some surprise as the ball whizzed along its backbone and the old man's crabbed features relaxed into the semblance of a smile.

'By gaw, vitnery,' he said, looking over at me, 'ah damn near made a bit of work for tha there.' He eyed me impassively for a moment. 'Ah reckon tha's never took a cricket ball out of a cow's arse afore, eh?'

Len returned to the job in hand and proved a difficult man to dislodge. But it was the batsman at the other end who was worrying Tom Willis. He had come in first wicket down, a ruddy faced lad of about nineteen wearing a blue shirt and he was still there piling on the runs.

At the end of the over, Tom came up to me. 'Fancy turning your arm over, Mr Herriot?' he enquired gravely.

'Huh?'

'Would you like a bowl? A fresh man might just unsettle this feller.'

'Well . . . er . . .' I didn't know what to say. The idea of me bowling in a real match was unthinkable. Tom made up my mind by throwing me the ball.

Clasping it in a clammy hand I trotted up to the wicket while the lad in the blue shirt crouched intently over his bat. All the other bowlers had hurled their missiles down at top speed but as I ambled forward it burst on me that if I tried that I would be miles off my target. Accuracy, I decided, must be my watchword and I sent a gentle lob in the direction of the wicket. The batsman, obviously convinced that such a slow ball must be laden with hidden malice, followed its course with deep suspicion and smothered it as soon as it arrived. He did the same with the second but that was enough for him to divine that I wasn't bowling off breaks, leg breaks or googlies but simply little dollies and he struck the third ball smartly into the ravine.

There was a universal cry of '*Maurice!*' from our team because Maurice Briggs, the Rainby blacksmith was fielding down there and since he couldn't see the wicket he had to be warned. In due course the ball soared back from the depths, propelled no doubt by Maurice's strong right arm, and I recommenced my attack. The lad in blue thumped my remaining three deliveries effortlessly for six. The first flew straight over the wall and the row of cars into the adjoining field, the next landed in the farmyard and the third climbed in a tremendous arc away above the ravine and I heard it splash into the beck whence it was retrieved with a certain amount of profanity by the invisible Maurice.

An old farm man once said to me when describing a moment of embarrassment, 'Ah could've got down a mouse 'ole.' And as I returned to my place in the field I knew just what he meant. In fact the bowler at the other end got through his over almost without my noticing it and I was still shrunk in my cocoon of shame when I saw Tom Willis signalling to me.

I couldn't believe it. He was throwing me the ball again. It was a typically magnanimous gesture, a generous attempt to assure me that I had done well enough to have another go.

Again I shambled forward and the blue-shirted lad awaited me, almost licking his lips. He had never come across anyone like me before and it seemed too good to be true that I should be given another over; but there I was, and he climbed gratefully into each ball I sent down and laid into it in a kind of ecstasy with the full meat of the bat.

I would rather not go into details. Sufficient to say that I have a vivid memory of his red face and blue shirt and of the ball whistling back over my head after each delivery and of the almost berserk yells

9

of the spectators. But he didn't hit every ball for six. In fact there were two moments of light relief in my torment; one when the ball smashed into the oak tree, ricocheted and almost decapitated old Len at the other end; the other when a ball snicked off the edge of the bat and ploughed through a very large cow pat, sending up a noisome spray along its course. It finished at the feet of Mr Blenkinsopp and the poor man was clearly in a dilemma. For the last hour he had been swooping on everything that came near him with the grace of the born cricketer.

But now he hovered over the unclean object, gingerly extending a hand then withdrawing it as his earthier colleagues in the team watched in wonder. The batsmen were galloping up and down, the crowd was roaring but the curate made no move. Finally he picked the thing up with the utmost daintiness in two fingers, regarded it distastefully for a few moments and carried it to the wicketkeeper who was ready with a handful of grass in his big gloves.

At the end of the over Tom came up to me. 'Thank ye, Mr Herriot, but I'm afraid I'll have to take you off now. This wicket's not suited to your type of bowling – not takin' spin at all.' He shook his head in his solemn way.

I nodded thankfully and Tom went on. 'Tell ye what, go down and relieve that man in the outfield. We could do wi' a safe pair of hands down there.'

I was not troubled further in the innings. We never did get blue-shirt out and he had an unbeaten sixty-two at the close. The Hedwick score was a hundred and fifty-four, a very useful total in village cricket.

There was a ten minute interval while two of our players donned the umpires' coats and our openers strapped on their pads. Tom Willis showed me the batting list he had drawn up and I saw without surprise that I was last man in.

'Our team's packed with batting, Mr Herriot,' he said seriously. 'I couldn't find a place for you higher up the order.'

Mr Blenkinsopp, preparing to receive the first ball, really looked the part, gay cap pulled well down, college colours bright on the broad V of his sweater. But in this particular situation he had one big disadvantage; he was too good.

All the coaching he had received had been aimed at keeping the ball down. An 'uppish' stroke was to be deplored. But everything had to be uppish on this pitch.

As I watched from my place on the form he stepped out and executed a flawless cover drive. At Headingley the ball would have rattled against the boards for four but here it travelled approximately two and a half feet and the fat lad stooped carelessly, lifted it from the dense vegetation and threw it back to the bowler. The next one the curate picked beautifully off his toes and flicked it to square leg for what would certainly have been another four anywhere else. This one went for about a yard before the jungle claimed it.

It saddened me to watch him having to resort to swiping tactics which were clearly foreign to him. He did manage to get in a few telling blows but was caught on the boundary for twelve.

It was a bad start for Rainby with that large total facing them and the two Hedwick fast bowlers looked very formidable. One of them in particular, a gangling youth with great long arms and a shock of red hair, seemed to fire his missiles with the speed of light, making the batsmen duck and dodge as the ball flew around their ears.

'That's Tagger Hird,' explained my nearest team mate on the bench. 'By gaw 'e does chuck 'em down. It's a bugger facin' him when the light's getting bad.'

I nodded in silence. I wasn't looking forward to facing him at all, in any kind of light. In fact I was dreading any further display of my shortcomings and I had the feeling that walking out there to the middle was going to be the worst part of all.

But meanwhile I couldn't help responding to the gallant fight Rainby were putting up. As the match went on I found we had some stalwarts in our ranks. Bert Chapman the council roadman and an old acquaintance of mine strode out with his ever-present wide grin splitting his brick-red face and began to hoist the ball all over the field. At the other end Maurice Briggs the blacksmith, sleeves rolled high over his mighty biceps and the bat looking like a Woolworths toy in his huge hands, clouted six after six, showing a marked preference for the ravine where there now lurked some hapless member of the other team. I felt for him, whoever it was down there; the sun had gone behind the hills and the light was fading and it must have been desperately gloomy in those humid depths.

And then when Tom came in he showed the true strategical sense of a captain. When Hedwick were batting it had not escaped his notice that they aimed a lot of their shots at a broad patch of particularly impenetrable vegetation, a mato grosso of rank verdure containing not only tangled grasses but nettles, thistles and an

11

abundance of nameless flora. The memory of the Hedwick batsmen running up and down while his fielders thrashed about in there was fresh in his mind as he batted, and at every opportunity he popped one with the greatest accuracy into the jungle himself.

It was the kind of innings you would expect from him; not spectacular, but thoughtful and methodical. After one well-placed drive he ran seventeen while the fielders clawed at the undergrowth and the yells from the wall took on a frantic note.

And all the time we were creeping nearer to the total. When eight wickets had fallen we had reached a hundred and forty and our bats-men were running whether they hit the ball or not. It was too dark by now, to see, in any case, with great black banks of cloud driving over the fell top and the beginnings of a faint drizzle in the air.

In the gathering gloom I watched as the batsman swung, but only managed to push the ball a few yards up the pitch. Nevertheless he broke into a full gallop and collided with his partner who was roaring up from the other end. They fell in a heap with the ball underneath and the wicket-keeper, in an attempt at a run-out, dived among the bodies and scrabbled desperately for the ball. Animal cries broke out from the heads on the wall, the players were all bellowing at each other and at that moment I think the last of my romantic illusions about cricket slipped quietly away.

But soon I had no more time to think about such things. There was an eldritch scream from the bowler and our man was out lbw. It was my turn to bat.

Our score was a hundred and forty-five and as, dry-mouthed, I buckled on my pads, the lines of the poem came back to me, 'Ten to win and the last man in.' But I had never dreamed that my first innings in a cricket match would be like this, with the rain pattering steadily on the grass and the oil lamps on the farm winking through the darkness.

Pacing my way to the wicket I passed close by Tagger Hird who eyed me expressionlessly, tossing the ball from one meaty hand to another and whistling softly to himself. As I took guard he began his pounding run up and I braced myself. He had already dropped two of our batsmen in groaning heaps and I realised I had small hope of even seeing the ball.

But I had decided on one thing! I wasn't going to just stand there and take it. I wasn't a cricketer but I was going to try to hit the ball. And as Tagger arrived at full gallop and brought his arm over I stepped out and aimed a violent lunge at where I thought the thing might be. Nothing happened. I heard the smack on the sodden turf and the thud into the wicket-keeper's gloves, that was all.

The same thing happened with the next two deliveries. Great flailing blows which nearly swung me off my feet but nothing besides the smack and the thud. As Tagger ran up the fourth time I was breathless and my heart was thumping. I was playing a whirlwind innings except that I hadn't managed to make contact so far.

Again the arm came over and again I leapt out. And this time there was a sharp crack. I had got a touch but I had no idea where the ball had gone. I was standing gazing stupidly around me when I heard a bellowed '*Come on!*' and saw my partner thundering towards me. At the same time I spotted a couple of fielders running after something away down on my left and then the umpire made a signal. I had scored a four.

With the fifth ball I did the same thing and heard another crack, but this time, as I glared wildly about me I saw there was activity somewhere behind me on my right. We ran three and I had made seven.

There had been a no-ball somewhere and with the extra delivery Tagger scattered my partner's stumps and the match was over. We had lost by two runs.

'A merry knock, Mr Herriot,' Tom said, as I marched from the arena. 'Just for a minute I was beginnin' to think you were goin' to pull it off for us there.'

JAMES HERRIOT, Vet in Harness, 1976

Neither the village game nor that played in the backstreets is for saints. A defeat by two runs is the cruellest of results, especially in local games. For one whole year the actors have to ponder the misfield, the long hop bowled or missed which contributed to the diminution of the eleven. Chance encounters with the victors in a pub or in the street bring a reddening to the cheek and bile to the throat. Even when they get the chance to right the wrong, the result may not go their way. Rivalries nourish, and in rivalry is born rancour.

Herecombe *v.* Therecombe

S HARP practice in our national game is probably a good deal
more common than most Englishmen would care to admit.
Although it is true that the other side is seldom openly accused of
cheating, there can be hardly a pavilion in the country which has not
at some time in its existence creaked with dark whisperings against
the impartiality of umpires from men who have been given out lbw,
or against the honour of wicket-keepers from men who cannot bring
themselves to believe that such a ball could possibly have hit the
stumps. League cricket in particular produces complaints from batsmen who are convinced that they are not really so much bowled or
caught or stumped as tricked out. Yet I question whether any match
has ever been conducted in a more thoroughly unsportsmanlike
manner than a certain officially 'friendly' match between the
old-world villages of Herecombe and Therecombe. In the annals
of the game it will, I imagine, stand for all time as the only match
in which, although there was not a drop of rain, although play
continued uninterrupted through the whole afternoon, and
although both sides had a knock, only two balls were bowled. That,
I feel sure, must be one of the most remarkable of all the records
unchronicled in the pages of *Wisden*.

Herecombe and Therecombe were old antagonists. For some
reason, as irrelevant as it is mysterious, there was no love lost
between them. The Feud, I believe, went deeper (if anything can)
than cricket. But after the sensational tie in which a Herecombe
batsman, backing up, was run out before the delivery of the ball, and
a Therecombe batsman, politely rolling the ball back to the bowler,
was successfully appealed against for 'handling', small wonder that
each side vowed to win the next encounter by hook or crook. And
small wonder, perhaps, that even the winning of the toss by
Herecombe was viewed by Therecombe with deep suspicion.

The Herecombe captain elected to bat. Of course, he had no
idea when he marched to the wicket to open the innings that it
would be over in one ball. It was an astonishing ball, striking a flint
– the ground was like that – and skidding at right angles to square
leg.

The Herecombe captain slashed at it, missed it, was dumbfounded, and audibly ejaculated 'Well, I declare!' Everybody on the ground heard him, including the Therecombe captain. And the Therecombe captain was not slow to seize his opportunity.

'Come along, boys!' shouted the Therecombe captain, and made for the pavilion. His boys followed him. Nobody, with the exception of the Therecombe captain, knew quite what was happening. An explanation was demanded. The explanation was given.

'Didn't your captain say he declared?' asked the Therecombe captain. 'Very well, then. Us to bat, boys, and one run to win!'

A heated discussion ensued. Everybody called everybody else a dirty swindler. Threats were levelled, fists were shaken. The umpires read the Laws of Cricket through three times. In the end they decided that the Herecombe captain had inescapably, if unintentionally, declared. The Herecombe team thereupon proposed to chuck it.

But suddenly the light of battle glinted in the eye of the Herecombe captain.

'All right,' he said to the Therecombe captain, 'we're game! You go in and win if you can!'

Then he led his men on to the field, handed the ball to little Smith, who had never bowled in a match in his life but who had once won a local Marathon race, and whispered a few words of command in his ear.

The Therecombe batsmen came out. The umpire called 'Play!' Little Smith began a long, zig-zag run up to the wicket.

But before Little Smith reached the bowling-crease a queer thing happened. He doubled back. Then, like a dog after its tail, he began running in circles.

What, gasped the spectators, was up with little Smith? Had he gone stark, staring mad? There he was – turning and twisting – twisting and turning – darting this way and that – hopping, skipping, jumping – a most eccentric run, indeed – but never delivering the ball.

'Hi!' growled the Therecombe batsman, 'what's your bowler think he's doing?'

'Oh,' drawled the Herecombe captain, grinning, 'just playing out time, you know, playing out time –'

So that was it! Another heated discussion now arose. Crowds congregated round the umpires, who read the Laws of Cricket all over again, while little Smith kept on running. But they could find nothing in the Laws of Cricket limiting the length of a bowler's run.

Apparently a bowler could run all day before delivering the ball, and apparently he meant to.

Hour after hour little Smith kept up his capering – a noble effort – the batsman sternly refusing to leave the wicket lest he should be bowled in his absence. The fieldsmen lay down at full length on the ground. Spectators went away and back again, to find little Smith still running. Longer and longer grew his shadow as the sun travelled into the west. The clock on the old church tower chimed five, then six, then seven.

And now a new point of discussion arose. It had been agreed that at seven o'clock stumps should be drawn. But was it legal to draw stumps in the middle of a ball? The umpires got together again and, after much cogitation, decided that it would not be legal.

Then things became really exciting.

Little Smith shouted that if that was so, then dang him if he would deliver the ball till it was pitch dark. Still the batsman stood grimly on guard, determined if possible to make a winning swipe when the chance came at last. Again the spectators departed – this time for supper. Again they returned – this time under a harvest moon.

And there were the fieldsmen still lying on the grass, there was the batsman still standing at the wicket, and there was little Smith, still running.

At ten o'clock came the climax. It was dark. The moon had disappeared behind a cloud. Half a dozen of the fieldsmen had taken up positions beside the wicket-keeper behind the stumps to prevent an untimely bye. Little Smith let fly.

The Therecombe batsman screwed up his eyes to pierce the gloom. He struck. He missed.

'Match drawn!' shouted the Herecombe captain.

It was not quite the end. During his long vigil, the batsman had been doing a bit of thinking. He now protested that if stumps could not be drawn in the middle of a ball neither could they be drawn in the middle of an over. The umpires started to consider the latest point. But while they were debating, the Herecombe captain put an end to doubt by appealing against the light – a rare thing indeed for a fielding side to do – the umpires allowed the appeal, and the game was over.

Whether the umpires were right in all their rulings may be open to question. I think they were. In any case, it must be conceded that they had some very knotty points to solve, and that on the whole they appear to have discharged their duties conscientously.

HERBERT FARJEON, *Cricket Bag*, 1946

It doesn't always get as bad. As serious, very possibly, as was evident when Australia's Tim Chappell bowled his infamous daisy cutter at the end of a one-day international on the orders of elder brother Ian. As hard, certainly, as those who felt the weight of John Snow's shoulder would testify. Or even as crafty, as the late Willie Rushton testified.

Gamesmanship

NOW cheating, to coin a phrase, ain't cricket. The fact that if you snick the ball to the wicket-keeper and set off regardless and at once for the pavilion or whatever, you are viewed as a fool and a ninny lowers the tone considerably. If you're out, you should leave. W. G. Grace apparently rarely paid much attention to the umpire, and was given to replacing the bails after being comprehensively bowled, and remarking loudly on the windy nature of the day. Don Bradman would never budge, until the finger had been up for some minutes. Even so, there is a code. I think, however, that anyone is entitled to question an lbw decision. I have never to my certain knowledge been out leg before wicket.

A little gamesmanship can be permissible. *Private Eye* were playing *The Times* a couple of years ago, and *The Times* had introduced a club cricketer of note, in I Zingari hat and Free Foresters sweater, clearly to grind our noses into the dust. He was into his 20s in no time at all and treating our bowling with casual disdain. I was keeping wicket, and grasping at straws, as he let one pass on the off-side, the slips appealed with vigour. 'Not out!' I cried 'You will note,' I said to the umpire at the end of the over, 'that I was not amongst those bothering you with unnecessary questions. *I* only appeal when it's out. Umpiring is no sinecure. We should do all we can to help.' I think he was quite touched. An over later, I organised the slips, clearly this elegant club man with gleaming pads was good for a century or two and we couldn't cope with that sort of target. 'Next time,' I said, 'it passes his bat, everybody up. The bowler,' I tapped

17

my nose knowingly, 'is already primed.' Next ball it was, our Raffles left it alone with Woolley-like grandeur and the entire orchestra and chorus raised a 'How was that then?' that caused earth to move near Droitwich, while I held the ball aloft and registered my own plea, both lungs in fourth. Up went the finger and exit left a louring batsman. 'Pick on someone your own size next time,' we scoffed. There are, as I said, times when needs must.

I draw the line at 'sledging'. This started as a baseball term. In baseball, apparently, it is perfectly acceptable for the players to mount the coaching mound and pour the most appalling insults and vilifications upon the opposition. Quite often, this ends in fisticuffs, but that is baseball, and there it is and none the worse for that. They *are* foreign, a point people frequently miss when contemplating Americans. Alas, this has now permeated the cricket field, and it is, one gathers, quite acceptable for the close fielders and the wicket-keeper to pour scorn on the batsman in the foulest of language. There's also a deal too much gesturing and histrionics. I have no objection whatsoever to footballers hugging and caressing after scoring a goal, it shows they care, in many cases it is the only evidence of this, you frequently get the impression that their minds are more occupied with their shirt emporiums or hairdressing salons than the game in hand or the side they're playing for. It may not be the side they were playing for last week anyway, loyalty must be hard to come by, and footballers by the very nature of football, a mixture of the slave trade and Hollywood in the thirties, breeds mercenaries. Not so cricket, and anyway it's played in long trousers at the time of writing and what we need is a little more of what Jack Fingleton has referred to as 'the old charm, the grace and gentility'.

Of course, you can still chat up the batsman. I remember impressing dour northern cricket writer Michael Parkinson with a little touch of southern *savoir-faire*. A side I'd raised was playing against the charming village of Aldworth in Berkshire on their pretty ground surrounded by three rows of elm. For some reason I was an hour late and when I arrived Parkinson, who had taken up the reins of office in my absence, had let the game already slip sadly away. The village was 120-odd for no wicket, and Charlie, their bold, bald opener, I gathered from the score-book, was on 94. I was on the pitch in an instant and realised at once that Charlie had no idea his century was in the offing. 'What a famous way to go to a 100, Charlie', I cried, 'with a mighty sixer'. I could see the lust gleam in his eye. 'Toss one up, Parky', I murmured, 'and he's yours'. And he was, gone with one wild heave and the clack of falling wickets. 'You're a bit of a bastard', said Parky, which I took as something of a compliment. 'It's our ruthless southern ways you'll never get used to', I said.

WILLIE RUSHTON, *Pigsticking,* 1977

Sometimes, even the umpires - impartial arbiters of justice at the higher levels but often a twelfth man for the village at the grass roots – get involved.

A VILLAGE CRICKET MATCH

A True Story

One day a friend of mine was playing cricket,
   And came in last with 'one' required to tie;
A single; he was 'home' beyond the wicket,
   As anyone could see with half an eye.

That he was 'in' the batsman never doubted,
   Delighted he'd escaped the dreaded 'blob' –
When suddenly 'How's that?' was loudly shouted;
   The umpire answered, 'Out! *I wins five bob!*'

W. N. COBBOLD

Occasionally, cricket is played in the spirit in which the game was intended, with good grace and sportsmanship, by amateurs from many a field, even that of literature.

LINES ON A CRICKET MATCH

How was my spirit torn in twain
When on the field arrayed
My neighbours with my comrades strove –
My town against my trade.

And are the penmen players all?
Did Shakespeare shine at cricket?
And in what hour did Bunyan wait
Like Christian at the wicket?

When did domestic Dickens stand
A fireside willow wielding?
And playing cricket – on the hearth,
And where was Henry Fielding?

Is Kipling, as a flannelled fool,
Or Belloc, bowling guns,
The name that he who runs may read
By reading of his runs?

Come all; our land hath laurels too,
While round our beech-tree grows
The shamrock of the exiled Burke
Or Waller's lovely rose.

Who ever win or lose, our flags
Of fun and honour furled,
The glory of the game shall stand
Stonewalling all the world.

While those historic types survive
For England to admire,
Twin pillars of the storied past,
The Burgess and the Squire.

G. K. CHESTERTON

Chesterton takes us back to the Edwardian game, an era which has now taken on the sepia-coloured hues of the photographs of that time. But whatever the circumstances, whatever the era, cricket is played with enthusiasm. As Chesterton points out, whether it be graced with aptitude is another matter. Some of us can only marvel at the grace which a Gower can bring to the game. Others, despite all evidence to the contrary, believe that there is a latent Gower within, straining to unleash itself but denied from dazzling the crowd by circumstance. Such a man was Bob, narrator of this tale of hapless infatuation.

An Infant Prodigy

F ROM my tenderest infancy I have always had a *penchant* for the noble game of cricket, and I attribute the fact that I am not at this moment a brilliant light in the cricketing world, solely to parental repression in my youthful days. When, at the ripe age of seven, my mother caught me in company with two extremely dirty little votaries of the manly sport, making prodigious scores with her frying-pan for a bat, and a bundle of rag-stuff for a ball, she banged my head, and took the implements away from us. This discouraged me – it is wonderful what a lot of discouragement can be conveyed in this simple manner – and it was nearly two years later before I again took what you could call an active interest in the game. Then I came into possession of a bat valued at about two-and-sixpence, and an india-rubber ball probably costing another sixpence. It was not an expensive outfit; but I managed to extract a considerable amount of enjoyment from it while in my possession.

I would invite a few particular friends in, and we would chalk-mark the wall immediately under the scullery window for our stumps, and play cricket to the extent of about three panes of glass per game. We usually left off at the third pane. I don't know why. Perhaps because there were no other windows within reach for us to break, and the game got monotonous without an object.

Sometimes, and not infrequently either, we broke each other. One man, who formed one of my party of playfellows in those days, still bears witness, in the shape of two missing teeth and a scarred lip, to the excitement and severity of our backyard cricketing. We had played several games and were quite making the fortune of our local glazier when, one morning, on assembling as usual, I could nowhere find my bat and ball. I was much troubled, I remember, at the time, and made diligent and exhaustive search for the missing goods; but without result. Subsequently I discovered that my worthy papa had marked his displeasure at the growing frequency of bills for broken glass, by converting my bat into fuel, and shying my ball out of the railway-carriage window on his way up to town. Thus was my blossoming talent nipped in the bud, and some years passed before I again essayed cricket, when I joined our local club and played it in a grown-up style, with proper implements, and on a proper ground. But there was a lack of my old enthusiasm that prevented me from ever becoming a shining light, and for this I think my parents are to blame. Surely it were better to sacrifice a whole Crystal Palace than to smother with the iron hand of parental repression a possible rival to Grace or Shrewsbury, a noble upholder of the manly old English sport, professional probably, who would play the game for the honour and glory of cricket, together with two pounds a match and a percentage of the gate money!

R. ANDOM, *We Three and Troddles*

It is a harsh world, that of childhood and schoolboy cricket, even for the masters who supervise the sport. John Betjeman, for whom Corinthians came in columns and bibles rather than sports fields, was worsted by the game.

CRICKET MASTER

(An Incident)

My undergraduate eyes beholding,
    As I climbed your slope, Cat Hill:
Emerald chestnut fans unfolding,
    Symbols of my hope, Cat Hill.

What cared I for past disaster,
Applicant for cricket master,
Nothing much of cricket knowing,
Conscious but of money owing?
    Somehow I would cope, Cat Hill.

'The sort of man we want must be prepared
To take our first eleven. Many boys
From last year's team are with us. You will find
Their bowling's pretty good and they are keen.'
'And so am I, Sir, very keen indeed.'
Oh where's mid-on? And what is silly point?
Do six balls make an over? Help me, God!
'Of course you'll get some first class cricket too;
The MCC send down an A team here.'
My bluff had worked. I sought the common-room,
Of last term's pipe-smoke faintly redolent.
It waited empty with its worn arm-chairs
For senior bums to mine, when in there came
A fierce old eagle in whose piercing eye
I saw that instant-registered dislike
Of all unhealthy aesthetes such as me.
'I'm Winters – you're our other new recruit
And here's another new man – Barnstaple.'
He introduced a thick Devonian.
'Let's go and have some practice in the nets.
You'd better go in first.' With but one pad,
No gloves, and knees that knocked in utter fright,
Vainly I tried to fend the hail of balls
Hurled at my head by brutal Barnstaple
And at my shins by Winters. Nasty quiet
Followed my poor performance. When the sun
Had sunk behind the fringe of Hadley Wood
And Barnstaple and I were left alone
Among the ash-trays of the common-room,
He murmured in his soft West-Country tones:
'D'you know what Winters told me, Betjeman?
He didn't think you'd ever held a bat.'
    The trusting boys returned. 'We're jolly glad
You're on our side, Sir, in the trial match.'
'But I'm no good at all.' 'Oh yes, you are.'

When I was out first ball, they said 'Bad luck!
You hadn't got your eye in.' Still I see
Barnstaple's smile of undisguised contempt,
Still feel the sting of Winters' silent sneer.
Disgraced, demoted to the seventh game,
Even the boys had lost their faith in me.

JOHN BETJEMAN,
from Summoned by Bells, 1960

In time, we acknowledge that the Gower within will never out, that the hours of Bob Willis impersonations will never recreate Headingley 1981 on the local pitch and the hour to withdraw to the other side of the boundary ropes is nigh. It is a bitter moment, as one anonymous Brigadier recalled in a letter to The Times.

The Last Innings

The Brigadier's Exit

THERE comes a time when a man begins to realise that his cricket days are over. The thing first began to dawn on me when I noticed that the captain of the side, whenever he started to set his fielders, invariably began by saying, 'General, will you go point?' So I decided to chuck it; but I would go down with colours flying; I would get up a side, I would captain it, I would play a captain's innings, and then I would retire 'to make room for younger men'. Accordingly I decided to challenge one of the battalions of the brigade to a match. It gratefully accepted the honour. What else could it do? And when the great day came I had collected a very useful side, including several of the star turns of the garrison. It was a bright, sunny day; rather warm perhaps; but this is to be expected at the beginning of the hot weather in India. I made an initial error of a kind a captain should never make: I lost the toss. The battalion batted first. It made 101 runs, about 18 of which were the result of my non-bending. I also missed catching the best batsman before he had scored; he then proceeded to make 37. I thought it a difficult catch, and there were sympathetic remarks of 'hard luck' from two or three soldiers who were included in my side; but from a chance remark from a subaltern which I happened to overhear later on, my opinion as to the difficulty of the catch was not shared by some of my side.

We started well. Fifty was up on the board before a wicket had fallen. With the abnegation of the great man, I had put myself in last, and it now looked as if I should not get an innings at all. But a new bowler was put on, one of the last draft just out from home, who was reported to be useful. He clean bowled two of my best bats in his first over and three more in his next. Five for 53. Then we pulled ourselves together and the score laboriously mounted up. But wickets continued to fall. We reached 100, but the ninth wicket fell next ball. Two runs to get to win and one wicket to fall, and I was that wicket. I confess my heart bumped; but here was the chance I had asked for – the captain's innings.

As I strode out into the bright light which beats upon a batsman in India my courage returned. At any rate, I felt, I looked the part. I was wearing a dazzlingly white polo helmet: I remembered that at the time of purchase I resented paying £3 for this hat; now I felt that it was worth it. My shirt was a wonderful creation cut short above the elbows and made of some patent stuff full of small holes. My trousers were a dream of creaminess and creases. My socks were – (but no one could see them, so that was all right). My boots were simply 'It'. I had borrowed pads and gloves, but not before I had noted they were of the best make; the gloves were covered with a sort of Chevaux-de-frise of black indiarubber and had the right military touch. My borrowed bat had some sticking-plaster in the correct place and the autograph of a famous cricketer and about umpteen crosses on its face; these, for some reason, suddenly reminded me of the marks put at the end of most of the soldiers' letters which I had to censor in France years ago.

I reached the wicket. The umpire obligingly told me my bat was covering middle and leg. Taking the lump of chalk from behind the wicket, I drew a beautiful straight line along the coconut matting from the bat to the wicket. At any rate my hand was steady. I had a look round at the position of the fielders. I noticed with satisfaction that there was no one on the boundary between short-leg and mid-on; that is my favourite place for a drive in the air, which I confess, however, has many times caused my downfall. One run to tie, two to

25

win. I faced the bowler. I felt my stance was all that it should be, and I did not forget to raise my left toe from the ground. The bowler was the successful last-drafter; but what matter? A two is an easy thing to get. The last-drafter took a longish run and then flung the ball at me. Long before the ball left his hand I had quite decided that whatever sort of ball it was, it was to go to my favourite place on the boundary.

The ball hit the bat. At such moments thoughts come like a flash; my flash was a hope that somebody in the crowd of spectators had one of those long-distance high-velocity cameras which photograph cricketers in action; this great shot of mine, I felt, was one which should be recorded. Then an extraordinary thing happened. The ball was not taking its proper course to the boundary; it was going slowly, but beautifully straight, direct to mid-on. Unless anything unforeseen happened to it, it would hit him full in the stomach. Alas! Something did happen to it. The fielder, no doubt as self-protection, put his hands in the course of the ball. The ball stayed in his hands. I was out. The match was lost.

Speechless, I walked back to the tent, accompanied by the batsman from the other end. We were received with respectful cheers; at least I think they were cheers. I sat down and took off my armour. The soldier audience was moving away behind the tent. I heard a man say, ''Bout time Brigadier give oop cricket'. He has done so.

The Times, 30 April, 1930

'*There's some idiot moving about behind the bowler's arm*'

THE ASHES

The little urn of burnt bails may no longer have the mystical quality of old – indeed, they now say the ashes are those of a veil, not a bail – but it still represents the pinnacle of the game in England and Australia. An Ashes year is special, the oldest of competitions in the international calendar. Tradition takes us back to a tour by a mediocre England XI in 1858–9, whose success encouraged cricket entrepreneurs to send over stronger, if not representative, teams over later winters. In 1876, Alfred Shaw made the journey on the fourth touring party, and committed to paper his memories of the winter including those of the first first proper Test match between the two countries.

The 1876–77 Tour

IN the winter of 1876–77 I was one of the fourth team of English cricketers to visit Australia. James Lillywhite was the promoter and manager. I had been asked to make one of the combination taken out in 1873–74 by Mr W. G. Grace, but I declined. The conditions offered for that tour to the professional members were £150 and second-class passage, travelling, and hotel expenses, the latter item being fixed, where possible, at 7s. 6d. a day. I declined the offer, chiefly because I objected to the second-class proviso. From what I learned subsequently, I had no reason to regret my refusal.

For the 1876 trip the general terms were £150 and first-class passage. I received £300, a figure which in subsequent years was allowed to the members of the Anglo-Australian teams in whose management I had a share.

It is doubtful if there has ever been a cricket tour in Southern climes so full of incident as this visit of Lillywhite's team to Australia in 1876. Our party was made up of the following twelve – J. Lillywhite (captain) and H. Charlwood (Sussex), H. Jupp, J. Southerton and E. Pooley (Surrey), Andrew Greenwood, T. Armitage, Tom Emmett, A. Hill and George Ulyett (Yorkshire), and J. Selby and myself (Notts). The team was described at the time as the finest combination of professional cricketers that had ever left England. This estimate was not, I think, an exaggeration. Lillywhite, Greenwood, Jupp, and Southerton had been members of Mr Grace's team; the others were paying their first visit to the land of the golden fleece.

My first practical acquaintance with an Australian wicket was at Adelaide on November 16th, 1876. Remembering the quality of the Adelaide wickets now, it is curious to recall the notions of wicket preparing that prevailed when I first appeared there. The Adelaide Cricket Association had been afraid to use the roller for fear it would bruise and kill the grass! They dumbfounded when they saw Southerton's preparations. He got them to borrow the Corporation roller, and then he took one of the four horses by the head and led the team right across the centre of the ground. Perhaps it was not singular that on a wicket that had received so little preparation I should have been able to claim an analysis of 226 balls, 46 maidens, 12 runs, 14 wickets, at my first turn with the ball.

What a sensation such a bowling start would make in Australia now! But the conditions of this day make such a performance impossible. Cricketers who have visited Australia in recent years can scarcely have a conception of the difference in the state of the wickets between 1876 and now.

It is not my intention to refer in detail to all the matches played on this, my first, visit to Australia, nor to those of subsequent visits. The results are to be found in the statistical records of cricket by all who desire to know them. There is one match, of such vital importance in the influence it has had upon Anglo-Australian cricket, that no excuse need be offered for reproducing the full score here. This is the match at Melbourne on March 15th, 16th, and 17th, 1877, in which a combined Australian team, playing on level terms, won the first victory over an English Eleven. The full score is as follows:–

Lillywhite's Team *v.* Australia

Australia

C. Bannerman (N.S.W.), retired hurt	165	b Ulyett	4
N. Thompson (N.S.W.) b Hill	1	c Emmett, b Shaw	7
T. Horan (V.), c Hill, b Shaw	12	c Selby, b Ulyett	20
D. W. Gregory (N.S.W.), run out	1	b Shaw	3
B. B. Cooper (V.), b Southerton	15	b Shaw	3
W. Midwinter (V.) c Ulyett, b Southerton	5	c Southerton, b Ulyett	17
E. Gregory (N.S.W.), c Greenwood, b Lillywhite	0	c Emmett, b Ulyett	11
J. M. Blackburn (V.), b Southerton	17	lbw, b Shaw	6
T. W. Garrett (N.S.W.), not out	19	c Emmett, b Shaw	0
T. Kendall (V.), c Southerton, b Shaw	3	not out	17
J. Hodges (V.), b Shaw	0	b Lillywhite	8
Extras	7	Extras	8
Total	245	Total	104

Lillywhite's Team

H. Jupp, lbw, b Garrett	63	lbw, b Midwinter	4
J. Selby, c Cooper, b Hodges	7	c Horan, b Hodges	38
H. Charlwood, c Blackham, b Midwinter	36	b Kendall	13
G. Ulyett, lbw, b Thompson	10	b Kendall	24
A. Greenwood, c E. Gregory, b Midwinter	1	c Midwinter, b Kendall	5
T. Armitage, c Blackburn, b Midwinter	9	c Blackham, b Kendall	3
A. Shaw, b Midwinter	10	st Blackham, b Kendall	2
T. Emmett, b Midwinter	8	b Kendall	9
A. Hill, not out	35	c Thompson, b Kendall	0
J. Lillywhite, c & b Kendall	10	b Hodges	4
J. Southerton, c Cooper, b Garrett	6	not out	3
Extras	1	Extras	5
Total	196	Total	108

Lillywhite's Team Bowling

	O.	M.	R.	W.
Armitage	11	6	15	0
Emmett	10	7	15	0
Hill	37	16	60	1
Lillywhite	15	5	20	2
Shaw	87.2	50	89	8
Southerton	37	11	61	3
Ulyett	44	19	75	4

Australian Bowling

	O.	M.	R.	W.
Garrett	20.1	10	31	2
D. W. Gregory	5	1	9	0
Hodges	28.2	5	34	3
Kendall	71.1	28	109	8
Midwinter	70.2	30	102	6
Thompson	17	10	14	1

Result – Australia won by 45 runs

This was the first victory secured by an Australian Team playing on even terms against an English Team.

C. Bannerman's innings of 165 was the first three-figure innings scored by any Australian batsman against an English Team.

The success of the Australians created immense jubilation in Melbourne and other Colonial centres. It would have been strange, indeed, had the effect been otherwise. For the time being the defeated Englishmen and their associates in the Colonies had to be content to eat humble pie – sweetened, it is true, with the thought that it was members of their own race who had offered it – but humble pie all the same.

We were counselled that in the arrangement of future tours it should be borne in mind that Colonial cricket had improved (a statement that was perfectly true), and that 'instead of eight out of every ten players, on emerging from the pavilion, leaving their hearts behind them, or allowing that necessary organ to subside into their boots,' they had acquired more nerve as well as increased skill.

The Australasian also told us we were the weakest side by a long way that had ever played in the Colonies, 'notwithstanding the presence among them of Shaw, who is termed the premier bowler of England.' It added, 'If Ulyett, Emmett and Hill are fair specimens of the best fast bowling in England, all we can say is, either they have not been in their proper form in this Colony or British bowling has sadly deteriorated.'

But what were the facts? We had only landed the day before the match commenced from our New Zealand trip. . . . Not one of us was fit to play cricket. We had arranged the match for a date that should have given us plenty of time for rest, but we were delayed on the voyage, and the accommodation on shipboard was so bad that some of us had to sleep on deck. I was simply spun out myself.

Others of our bowlers were also completely knocked up. Armitage, in trying to bowl C. Bannerman, tossed one ball wide over the batsman's head – a delivery which brought forth the remark that the Australians could not reach Armitage's bowling with a clothes prop! The next ball he rolled along the ground. Another delivery went wide over the heads of both batsman and wicket-keeper, and was called a wide by the umpire.

Bannerman, whose 165 was the first three-figure innings scored by an Australian batsman against an English team, was missed by Armitage at mid-off before reaching double figures. I was the bowler, and the ball lobbed up in the simplest fashion, and struck Armitage in the stomach. As Australia only won by 45 runs, it will be seen this mistake cost England the match. Bannerman hit splendidly after receiving the 'life'. He gave no other chance, and his retirement was due to an accident, a ball from Ulyett damaging one of his fingers.

After the criticism we had received, all our fellows were eager to arrange another match on even terms. This was done, and on Saturday, March 31st, 1877, and the Monday, Tuesday, and Wednesday following, we again met the combined Australians on the Melbourne ground. This time Mr F. R. Spofforth, who had not played in the first match, was in the Australian team. With this addition to the team's ranks the local public confidently predicted a second victory. But we won by four wickets, thanks mainly to the magnificent batting of George Ulyett, who scored 52 in the first innings and 63 the next.

Our defeat on level terms at Melbourne in mid-March was the last encouragement that our Australian friends needed to embark upon a first visit to England. Lillywhite and I had done our best to induce them to tackle the enterprise. We even offered to undertake the financial responsibility of the tour, which we had confidence would be a success. It was not until the victory alluded to that the decision to visit England was come to. Then it was an Australian enterprise in a financial sense, as it was quite right it should be. A year later the first Australian visit was paid, and the cricket world was agape with astonishment at the most powerful side that the MCC could select being put out twice in one day for scores of 33 and 19. Equality and fraternity between England and her Colonies are now established with a completeness that is at once the astonishment and the envy of the other nations of the world. Let it not be forgotten that cricket has played a most important part in this happy concord, and that the two events which marked its origin were the matches that James Lillywhite and his men played in March and April, A.D. 1877 at Melbourne.

ALFRED SHAW, *Cricket Reminiscences*

The match was the first eleven-a-side game between the two countries and thus the first Test match. That Australia beat a substandard England team has set the pattern for the rest of time. The first Australian team proper – excluding the aboriginal team that toured England in 1868 – came to England in 1878, encouraged by Bannerman's century and the 45-run victory. On home territory and with W. G. Grace, England were confident of victory. But, again, they were disabused of their feeling of superiority when the 'Demon' Spofforth rattled them out, Grace and all, twice in one day, to give Australia a nine-wicket victory.

A follow-up success at the Oval in 1882 prompted the Sporting Times *to write the first of many obituaries of English cricket.*

In affectionate remembrance
of
English cricket
which died at the Oval 29th August 1882
deeply lamented by a large circle of sorrowmg
friends and acquaintances
RIP
NB The body will be cremated and
the Ashes taken to Australia

The Ashes themselves were cremated after a victorious tour of Australia the following winter by the Hon. Ivo Bligh. He was presented with an urn which supposedly contained the ashes of two bails, although recent research suggests it could hold an incinerated veil belonging to Bligh's future wife. From 1883 to the end of the First World War, England held the ascendancy and the Ashes, though not always. Around the turn of the century, Australia marshalled a world class team to tour England in 1902 in one of the best contests for the Ashes.

The 1902 Tour and Jessop's Match

THE Australian invasion of 1902 was again led by Joe Darling. The England captain was again A. C. MacLaren. The series of Test Matches was won by Australia by two to one, with two matches drawn, both washed out by rain, one of which England had in her pocket. Compared with modern figures, the totals for completed innings seemed small. Out of thirteen completed innings three were under 100, seven under 200, and only two over 300.

It is strange that England should have lost the rubber, because the eleven who took the field in the first match at Edgbaston is generally agreed to have been the strongest that ever at any time represented us. The batting order was: A. C. MacLaren, C. B. Fry, K. S. Ranjitsinhji, F. S. Jackson, J. T. Tyldesley, A. A. Lilley, G. H. Hirst, G. L. Jessop, L. C. Braund, W. H. Lockwood, W. Rhodes. Lilley, who went in fourth wicket down, had been a successful batsman in Test Matches. Wilfred Rhodes, who went in last man, was even then as good a batsman as he was when later on he went in first with Jack Hobbs for England and created history. Lockwood, last but one, was a fine bat who went in high up for Surrey. Braund, last but two, was a century maker in Test Matches. But it was not merely the strength of the batting which distinguished this eleven. We had four bowlers, each of them with fair claims in his own style to have been the best ever. Lockwood among cricketers would be at the top of the poll for the best genuine fast bowler in the history of the game. George Hirst would at any rate be near the top as a fast left-hand bowler. Similarly Wilfred Rhodes as a slow left-hand bowler. And certainly Braund has claims as one of the three or four best leg-break bowlers. I myself consider Braund as good a leg-break bowler as I ever played; none has ever been more accurate in length: not even Grimmett. It was not merely the class of these bowlers; it was the combination of ideal variety which they presented. In addition we had F. S. Jackson, and he proved to be one of our very best bowlers in Test Matches. Then there was Gilbert Jessop, a good enough fast bowler to have been chosen on that account alone for England. Jessop could also bowl good medium-pace stuff. Thus the side contained no less than six top-notch all-rounders. Nor was this all. We had a competent fielder for every place in the field and at least seven exceptionals. We had five men who could field in any position whatever with credit. We had three superb slips in MacLaren, Ranji, and Braund. In a Test Match Braund at first slip made a catch at fine leg off Hirst. Not a cocked-up catch, but one slick off the edge of the bat. He anticipated it, of course. There has never been a better first slip than Leonard Braund.

We started off at Birmingham by scoring 376 for 9 wickets declared. The chief scorer was Tyldesley with 138. Jackson and Lockwood made 50 each; and Hirst and Rhodes scored well. I made 0; MacLaren, Ranji, Lilley, Jessop, and Braund were got rid of much under their value in runs. It rained during the night. We then proceeded on an unpleasant but not too terrible wicket to evict Australia for the exiguous total of 36. Of this Trumper made 18, and no other batsman more than 5. Hirst got 3 wickets for 15 runs, Rhodes 7 for 17. Curiously enough, it was Hirst who was most troublesome to the Australians; their batsmen hurried to the other end and tried to hit Rhodes, without success. Well as Rhodes bowled, it was Hirst who was responsible for the debacle. This is the best instance I know of the bowler at the other end getting wickets for his colleague. But this often happens. In the second innings we had 2 of their wickets down for 46, and the whole side would have been out for about 130 at most. But rain interfered and finally washed the match out.

The next match at Lord's was a complete wash-out. The only feature was that both Ranji and I were out for 0 in a couple of overs. The ground had been too wet for play, and most of us had gone to our hotels. At about five o'clock we were telephoned for. We won the toss, and what upset the apple-cart was that Joe Darling, for some reason which he could never explain, started with a bowler named

A. J. Hopkins, when, in addition to Ernest Jones, he had declared good bowlers on his side in Noble, Armstrong, and J. Saunders, the latter a left-hander specially suited to a wet pitch. I had never seen Hopkins, who was a fair bowler of the practice description, but in his first over I was caught at fine leg by Clem Hill, who was on his way from second slip to square leg by the umpire. The ball and he happened to coincide in transgression. In came Ranji, and he was promptly bowled by an innocent straight ball from Hopkins, which the bowler had endeavoured to break back with a prodigious amount of finger-work. After that MacLaren and Jackson played out time with the greatest of ease, although against them Joe Darling tried all his six bowlers. It was a dead easy wicket. They scored 100 runs in 100 minutes. The rest of the match was a flood.

In July the Australians beat us fair and square at Sheffield by 143 runs. We were short of Ranjitsinhji and Lockwood, both damaged, though this time Ranji had not trodden on a nail. But we had Sidney Barnes, and he took 7 wickets in the match for 99 runs. The Australian advantage in runs was due to Monty Noble and Hugh Trumble in their first innings, and Trumper, Clem Hill, and Hopkins in their second. Clem played a grand innings of 119, and Trumper made a brilliant 62. Only two batsmen on our side did any good – MacLaren and Jessop. The former played finely for 31 and 63; and in our second innings Jessop punched a redoubtable 55. With the exception of Bobby Abel and Tyldesley in our first innings, no one on our side scored 20 runs. During our innings it happened that the light was atrocious. When I was stumped in the first innings I literally saw no ball at all to play at. The Sheffield smoke-stacks were in fine form, and the light was otherwise grim. Gilbert Jessop was l.b.w. to Hugh Trumble to a ball which hit him in the middle of his chest on the lower shirt button; he was trying to hit a straight ball to square leg from the position of a doormat. For us, besides Sidney Barnes, Wilfred Rhodes bowled well. For the Australians, Noble and Saunders were well on the spot in first innings, and Hugh Trumble and Noble in the second. Noble took 11 wickets for 103 runs; he bowled beautifully.

The result at Sheffield disturbed the Selection Committee, they began changing the team. This resulted in the historic victory for Australia by 3 runs at Manchester in the match known as Fred Tate's. Had it not rained overnight for our second innings we should have won the match with ease. The Australians scored 299, due to a lovely century by Trumper, and good scores by Duff, Clem Hill, and

Joe Darling. We replied with 262, of which F. S. Jackson scored a splendid 128 and Braund a fine 65. Then we got them out for a paltry 86 on an easy wicket. Lockwood had taken 6 wickets for 48 runs in the first innings. In the second he did one of the finest bowling performances in the history of Test Matches by taking 5 for 28. His bowling was truly magnificent; the more so as the ground was so wet that no other fast bowler I have ever known could have found a foothold. His beautiful bowling in the circumstances proved how perfect were his swing and control; a mere strong-man bowler would have been sliding all over the place. So we had 124 runs to make in our second innings. Of these 89 were made by our first four batsmen, but after MacLaren got out for 35 no one made another double figure. Hugh Trumble did the damage.

Why Fred Tate's match? Because the unlucky Fred Tate had to walk in last with 8 runs wanted to win. He snicked an uncomfortable fourer between legs and wicket. Then the rain came, and he had to sit in the pavilion for three-quarters of an hour before again facing fate. This time Saunders, the Australian left-hander, sent his off-stump flying, and Australia won by 3 runs. But Fred Tate was otherwise unlucky. In the Sussex eleven he never fielded anywhere but in the slips. The difficulty of providing for the deep-field with a right-hander and a left-hander when Joe Darling was in with Gregory caused MacLaren to put the unfortunate out in the country at deep square leg. Joe Darling immediately hit a colossal skier. Fred Tate, on the boundary near Old Trafford Station, carded wool beneath it. The ball hit his chest. This miss really lost the match. But another chance which was held really won it when Clem Hill brought off a miraculous running catch along the pavilion rails at deep square leg, to the detriment of Lilley off Trumble.

Now I must tell you that the only reason that Fred Tate was playing at all was that at the Selection Committee before the match Lord Hawke objected to our taking Schofield Haigh, of Yorkshire, as one of our thirteen and as the proposed wet-wicket bowler. It was gorgeous sunshine at the time the selectors met, and we had chosen Rhodes and George Hirst as well as Stanley Jackson from the Yorkshire side. It seemed as if Schofield Haigh would be a mere twelfth man, *honoris causa*. When someone proposed Fred Tate instead of Schofield Haigh, I distinctly told my colleagues that Fred Tate could not field anywhere except at slip, and that, though he was a careful slip in a county side, he was not up to the standard required in a Test Match. Lord Hawke was huffy, and we gave way to him, me protesting. So the truth is that this remarkable match ought to be called Lord Hawke's match. But there is more to say. When we got to Manchester and rain was in question, Archie MacLaren decided to leave out George Hirst of all people, a strong bat and prospectively the most dangerous wet-wicket bowler we had. So Fred Tate, whose forte was medium-pace bowling on fast, dry wickets, though no doubt he was useful in county cricket on wet ones, was included instead of George Hirst; because Archie MacLaren was pardonably annoyed with Lord Hawke for, as he said, foisting Fred Tate on him as a wet-wicket bowler. Archie said, 'Martin chose Fred Tate for a wet wicket, and it will rain.' In addition, the selectors left me out in favour of Bobby Abel. This was all right because I had not been making runs. But as it happens I was for value at least 25 per cent a better batsman on a wet wicket than on a dry, whereas Abel was preferably a dry-wicket batsman.

The events of this match in combination with others are the origin of the caustic saying that Lord Hawke lost more Test Matches than anyone who never played for England. This is rather severe. Lord Hawke was chairman of the selectors from 1899 to 1909, and again in 1933. He was not a good chairman. He was too much concerned with the fortunes of Yorkshire; he regarded the Test Matches as spoiling the county championship, and he was much too observant of what he thought was public opinion. He has been much misrepresented as a strong man of cricket.

Whoever's name ought to be allotted to the fatal Manchester match, there is no doubt about whose name should distinguish the fifth Test Match at the Oval that year. This, the most dramatic game ever played between England and Australia, was won by Jessop's hurricane century. I have seen the spectators at Test Matches strained and excited, but this is the only Test Match in which I have seen a spectator burst into tears when the winning run was scored. The Australians won the toss and played a fine first innings against fine bowling by Lockwood, Hirst, Braund, and F. S. Jackson. They scored 324, and against such bowling this was a performance. Hugh Trumble with Trumper and Noble were the chief scorers. George Hirst took 5 wickets for 77, and I never saw him bowl better. England followed with the poor total of 183, but the wicket had been damaged by rain. Trumble took 8 of our wickets for 65 runs – a masterly piece of bowling. He was also top scorer with 43. We then shot out the Australians for the small total of 121. Lockwood bowled at his best, taking 5 wickets for 45. Only Clem Hill and Warwick

Armstrong scored over 20 runs. So we were left with 263 runs to get on a wet wicket. A. C. MacLaren, L. C. H. Palairet, Tyldesley, Hayward, and Braund were all out for less than double figures each. Stanley Jackson, however, played a fine innings of 49. His certainty on an unpleasant wicket was superlative. Then Jessop let himself loose like a catapult at the bowling and scattered it to smithereens. He offered one scanty chance in the deep off a giant drive. If ever an innings ought to have been filmed, that was the one. I should say that Jessop's 104 must rank as the greatest innings by a pure hitter ever played. The other batsman who made a difference was George Hirst with a brave and skilful 58 not out. The match was pulled out of a very wet fire. I am bound to say that when our last two men were in Hugh Trumble planted a likely-looking l.b.w. on George Hirst. He was bowling round the wicket, and there was a scintilla of doubt, but I have never been able to feel comfortable about that decision. Hugh Trumble picked up the ball without a sign of discontent.

C. B. FRY, *Life Worth Living*, 1939

Edwardian cricket was the era of golden names whose deeds are recorded in the frowsty pages of old Wisdens and in the reminiscences of the oldest members of the MCC. The lustre of their deeds lives on: only recently Londoners said one of the sporting events they most wished they had attended was the last of the matches described above by Charles Fry, known now as 'Jessop's match'. After that series the ascendancy passed to England until the First World War, then swung back to Australia and Warwick Armstrong's great team of 1920 then back to England until the arrival of one Donald Bradman. In twenty years, Bradman rewrote the record book quite as determinedly as 'W.G.' had done half a century before him. In the next piece, Bradman scores but one, but then he had already done the damage with a first innings score of 254. The day's play at Lord's in July 1930 is described by the doyen of cricket reporters, Sir Neville Cardus.

Lord's, 1930

THERE is a passage in 'Tom Jones', greatest of English novels, where Henry Fielding, having got his plot terribly compli- cated, calls on all the high Muses, in person and severally, for aid, because, as he tells us, without their guidance 'I do not know how I am going to bring my story to a successful conclusion.' As I write these lines, after a day of wonderful cricket, I feel also the need of inspired and kindly forces. The day's play, in the old term, simply beggars description. England lost the match at noon, nearly won it again at the last hour, and lowered the flag only when forced down by sheer odds.

When twelve o'clock struck in the clock covered with ivy near the nursery, England were 147 for five, with Hobbs, Woolley, Hammond, Duleepsinhji, and Hendren all gone and 157 still needed to save themselves from defeat by an innings. Grimmett was master. Against his spin Hammond, Duleepsinhji, and Hendren had been batsmen sorely troubled and helpless. Now Chapman came in, and before making a run he mis-hit Grimmett's spin and sent the easiest of catches conceivable in a Test match. Victor Richardson seemed to lose sight of the ball, which fell to the grass. Chapman's lucky star has never shone with today's brightness; he lived to play one of the most astonishing innings I have ever seen. Allen helped him in a stand which, coming as it did after the impotence of Hammond and Hendren, was incredibly secure once Chapman had found that he could kick Grimmett's breakaway with legs and pads which were quite indecently unconcerned with any academic relationship between a batsman's footwork and his bat. Chapman and Allen were undefeated at lunch, by which time they had taken England's score from 147 for 5 to 262 for 5. After the interval Grimmett's straight ball baffled Allen at 272. The sixth English wicket scored 125 in 95 minutes.

Allen's courage and his trustfulness in the forward stroke, defensively and offensively, put rather to shame the aimlessness and shiftlessness which we had witnessed (very painfully) when some of his superiors in technique were at the wicket. The day indeed was a triumph for courage and optimism – and an exposure of that professionalism which is too often content to work according to its own routined machinery and has too little use for the influences of imagination. Chapman's innings was no doubt technically very bad at parts, but probably the hardened county expert was inclined to look indulgently upon Chapman's many and fortunate mis-hits. But if Chapman's innings could not be called batmanship in the strict technical sense, it was something better than that in the eyes of Providence – it was an act of faith and cheerfulness. Before Chapman arrived at the wicket technique (of a sort) had proved useless for England in a dark hour – useless because it was technique and nothing else, lacking as it did the beard of men determined not to look at difficulties save to see them as hills that could be scaled granted the effort and the risk.

While Hammond and Hendren tried to tackle Grimmett, you would have sworn the wicket was sticky; each batsman thrust out a bat protectively and groped for the ball. Hendren, true, hit a beautiful four through the covers and a desperate on-drive against the spin, but the stroke which got him caught at 'silly' mid-off was a purely speculative stab in the dark. Hendren's innings was distressingly touched with mortality and not worthy of a Test match player.

After Allen's wicket fell, Chapman's innings went gloriously insane, yet retained some method in its madness. No cricketer, no matter how blessed by the gods, can hope to hit Grimmett simply by fling-ing his bat at the air. As a fact, Chapman by a curious compound of push work with his pads and a delayed forward stroke, quite upset Grimmett's tactics at the beginning of his innings, even while England's position was at its worst. Grimmett packed the off-side field to Chapman, and pitched his leg break wide of the off stump. As soon as Chapman had got sight of the ball, he pulled Grimmett round to the on, often in the grand manner, and sometimes sending the ball to fine leg with a very likeable lack of intent. Three times he achieved colossal on-drives from Grimmett for six. When his score was in the nineties and everybody on the ground save Chapman in a state of proud and affectionate anxiety, Chapman gorgeously mis-hit a ball over the slips for four, and he seemed to enjoy the escapade even more than he enjoyed those of his hits which observed the unities.

In an hour after lunch Chapman plundered 69 runs from the Australian attack, and his most remunerative, if not his most violent strokes were square-leg hits from Grimmett, a straight drive from Grimmett, a clout into the people on the mound stand from Grimmett, a hit to long leg from Grimmett, a pull toward leg from Hornibrook, another clout into the mound stand, a drive to long-on from Hornibrook, a thoroughly characteristic snick from Hornibrook, and then another six, all the more delightful because four of the runs were given away for nothing by overthrows which sent the crowd into fits of laughter and applause. Seldom can an innings in a Test match have caused more jubilation and hubbub amongst a crowd. Probably we should have to go as far back as Jessop's great routing of the Australians in 1902 to find an equal to this innings by Chapman – that is, an equal as far as animal spirits are concerned, for of course Jessop's greatest innings was not only energy, strong and fearless, but energy concentrated and made whole by a masterful range of strokes all over the field. Nearly all of Chapman's major strokes today were drives theoretically or in practice. He came to the wicket when most of us were looking up trains for home. By the time he had been batting two hours we were as busy ringing up our hotels asking for a room for one night longer. Chapman fell to a clever catch by Oldfield at 354. In two hours and a half he made 121 out of a total of 207 scored while he was at the wicket.

It was not good bowling but marvellous fielding that captured the second Australian wicket at 17. Bradman cut Tate magnificently; it was one of the best strokes of the match. The ball flashed hard toward the ground quicker than sight could follow. The crack of the bat was triumphant. Chapman took the ball at his feet with both hands and threw it in the air almost before we knew what had happened. I have never seen a finer catch or a more beautiful one for that matter, and I have never seen a finer or more beautiful fieldsman than Chapman. Bradman could scarcely believe his eyes, and he walked slowly back to the pavilion. The ovation to Chapman was probably heard a mile away.

Then came another of those dramatic silences which fall on a cricket field after a moment of tumult. Robins bowled Kippax, the ball spun, and Kippax tried a cut. Duckworth's clamant crow split the skies, and another roar from the crowd went up as the finger of the umpire was seen pointing on high. The appeal of Duckworth was worthy of the word great; the occasion demanded it. His catch was a masterpiece of clean alacrity. And now Australia were 22 for 3 and the whole of Lord's was a bedlam, the heat of the afternoon was as though thrown out from action. Voices everywhere were asking could England, after all, win? Was it possible? 'You never know,' said a man in white spats non-committally. And he added, as though discovering an entirely new and original thought, 'It's a funny game is cricket.' When McCabe came in Woodfull went towards him to meet him. Words were spoken. The scene and the occasion were obviously trying to Woodfull himself let alone to a young cricketer with his spurs still to win. Woodfull again was Australia's good anchor. He watched Robins's spin to his bat, yet had one or two narrow escapes from edged strokes through the slips. McCabe, reliant as Woodfull, playing finely, meeting the ball cleanly and confidently. Here is another great batsman in the making.

Sad to say the end was anticlimax. Robins raised our hopes by a spell of bowling clever and as waspish of spin as anything achieved in the match by Grimmett. Then, with a quite sickening suddenness, his length went to pieces. Thirteen were hit from one over – and once again the Australians' crown on the stand lifted up heart and voice. The winning hit was made at five o'clock, and a memorable day was at an end.

As the cricketers came from the field sunshine fell on them, touching them with a lovely light. It might well have been a light cast by immortality, for this match will certainly never be forgotten. Australia won against a first innings score of 425; England, though compelled to bat needing 304 to avoid defeat in an innings, made 375 on the fourth day of a match played at Lord's in dry weather – a gallant performance. Victors and vanquished emerge from the game the better and the more historical for it. The finish when Australia were sweating by the brow to score 72 for victory was ironical. Only the day before they had waxed fat to the strength of 729 for six. The game of cricket played by men of true sport is incomparable.

Perhaps in years to come this match will be known as Chapman's match. Though for the first time he is a defeated English captain, his renown has been increased thereby, and not only because of a lion-hearted century. The match's greatest cricket was Chapman's fielding; it was fielding unparalleled. The catch that dismissed Bradman was a good crown for work which, by its swiftness, its accuracy, and for its beauty, will assuredly go down for good and all in the most precious annals of the game.

Final Scores

England – First Innings

Hobbs, c Oldfield, b Fairfax	1
Woolley, c Wall, b Fairfax	41
Hammond, b Grimmett	38
K. S. Duleepsinhji, c Bradman, b Grimmett	173
Hendren, c McCabe, b Fairfax	48
A. P. F. Chapman, c Oldfield, b Wall	11
G. O. Allen, b Fairfax	3
Tate, c McCabe, b Wall	54
R. W. V. Robins, c Oldfield, b Hornibrook	5
J. C. White, not out	23
Duckworth, c Oldfield, b Wall	18
Extras	10
Total	425

Fall of wickets: 1-13, 2-53, 3-105, 4-209, 5-236, 6-239, 7-337, 8-383, 9-387, 10-425

Bowling: Wall 29.4-2-118-3, Grimmett 33-4-105-2, Fairfax 31-6-101-4, Hornibrook 26-6-62-1, McCabe 9-1-29-0

Australia – First Innings

Woodfull, st Duckworth, b Robins	155
Ponsford, c Hammond, b White	81
Bradman, c Chapman, b White	254
Kippax, b White	83
McCabe, c Woolley, b Hammond	44
Richardson, c Hobbs, b Tate	30
Oldfield, not out	43
Fairfax, not out	20
Extras (b 6, lb 8, w 5)	19
Total (6 wkts dec.)	729

Fall of wickets: 1-162, 2-393, 3-585, 4-588, 5-643, 6-672

Bowling: Allen 34-7-115-0, Tate 64-18-148-1, White 51-7-158-3, Robins 42-1-172-1, Hammond 35-8-82-1, Woolley 6-0-35-0

England – Second Innings

Hobbs, b Grimmett	19
Woolley, hit wkt, b Grimmett	28
Hammond, c Fairfax, b Grimmett	32
Duleepsinhji, c Oldfield, b Hornibrook	48
Hendren, c Richardson, b Grimmett	9
Chapman, c Oldfield, b Fairfax	121
Allen, lbw, b Grimmett	57
Tate, c Ponsford, b Grimmett	10
Robins, not out	11
White, run out	10
Duckworth, lbw, b Fairfax	0
Extras (b 16, lb 13, w 1)	30
Total	375

Fall of wickets: 1-45, 2-58, 3-129, 4-141, 5-147, 6-272, 7-329, 8-354, 9-372, 10-375

Bowling: Wall 25-2-80-0, Fairfax 12.4-2-37-2, Grimmett 58-13-167-6, Hornibrook 22-6-49-1, Bradman 1-0-1-0, McCabe 3-1-11-0

Australia – Second Innings

Woodfull, not out	26
Ponsford, b Robins	14
Bradman, c Chapman, b Tate	1
Kippax, c Duckworth, b Robins	3
McCabe, not out	25
Extras (b 1, lb 2)	3
Total (3 wkts)	72

Fall of wickets: 1-16, 2-17, 3-22

Bowling: Tate 13-6-21-1, Hammond 4.2-1-6-0, Robins 9-1-34-2, White 2-0-8-0

NEVILLE CARDUS, *The Manchester Guardian*, 1930

During the 1930 series, Bradman scored 974 runs at an average of 139.14, winning the series for Australia by setting the home side first innings totals of such daunting scale that they faltered in the chase. Before the 1932–3 tour of Australia, England and its captain, Douglas Jardine, accepted they had to find a way to disrupt the Bradman run machine. His preferred method was leg theory, or as it is better known, bodyline.

Bodyline

E VEN some of the players hardly knew what to make of it at first. Of the 53,916 people in the Melbourne Cricket Ground that afternoon of Nov. 19, 1932, I doubt whether two dozen had not an ingrained belief that Don Bradman was the master of every bowler alive.

It was not as if some new-risen destroyer had emerged, surpassing those who had been unable to prevent Bradman from scoring 1,442 runs in his first 15 Test innings. Plainly none of the newcomers was a better bowler than Harold Larwood. And Larwood, 28, had been through four years of a fast bowler's wear and tear since they last met in Australia. In all, Bradman had batted in 17 innings in which Larwood was a bowler and had been run down only once by the Notts Express – bowled for 232 at the Oval, 1930.

With such thoughts at the back of their minds, few sensed the true import of what happened that afternoon, a fortnight before the first Test match. The onlookers were either mystified or amused. Bradman shared neither of those feelings. Poor Don! He had suddenly discovered that the game of cricket, which had been such fun, could be made harsh and bitter. Quick on the uptake, he probably had formed some idea of what to expect when he heard that England was sending four fast bowlers out – one of them, Bowes, having been added to the team four days before the ship sailed. Bradman realised that things were going to be much tougher than he had expected when, about an hour before he came in that afternoon, he saw one of Larwood's bumpers strike Woodfull a sickening blow over the heart.

When Bowes and Voce lumbered up and bounced the ball at Bradman the record-breaker played strokes as much like a carpet-beater's as a batsman's – what's more, a carpet-beater in a hurry to get through with the job. This sure-footed cricketer, noted for his balance, once got into such a tangle that he fell, landed in a sitting position, waved the bat above his head like a semaphore and - so remarkable is his eye – scored a run. When Larwood came on, with the new field-setting he had used against Woodfull (one slip, five leg-fielders) Bradman lashed at the bumpers, if they were straight;

when they bounded at him he skipped back or tumbled out of harm's way outside the off stump, reminding one of the hare which can look backward for danger while fleeing.

Gusts of mirth came from those in the crowd who imagined Don was putting on a jitterbug turn to entertain them, or to make the English bowlers look cheap. The tragi-comedy lasted 45 minutes in which he scored 36. The odds are that nobody else using the same methods could have stayed in half as long or scored half as many.

Some of the Australian players who watched the performance found it difficult to believe that Bradman's actions were caused by alarm or his determination to live to fight another day. Knowing he was about as deep as the Pacific Ocean and that he had fed voraciously on short balls in the past, a few half-suspected a more artful motive. Vernon Nagel, Victorian fast bowler who had played against the Englishmen in the preceding match, put it in words by asking: 'Is he trying to kid them into serving him up a lot of short stuff in the Tests?'

The truth was that the match (an Australian XI v. England) gave us a preview of the pattern of the way Bradman was to bat against bodyline in the Test matches. In the second innings he backed away to leg from a straight ball from Larwood, gambling on its rearing higher than the stumps and ready to cut it as it careered by. But the ball skidded through to find an unguarded wicket. Next match it was Voce who hit an untenanted wicket, in New South Wales's second innings. That time Bradman evacuated his position in the opposite direction: expecting another bumper he hunched down and scuttled to the off without attempting a stroke at the ball.

As Bradman was not fit to play in the first Test of the series, further examination of his ability to counter Jardine's leg theory had to wait another two and a half weeks.

On medical advice, Bradman spent a fortnight at a seaside holiday camp because of his run-down condition, then played in the second Test. To the first ball he received he played an uncharacteristic, convulsive stroke, the sort of shot suitable for impromptu beach baseball when they're making wicky-wacky down at Waikiki. As Bowes bounced the ball toward his left shoulder he skipped to the off and lashed out with a hasty hook which dragged the ball down behind him into his wicket.

After all that had gone before, the strain on Bradman must have been almost unbearable when he walked out in second innings before an unprecedented crowd of 68,000. I rank that day's 103 not out (of Australia's 191) as the innings of his life, though it was not technically as flawless as other innings two or three times larger when the going was easier. For he was playing not only the three bodyline bowlers and Allen and Hammond but to reinstate himself in the estimation of the public and his team-mates, watching sceptically from their foxholes beneath the Grey-Smith stand.

After a few gimcrack shots his batting showed few signs of anxiety. He realised that the Melbourne wicket was not true to label (Australia's best for fast bowlers). Larwood, Bowes and Voce found it difficult to make the ball fly quickly and Bradman, with his unrivalled quickness, often had time to play with certainty his newly-patented tennis-like stroke (All Rights Reserved) in which he depended on forearm power to swat the ball down through the packed leg field. (To commemorate Don's great innings admirers presented a piano to his charming wife. That was about the only harmonious note in a jangling season.)

That innings was the only real setback Jardine suffered at Bradman's hands in his war of nerves against Australia's batsmen. Though Don was seldom dismissed for a low score all his other innings against bodyline were marked by an agitation which showed itself in overtones of rashness and an undertone of uneasiness, as if he were jittery – as he had ample cause to be, for that matter. It was most evident in his retreats to a new line, wide of the leg stump. A more nervous short-leg fieldsman than Jardine might have felt concerned lest his toes be trodden on.

From his remote disadvantage-point Bradman indulged in wishful thinking by attempting slashing square-cuts and cover-hits. His bat, so often described as a flashing broadsword, was used more like a harpoon. If, instead of a bodyliner, the ball happened to be straight, Whaler Bradman trusted to luck that it would clear his forsaken stumps. Though that ruinous manoeuvre was not always the immediate cause of his dismissal – as it was in both innings of the fourth Test (bowled, and caught at point) – it was the main factor in the insecurity which brought his downfall in other ways.

A secondary factor was his impetuosity on haymaking off other bowlers before the bodyliners could cloud out the sunshine. In the third Test, after bumpers from Larwood had struck Woodfull over the heart and Oldfield on the head in the first innings – casualties accidentally suffered under enemy action – Jardine did not consent to Larwood's appeals for the bodyline field-setting in the second innings until Australia's score was 75 (Bradman 46). Don then assailed Verity's bowling brilliantly and one of his threshing strokes – a six over long-on – struck a woman onlooker. But there was something feverish in the brilliance. It was as if he had pasted up one of those shop placards: *Great Fire Sale. Closing Down. Everything Must Go.* He jumped down the wicket to almost every ball until Verity caught a hard drive to dismiss him for 66, made in only 71 minutes. On entering the dressing-room Bradman was asked why he had not gone a little steadier and replied frankly: 'Oh, I wanted to hit one bowler before the other hit me.'

On the figures, a case could be made out that Bradman's methods were justified by the fact that he topped the Australian batting averages – with McCabe nearest (385 for nine times out). But any theory based solely on figures collides head-on with the fact that a run has no fixed value. Fifty of them can be beyond price or not worth a cracker. Everything depends on how much the team needs them and whether they are made in the way circumstances require. When H. L. Collins stayed in for 4¾ hours of match-saving vigil in the Manchester Test, 1921, whether he scored 40 or 140 in the time had little bearing on the result of the match; he was playing for minutes, not runs. So when runs are lumped together in dehydrated form in end-of-season tables of averages they sometimes lose their significance and can even be misleading.

Australia was always sorely in need of runs against Jardine's bowlers. Never throughout a Test season has a run been worth more. Without the influence of the 103 Bradman put on the board in the second Test it is unlikely that O'Reilly's artifice, Wall's speed and Ironmonger's left-hand spin could have won the match, even though Australia's winning margin was eight more than Bradman's total. In appraising the value of the other runs made by Bradman against that English team there was one over-riding factor: the effect his batting had on his opponents and on the morale of his own side.

If it is half the battle for a batsman to act as if he is master (or at least is gaining mastery) and never to betray himself to the bowler with signs of discomfiture, Bradman's battle was half lost in quick time. He could be likened to a boxer who, despairing of his chance of subduing his opponent, shut his eyes and lashed out indiscriminately, yet whose natural talent was so great that he landed enough blows to score a number of points before he took the count. Among those not fooled was his opponent, who knew to try the same kind of unsettling attack at their next encounter. Larwood's greatest encouragement was that Bradman, instead of trying to counter the rib-roasters by scientific adjustments to the technique which had humbled the world's best bowlers, switched to ersatz methods which had no chance of being an effective substitute. Being hit for half a dozen fours caused Larwood no distress while he had the comforting knowledge that his most dangerous opponent was insecure and, botanically speaking, had almost no prospect of becoming rooted.

I suspect that bodyline proved to be much more demoralising than its devisers had dared to hope. If Larwood, who had got Bradman only once before, ever paused to daydream on the bridge over the Trent he would scarcely have pictured himself dismissing the record-breaker in six of the nine innings in which he bowled at him in 1932–3. And if Woodfull's overdoses of dry ginger ale ever caused nightmare I doubt whether his sleep was ever oppressed by a vision that his greatest batsman would be out in three-quarters of an hour or less in seven of his 12 innings against bodyline and only twice would last longer than two hours.

The only time the Australians looked like overcoming bodyline was in the fourth Test which decided the rubber. They did not have to face it from both ends, as neither Voce nor Bowes was playing, but that brought scant relief to their ragged nerves because Larwood was by far the most terrifying. The batsmen had two telling allies in a heat wave and an exceptionally easy Brisbane wicket.

Bowling under a February sun at Brisbane – only four degrees outside the tropics, where only mad dogs and Englishmen venture out at midday – is always an ordeal for fast bowlers. Well aware of that, Woodfull knew soon after play began that if it were humanly possible to break bodyline's spell (and Larwood's heart) the heat and the wicket gave the shaken Australian team that chance. The purposeful captain had with him as opening partner valiant Victor Richardson, not the equal in technique of several other Australians who played in that Test season, but the one least daunted by bodyline (even such bold spirits as McCabe and Darling confessed that they were intimidated by Larwood's tactics). For the first time in the rubber Australia reached 40 without loss of a wicket.

For Larwood, all that offered was toil, sweat and jeers. Jardine tried him from each end, gave him sips of champagne to overcome his disinclination for food at lunch. Four times Jardine launched him against the pair, but they stood their ground. Richardson was circumspect until the score neared 100, then unchained his power-ful short-arm hook against Larwood's short ones. Two of the close leg-fielders, Allen and Leyland, were moved back to safer distance.

Woodfull walked along the pitch to remind Richardson that, above all else, Larwood must be denied the encouragement of a wicket, and that there would be time for belligerence after the tea interval. Richardson's reply: 'I'll show the beggar he can't bowl.'[1]

To those who knew how low the Australian team's spirits had been driven by bodyline the remark was astounding. Only the redoubtable Richardson could have made it. Next time Larwood pitched the ball up the South Australian jumped down the wicket and drove the fast bowler over mid-on to the boundary. Larwood was taken off, too dry to foam at the mouth. When Richardson was stumped off Hammond he had made 83 of the opening partnership's 133.

Richardson's lion-taming and the steadfastness of Woodfull (who defied the foe for five-sixths of the day) created a position of great possibilities, but Bradman was too taut-strung to show a firm front to Larwood, though the fast bowler was no longer able to get full steam up. Don batted well against the other bowlers and at the day's end was 71 not out. The Australians had built up a chance for victory by scoring 251 for three wickets and frustrating Larwood, who bowled 20 overs for 65 runs without a wicket. Woodfull knew that fast bowlers were never so fearsome when they came up for a second day's turn on the Brisbane griddle.

After a night's sweltering under mosquito-nets Larwood made a stout-hearted effort in his first few overs, on which the fate of the match hung. For the batsmen, one duty over-rode every other con-sideration: for the team's sake they must endure anything to thwart him in that critical period. The occasion demanded more than Bradman's state of mind allowed him to give. Though Larwood was palpably tiring, Don deserted his wicket and attempted a cross-bat cover-slash at a straight ball which uprooted his leg stump.

His sudden downfall altered the course of the match. That moment began the Englishmen's fighting recovery. How little more would have been necessary to shunt the Notts Express into a siding in that innings was evident before lunch: during a delay about a change of bowlers, coatless barrackers bawled to Jardine: 'Keep Larwood on!' But by then the backbone of the batting was broken. By day's end the Englishmen had determinedly laid the foundation for the victory which decided the rubber.

[1] Roughly speaking.

Don knew that in bodyline's pattern bombing he was No. 1 Target for Fright. It gave him no comfort that his opponents' resort to that alarming technique was a tribute to his superlative skill in conquering every kind of bowling known before. Nor did it lessen his anguish to know that he was not the sole target, that high on the list of objectives were Woodfull and Ponsford (after their record feat of first-wicket partnerships of 162, 106 and 159 in three of the four Tests in which they opened in 1930) and that McCabe, Fingleton, Richardson and other batsmen were added to that list. As it worked out in the Tests, Woodfull faced 201 more balls from the bodyline bowlers than Bradman, McCabe 94 more, Fingleton 58 more and Richardson 17 fewer.

Harness or no harness, Bradman was determined that as he had to be a target, he would be a moving target. He would not be sunk at his moorings. Any price the enemy had set on his head applied only while he was alive and kicking; he knew that, if laid aside by disablement, he would not be worth as much as a leg-bye to his team. His extraordinary quickness of foot put him in the first and foremost flight in preserving his gore, like that devastating calculating, palpitating paladin, the Duke of Plaza-Toro. Don might have died a thousand deaths during the ordeal but only once was the fugitive from injustice winged. In Australia's last innings of the season he was struck on the arm, outside the leg stump, by a ball from Larwood which he apparently tried to slash between point and cover. Next day Bromley fielded as a substitute for him.

Bodyline shook the nerves of all the Australian batsmen. It intimidated Bradman into putting the security of his wicket second to the safety of his body and head; self-preservation remains the first law of nature, even for a Test cricketer. But that does not confirm the conclusion that his cavortings were caused by 'sheer funk,' as Larwood's book asserts.

Above all, Bradman is a realist. As such, he recognised instantly that bodyline could not be mastered, that at most it could only be temporarily thwarted when conditions handicapped the bowlers. He could see no sense in getting himself knocked about in fruitless martyrdom for a hopeless cause.

Midway through the rubber he said he thought it practically impossible for even the leading batsmen to make runs against that type of attack without getting a least one or two severe cracks. After the Tests he said that, no matter what methods had been adopted, he could not conceive that Larwood's attack could possibly have been ineffective. I recall a compassionate comment by Hobbs: 'Bradman would have none of it. He was not going to be hit. He gave it up a little too early, I thought. He has my sympathy.'

RAY ROBINSON, *Between the Wickets*, 1946

With but that one setback, the Australian domination of England continued to the end of the Bradman era - which ended in the almighty triumph of the 1948 tourists whom he captained to a 4–1 win - and on into the beginning of the fifties. Then the worm turned. The Ashes were won back in 1953, and then, in 1956, an Englishman produced the greatest feat of bowling in Test cricket history.

19 for 90

Old Trafford, Fourth Test, last day

FOR many nervous hours since last Friday evening it has seemed that England would be robbed of victory in the Fourth Test match. But Manchester expiated its sins of weather this afternoon, and it was in bright sunshine tempering the wind that the game ended in an innings win, which meant the safe-keeping of the Ashes until MCC next sail in their defence two years from now. The only proper formal announcement of the result is that J. C. Laker defeated Australia by an innings and 170 runs. Unprecedented things are always happening in cricket because it is so charmingly unpredictable a pastime. But now and then occurs something of which one feels certain there can be no repetition or bettering. Laker followed his capture of nine first innings wickets with all 10 in the second. What is left in the vocabulary to describe and applaud such a *tour de force*? It is quite fabulous.

Laker's first innings performance was phenomenal enough, but its merit was perhaps clouded by the deficiencies of the Australian batting, as also by the palaver over the condition of the wicket.

There was no room whatever for argument regarding his bowling today. He bowled 36 overs, practically non-stop except for the taking of the new ball, all the time attacking the stumps and compelling the batsman to play, never wilting or falling short in terms either of length or direction. Nor was he mechanical. Each ball presented the batsman with a separate problem. Laker never let up and neither for an instant could his adversary.

It is, of course, scarcely less remarkable that while Laker was building up new heights of fame at one end Lock was toiling just as zealously, albeit fruitlessly, at the other. On a wicket on which one famous cricketer captured 19 wickets the other, scarcely less successful and dangerous, taking one day with another, in 69 overs had 1 for 106. Still, the comparison between the figures is in one sense unarguable evidence of Laker's great performance. If the wicket had been such a natural graveyard for batsmen it is inconceivable that Lock, even below his peak, even with the other arm tied to his side, would not have taken more than one wicket.

So long as McDonald was in the odds were still fairly balanced. When he was beaten at last directly after tea the latter-end batsmen carried on in the same spirit, and there was a bare hour to go when Maddocks, the No. 11, played back and slightly across to Laker, fell leg-before and advanced up the wicket to shake the hero by the hand. One of the Australian party summed up the day, as the crowd that massed round the pavilion dispersed and Laker, glass in hand, had turned from the balcony to the dressing-room by saying: 'Well, it was a good scrap after all.' There was relief in his voice, just as there was jubilation in the surrounding English faces.

The captains having formally disagreed, there was a delay of 10 minutes before play was continued this morning. The wicket was just about as sluggish as yesterday. McDonald and Craig, by high-class defensive play, withstood the session of an hour and 50 minutes without many moments of difficulty. Just before lunch Evans and Lock, those tireless propagandists, when the latter was bowling, tried their hardest by expression and gesture to suggest that the dormant pitch was stirring. But McDonald and Craig came in calm and unscathed, having incidentally added 28 runs.

There were early signs after lunch that the batsmanship might be more severely tested. Craig was twice beaten by lifting balls from Lock, who naturally enough was sharing the bowling with Laker. After quarter of an hour Craig went back to the latter and was lbw to an off-break. Thus he retired full of honour after an innings of 4 hours and 20 minutes, in which his stature had grown surely and steadily. The breaking of the stand was the signal for the second Australian collapse of the game. Within half an hour Mackay, Miller and Archer had all followed Craig, all to Laker, and all for ducks. Granted the ball was doing a little more during this phase in answer to bursts of sun, these batting failures underlined the worth and value of the third-wicket partnership. Where before the judgment of length and direction had been good enough to ensure a smooth, well-considered defensive stroke, now the new batsmen were floundering about and either using their pads or offering a last-minute jab. Mackay was surrounded by slips, silly mid-off, and short-legs, six in all within a five-yard radius. One could hardly see how he could survive, for in going forward he plays so far in front of the front leg. This had been evident against the slow bowlers even while he was putting up his celebrated resistance at Lord's. Now Mackay probed out, and edged a short sharp catch to Oakman, the middle of the slips. I have never seen a batsman whose value rose and fell so abruptly according to the state of the wicket. On a good one he wants blasting out. When the ball is doing anything it is hard to see how he can last five minutes. As it was, Mackay today, like Harvey on Friday, bagged a pair.

McDonald was seemingly impervious, immovable, and he and Benaud came in to tea, having stayed together an hour and 20 minutes. Australia were still breathing. But McDonald did not take root afterwards and it was the inevitable Laker who got the most valuable wicket of all. This was a sharp off-break which for once went too quickly for McDonald, who edged it to the sure hands of Oakman in the middle position just behind square. So ended a valiant effort lasting without a chance for more than five hours and a half.

Lindwall made a steady partner for Benaud and at five o'clock these two looked ominously settled and determined: there was still Johnson and Maddocks to come. It was not yet 'in the bag'. But Benaud now went back where he might have gone forward and was bowled midde-and-off stumps or thereabouts. Twenty minutes later Lindwall, like so many before him, fell in the leg-trap. Then, with Johnson looking on, Maddocks made his entry and speedy, gracious exit. So the game ended. The post-mortems no doubt will linger on. But whatever is added one thing cannot be gainsaid: Laker was magnificent.

England *v.* Australia, at Old Trafford, 26–31 July 1956. England 459 (Sheppard 113, Richardson 104, Cowdrey 80); Australia 84 (Laker 9 for 37) and 205 (McDonald 89, Laker 10 for 53). England won by an innings and 170 runs.

E. W. SWANTON, 1956

If that performance lives on in cricket history, a second, twenty-five years later, is the stuff of modern legend. Though it is Ian Botham's name which has become synonymous with that Headingley Test – his brazen gunslinger's innings that people recall when you mention the game – Paul Fitzpatrick describes the cleaning-up operation brilliantly performed by Bob Willis on the final day of that game.

Headingley, 1981

NOT since the golden age of cricket have England won a Test to compare with the one they won by 18 runs against Australia at Headingley yesterday.

Not since A. E. Stoddard led his side to victory by 10 runs in Sydney in 1894, the only previous instance of a Test side following on and winning the game, has an English cricket public been given quite such cause for celebration.

This third Cornhill Test will be remembered for many things – chiefly for the soaring performances of Ian Botham and the marvellous bowling yesterday of Bob Willis – but perhaps the thing that will give it an imperishable place in cricket history alongside the tied Test of Brisbane 1960 was the utter improbability of the victory.

England, it will be remembered, scored 174 to Australia's first innings 401 for nine declared; and at one stage on Monday they were still 92 runs short of making Australia bat again with only three second-innings wickets standing.

To be at Headingley yesterday was to be part of a drama as gripping as anything the fertile mind of Wilkie Collins could have dreamed of. It was impossible to take the eye away from a single delivery; every run that edged Australia towards their target of 130 heightened the anxiety of an absorbed crowd; every wicket England captured added another heartbeat of tension until by the time that Willis uprooted Bright's middle stump to end the game most nerves could have stood no more.

Only Test cricket could have produced such a fascinating plot as this; no other game could have allowed such an unlikely and outrageous swing of fortune as England experienced. Only a drama that is allowed to unfold over five days could permit such a twist in the plot so wild as to be almost unthinkable.

After three and a half days of largely dull preamble, England were finished, ready, it seemed, to subside to an innings defeat; ready, humiliatingly, to go 2–0 down in a series only three matches old. Kim Hughes already had visions of himself as the latest proud owner of the Ashes. With three matches still to go his dream is now a long way from realisation.

The man who did most to fling logic the full length of the Kirkstall Lane was Ian Botham, with an innings that was the modern embodiment of Jessop. That blistering sustained attack on the Australian bowling turned the game upside down on Monday afternoon, but in spite of its magnificence it seemed at best a heroic gesture. If England were to have the slightest hope of winning another 50 or 60 runs would be needed yesterday and with only Willis left to support Botham that seemed unlikely.

Botham struck another four, his 27th of an unforgettable innings of 149, but Willis was not able to keep him company for much longer yesterday. A push forward at Alderman, an outside edge, a catch to second slip and Willis's resistance had ended, leaving Australia to score a modest 130 runs to win . . . a target to be treated with respect but not one surely to perturb unduly pragmatic Australians.

The Headingley crowd had seen the rebirth of Botham. They now saw Bob Willis peel away the years and give a display of pace bowling culled from his youth before the days of suspect, creaking knees. No one has tried harder for his country over the years.

His performance surpassed anything that he has produced in Test cricket previously. Throughout his spell he found movement, bounce, life and pace; too much pace for eight Australians. No Englishman has ever returned a more impressive set of figures at Headingley – eight for 43, an analysis to give Willis a glow of pride when he is 'old and grey and nodding by the fire'.

Willis is a laconic chap, except it seems, when he is asked on the television to give his views on the English press. He weighs questions carefully, delays the answer until you think he is not going to answer at all, and then usually produces some telling or humorous comment.

Did he think he would ever play Test cricket again when he left the West Indies in February for repair to a troublesome knee? 'I never thought I'd play cricket again, let alone Test cricket,' he replied. What motivates him? 'I want to keep playing for England. That sounds phoney, I know, but it's the truth.' Who could doubt that yesterday?

The Warwickshire captain is used to reading his obituary notice in the columns of national newspapers. If England had lost this game he might have expected to see it there again. But his desire to keep playing for England will now be fulfilled for a few more Tests yet.

Young pace bowlers with aspiration to an England place – the Allotts, Hughses and Newmans – will have to look elsewhere for a possible opening. This vacancy is definitely filled. As Brearley said: 'I didn't think Willis could still bowl like that. He surpassed himself.'

Ron Allsop tried and failed to produce a wicket at Trent Bridge that was fair to both batsmen and bowlers but would produce exciting cricket; Keith Boyce adopted a similar policy at Headingley and he too failed.

Everyone agreed, Willis even, that the wicket was loaded in favour of the bowlers. 'If you hit the cracks,' Willis said, 'the ball either squatted or went vertical.' But although here was a track that no batsman could trust there were surely, as Dyson, Hughes, and Yallop, Botham and Dilley had proved, surely 130 runs in it.

There was really no one else to whom Brearley could have given the new ball. It had to be Botham. His rich vein had to be tapped as long as possible and sure enough Botham raised English spirits by having Wood, who struck the first two balls from the Somerset all-rounder for four, caught at the wicket in the third over.

But no sooner had a back bone been established than it was snapped by a furious spell of bowling that brought Willis three wickets in 11 balls without a run scored off him.

England for the first time could entertain the audacious thought of a win while Australia must have suffered their first serious misgivings.

An awkward lifting delivery to the outside edge of Chappell's bat gave Taylor the second of the four catches which brought him the world record number of dismissals. Hughes, never comfortable, could not keep down a rising delivery that caught the throat of his bat and brought Botham to a fine, tumbling catch at third slip.

Yallop, also unable to angle his bat enough over another ball of chest height, was caught alertly by Gatting at short leg. At 58 for four, Australia must have felt for the first time like unwilling victims in a plot they had no power to resist.

Border, getting an inside edge to a delivery from Old that uprooted his leg stump, became the third Australian batsman successively to collect a duck and when the obdurate Dyson after two hours' solid resistance fell trying to hook Willis, Australia were 68 for six and sliding fast. With Willis pounding in from the Kirkstall Lane end, a bounce in his step and bent on destruction, there was no respite either.

Marsh might so easily have done for Australia what Botham on a much grander scale had achieved for England. He is a batsman who could have put the game back into Australian hands wih a few powerful swings of his woodcutter's arms.

Swing he did but only high down to fine leg, where Dilley, glancing down swiftly to make sure his feet were firmly inside the boundary line, judged a difficult catch to perfection.

Lawson, a promising batsman but still young, had neither the nerve nor the experience for the occasion and plodded fatally at Willis. Only two wickets remained and now 55 runs were needed and England, it seemed, astonishingly, would win with something to spare.

The margin in the end, however, was a mere 18 runs, and English followers could have stood nothing closer. Bright is a sound bat, Lillee is experienced, and between them – Lillee by unorthodox but perfectly justifiable methods, Bright by more legitimate means – whittled away the deficit until Lillee tried to hook Willis to the mid-wicket area but succeeded only in loping the ball up to mid-on, where Gatting took his second outstanding catch of the innings.

Botham was brought back and watched Old drop Alderman twice in an over before Willis, fittingly Willis, ripped out Bright's middle stump.

PAUL FITZPATRICK, *The Guardian*, 27 July 1981

Since 1981, there have been few similar performances for Englishmen to cherish. The nadir came in 1993, a series which introduced Shane Warne to an English audience and which proved to be the final visit to this country by Allan Border, who captained the side twelve years after he was a footnote in Botham and Willis's triumph. This time, however, Border was in the ascendant as Botham and Willis watched from the press box. England were a mess.

England on the Rocks

COMPARING the hapless Taylor and Gooch with the helpless Tory Prime Minister became a commonplace. In the previous year [1992], sterling had crashed out of the European Exchange Rate Mechanism, the Maastricht Treaty had split the ruling party and the pit-closure plan had pushed the Murdoch press into backing the miners. Amid recession, unemployment, homelessness, rising crime, cynicism towards virtually everyone in authority flourished. Politicians were distrusted and disliked almost as much as journalists, and even more than High Court judges and police. Yet this was an electorate that had returned a Tory government for the fourth time in succession only a year before.

Failure in the Ashes became even more resonant because the nation's leader was a certain type of English cricket lover: a little in awe of the game and the players, 'considerably' impressed by its ruling personnel and traditions, acknowledging with arch self-deprecation the frivolity of his eccentric but 'very English' passion. The lodestar of John Major's cricket memory was the golden summer of 1953, Coronation Year, when as a small boy he watched England regain the Ashes at the Oval under Len Hutton's leadership. When he became Prime Minister in 1990, the MCC allowed him to jump the membership queue.

On St George's Day in April 1993, Major gave what was intended to be a patriotic speech to a group of disgruntled Tory Euro-MPs. Echoing George Orwell, with radically different intent, he invoked 'the long shadows falling across the county ground, the warm beer, the invincible green suburbs, dog lovers and pool fillers . . . old maids bicycling to Holy Communion through the morning mist'. As the British economy wrestled with the demands of a global market, Major offered the governing party shelter in the cosy old England of county cricket. This was an England that did not exist, except, powerfully, in people's heads.

Major's real audience was in the suburbs, among voters no longer convinced that they were 'invincible'. Here 'the county ground' and the traditions of country life, including cricket, were ideological mantras to ward off the demons encroaching ever more menacingly from the crime-ridden, multi-racial, dispossessed inner cities.

It was not, however, an opportune moment to ask Tory voters to take comfort in the continuity of English cricket. During the previous twelve months, the Test side had been defeated at home by Pakistan and abroad by India and Sri Lanka. Now they were being humiliated by the Australians.

It was not just that England were losing but the way they were losing. The sheer scale of the defeats – by 179 runs at Old Trafford, by an innings and 48 runs at Headingley, by 8 wickets at Edgbaston – told only part of the story. England's bowlers – fourteen were employed during the series – were drubbed. The Australian batsmen knocked up one huge total after another – 632 for 4 at Lord's and 653 for 4 declared at Headingley (where the pitch was supposed to favour English bowlers). Altogether, they struck ten centuries, including four that surpassed 150 and one from wicket-keeper Ian Healy. The top seven in the order all averaged over 40 for the series. England could boast three centuries, two by Gooch, and only four averages over 40. In light of the absence for most of the series of Australia's principal strike bowler, Craig McDermott, after the first Test, the failure of the England batsmen seemed abject.

As a deracinated Marxist of American Jewish background, success for 'England' means little to me. But this abysmal humiliation, though carrying a perverse frisson, undermined the theatrical and creative aspects of the game. No one will look back on England's neurotic and joyless performance of 1993, as John Arlott looked back on the Ashes defeat of 1920, and sigh with satisfaction: 'That was a great year. England were murdered by Australia.' In the *Observer*, Scyld Berry described the Test side as 'resigned, exuding non-commitment, misfielding, hoping not expecting, a group of individuals each wanting to do well without common purpose'. The England cricketers seemed bowed down not just by the burden of losing, but even more by the burden of representing their country.

The responses to the Ashes failure of 1993 were bewilderingly contradictory. What gripped me during that summer was the way the innumerable claims and counter-claims, often vehement and extreme, echoed larger arguments over the plight of the nation.

English cricket plunged into one of its periodic frenzied mass hunts for scapegoats and saviours. The media, of course, were at the head of the pack. Soon after his arrival in May, Allan Border had declared, 'The English media are pricks.' Unlike the Pakistanis the year before, his Australians were spared the full treatment as the 'pricks' trained their sights on the home side.

As always, the first targets were the biggest and most visible: chairman of selectors Ted Dexter, team manager Keith Fletcher and captain Graham Gooch. The *Mirror* dubbed them 'the three stooges' and *The Sunday Times* 'the Board of Misdirectors'. The *Mirror* replied with a Cromwellian, 'Go, in the name of God, Go'. There was more to this than the familiar tabloid exercise of 'building them up to knock them down'. It reflected a deeper quest for heroes, for individual solutions to collective problems.

Selection policy was pilloried. As so often in recent English Test history, it had been inconsistent, panic-driven, at times defying any intelligible logic. Announcing his squad for the first Test at Old Trafford, Dexter proclaimed, 'We don't envisage chopping and changing.' By the end of the series, he had called up twenty-four players to represent the country, only just short of the record-breaking twenty-nine he had employed in 1989, his first year at the helm.

The selection of Foster at Lord's and Emburey at Edgbaston (retrograde moves which betrayed a lack of confidence in younger players), the suspicion of spin and reliance on medium pace, the use of Alec Stewart as a batsman–wicket-keeper, all came in for sharp criticism. However, the selectors, as ever, did respond to the pressure of public opinion, as orchestrated by the media. Lathwell and Caddick were chosen after glowing early-season notices, then dropped. Later, Malcolm, Watkin and Maynard came in after sustained media promotion. But the selectors were not prepared to give in to popular demands for a recall of David Gower, whose omission throughout the summer seemed motivated mainly by a desire on their part to save face. Spurned by England, at the end of the season Gower announced a premature retirement.

Gower became a martyr in a popular crusade against the Dexter–Gooch–Fletcher triumvirate. What drove the press wild was not merely the failure of the England side, but the refusal of any of the triumvirate to acknowledge or take responsibility for mistakes – an uncanny reflection of the Major government's attitude to the country's economic woes. Dexter's supercilious remark after the Lord's defeat was the final straw: 'We may be in the wrong sign or something. Venus may be in the wrong juxtaposition to somewhere else.' In other circumstances the media might have found in Dexter's unflappable complacency the stuff of a typically English national hero. Instead, 'Lord Ted' became a symbol of the unaccountability of the English cricket establishment, sleepwalking, like the government, to oblivion. When his resignation from the £40,000-a-year part-time post was announced during the final day of the fifth Test, the Edgbaston crowd cheered. 'GOOD RIDDANCE,' whooped the *Mirror*, catching the mood. During his regime, England had won 9 Tests, lost 21 and drawn 4.

Gooch, England captain during most of that time, had resigned two weeks earlier. His route to the top had been halting and circuitous. When he finally seized the prize in 1990, after the failure of all the other leading cricketers of his generation, he surprised many by raising his own batting and leading England to respectable performances against the West Indies, India and New Zealand as well as the final of the 1992 World Cup. But this was a false dawn, one of many in English cricket since the Packer revolt. After a poor series in India, Gooch was initially appointed captain only for the first three Ashes Tests. After the loss of the first, he insisted to the press, 'I haven't considered resigning and I don't think this is the right time to do so.' The England Committee then extended his appointment to all six Tests. 'It is now up to the rest of the team to learn from his example,' explained Dexter. After defeat in the second Test Gooch spoke of resigning 'if things don't improve'. However, he remained in post, ever more lugubrious, until defeat in the fourth Test, which ensured that the Ashes would stay with Australia. Asked why England kept losing, he replied, 'We are not playing very good cricket.' It was neither stupid nor evasive. It was simply that Gooch, like Dexter, was baffled by failure.

This applied even more to Keith Fletcher, on a five-year contract worth £250,000. Fletcher spent much of the Ashes series (his first summer in charge) complaining about pitches, balls going soft, net conditions and injuries. He seemed bereft of strategy, falling back, in the absence of any other ideas, on the routines which had served him well in county cricket. Fletcher had been the chosen successor of Micky Stewart, the first-ever England team manager, who had also schemed to ensure Gooch's succession to the captaincy. For many commentators, Dexter's greatest crime was to have betrayed his own amateur, cavalier heritage by giving free rein to Stewart's hard-nosed professionalism. Obsessed with 'preparation', Stewart had assembled an apparatus of coaches, scouts and fitness trainers never before seen in English cricket. The lax, dilettante days of the old amateurism were declared at an end. On taking up his newly-created post in 1988, Stewart declared: 'Life is competitive. We talk too much about learning to be good losers.' By the end of his tenure in 1992, his main accomplishment, many thought, was to have taught England's cricketers to be bad losers.

The scientific claims of the Stewart regime had been made to look hollow by the technical deficiencies exposed at the highest level of English cricket. Above all, the English bowlers appeared to have forgotten how to swing the ball. Swing, after all, was a great English tradition, as much the hallmark of English cricket as pace was for the West Indies or spin for India. E. W. Swanton, the conservative doyen of the cricket media, argued that there had been 'too much fitness training and not enough practice in the nets'. Ray Illingworth wanted more and better coaches.

Against the leg-spin of Australia's Shane Warne (who took 34 wickets at 25.79 runs apiece in the course of the series), the English batsmen were at sea, as they had been against the spinners in India earlier in the year. Warne's success only rubbed in the mystery of England's technical inadequacies. The demise of the arcane craft of leg-spin had been lamented for years by pundits who blamed it on flat pitches, the lbw law, the one-day game or lower seams. Here it was being practised, with relentless exuberance, by an overweight, bleach-blond Aussie beach boy. Warne had been kicked out of the much-admired Adelaide Cricket Academy and had spent the previous English summer playing League cricket in the North of England, drinking the Accrington club bar dry. He listed his favourite cricketers as Rod Marsh, Ian Botham and Ian Chappell, his favourite TV shows as 'Get Smart' and 'Gilligan's Island' (both of which he could know only from daytime reruns), his favourite films as *Rocky III*, *Caddyshack* and *Rambo* and admitted to having no favourite books because 'I've never read anything but sports books'. Warne showed that leg-spinners could flourish in all types of cricket and on all types of pitches. The ever-frustrated left-arm spinner Tufnell, who took five wickets for 63.80 in two Test appearances that summer, made a telling contrast to the easy-going Warne, a sublimely uncomplicated maestro of an infinitely complicated art.

Clearly, this crisis required more radical remedies than mere changes in personnel or a technical fix. But there was little agreement about what these should be. The 'England Committee' system associated with Stewart and his retinue came under fierce attack. It was seen as the malformed offspring of the out-of-control monster which the Test and County Cricket Board (TCCB) had become. Tony Greig declared himself 'speechless' after watching England lose the Ashes. 'Who are these people running English cricket?' he demanded. 'The chairmen of the counties should demand that people are made accountable for their actions . . . the counties are merely rubber-stamping decisions taken by some TCCB committee . . . The trouble is the real villains don't show their faces.' They could rail at Dexter and Fletcher all they liked, but Dexter and Fletcher were accountable only to the inner circle of the England Committee. The new-model TCCB had proved as insular and unresponsive as the old-fashioned MCC.

But was the problem with the TCCB that it was too professional or not professional enough? Was it too autocratic or too bureau-cratic? For Tony Lewis, the centralised TCCB concentrated too much power in too few hands. 'The county teams are the focus of local inspiration,' he insisted, calling on cricket supporters to 'blow the bureaucratic centre out of the water'.

In contrast, the medium-paced bowler and sometime journalist, Simon Hughes, denounced 'cumbersome selection committees . . . assemblies of fuddy-duddies mulling over trivialities'. His alterna-tive to the fuddy-duddies was clear-cut central leadership. Not for the first time, national sporting failure had brought out the author-itarian in the English soul. What English cricket needed, it was argued, was 'a supremo'. The current crop of weaklings had to be replaced with a single, strong man enjoying unfettered powers. Geoff Boycott, of course, was an advocate. Make Stewart captain ('he's a no-nonsense type') and get a 'hands-on, full-time supremo' – provided he wasn't Keith Fletcher. The problem for the support-ers of the supremo-strategy was that none of them could agree on who the supremo should be. Robin Marlar, the former Sussex amateur and *Sunday Times* cricket columnist, went so far as to propose that Trevor Bailey, at the age of sixty-nine, 'should have been called up and charged with recovering national pride'.

Marlar, a right-wing Tory, saw the crisis in English cricket – 'more serious than any of us can remember' – as a replay of the dark days of the last Labour government. 'The TCCB reminds me of Jaguar in the mid-'70s.' He proposed that Norman Tebbit or Iain MacLaurin, Chairman of Tesco plc, should take over as TCCB chairman, with Ian Botham, of all people, as team manager. The new leadership would then be given *carte blanche* to refashion cricket on a corporate model, as Marlar's party had tried to refashion the country in the 1980s.

Marlar's contempt for the public sector was shared by many of his foes in the TCCB. The decline of cricket in state schools became another of the summer's recurring themes. Left-wing Labour local authorities, it was alleged, discouraged competitive sports and were hostile to individual excellence. Better-informed observers attributed the decline to other factors, not least among them Tory education policies – under-investment, the national curriculum, the steady alienation of the teaching profession and the selling off of local sports grounds.

But for others, the problem was that the money-maddened TCCB had cursed the English game with crass commercialism. Symbolising the sale of English cricket's soul to the highest bidder were the sponsor's logos painted on the outfield grass. 'These logos remain a damn eyesore,' complained Scyld Berry. 'I do wish English tolerance would not extend to letting them get away with it.' Yes, he recognised the financial argument, but cricket's 'whole *raison d'être* is violated by reality's intrusion into the escape world of the play'. He called for a boycott of the sponsors' products.

Along with the critique of commercialism and in reaction against the mechanistic hyper-professionalism of the Stewart regime, there emerged a call for a return to amateurism. Bill Deedes reminded *Telegraph* readers: 'It was the amateur in cricket who showed the young how to play the game for enjoyment and he has gone.'

Like Harold Macmillan decrying privatisation as 'selling off the family silver', Deedes lamented schools selling off playing fields. But the hankering after amateurism was not confined to the old Tory grandees. Even Brian Close, who had been a victim of the hypocrisies of the amateur brigade twenty-five years earlier, joined the chorus. As ever in England, escape from the dilemmas of the present is sought in the past.

MIKE MARQUSEE, *Anyone but England*, 1994

But it is easier to carp and cavil, as 'Giglamps' saw.

THE MEN WHO PLAY FOR ENGLAND

The men who play for England
    Are apt to make mistakes
Against O'Reilly and McCabe
    Or Grimmett's hidden breaks.
And when their innings closes
    They throw away the match
By bowling short or bowling wide,
And sometimes when the ball is skied
    They fail to make the catch.

The men who pick for England
    Are either fools or cranks.
They put in Binks of Middlesex
    Instead of Jinks of Lancs.
While those who captain England
    Are void of vital flair:
They get the bowling in a mess,
They place more slips instead of less –
    And long-stops far too square!

The men who write for England
    Are cast in finer mould.
They deal (what mastery of style!)
    With every ball that's bowled.
At once they place a fielder
    To counter Ponsford's glance,
And though the catching of the side
Is weak – 'just as I prophesied' –
    They never miss a chance.

THE ASHES

The men who bowl for England
  Are sometimes known to tire,
And under-pitch and over-toss
  And lack their early fire.
But those who write for England
  Go on from strength to strength;
They send us for the 'close of play'
Ten thousand words each blessed day,
  And never lose their length.

'GIGLAMPS',
The Morning Post, c.1934

*'I have again refused
an lbw appeal from
F. S. Trueman'*

THE GREATS

W. G. Grace

THROUGH W. G. Grace, cricket, the most complete expression of popular life in pre-industrial England, was incorporated into the life of the nation. As far as any social activity can be the work of any one man, he did it. Perhaps the best way to introduce him is to tabulate what he did. He did not merely bring over what he inherited. Directly and indirectly he took what he found and re-created it. It is not certain that the game would so easily and quickly have gained and held its place without the technical transformation and the *réclame* he gave to it. This total success might have come in a different way. It came his way, at the perfect historical moment, and it came completely. Any extended cricket analysis which is not based on historical facts or the technique of the game tells more about the writer than what he is writing about. Let us begin, therefore, unusually, with his influence on bowling.

It is a cricket commonplace that he killed the professional fast bowling of the sixties. For twenty years a line of fast bowlers dominated play. On the many rough wickets of the day they were often unplayable. W.G. so mastered them that after a time they were almost afraid to bowl within his reach. Looking back, one of the players wondered how he escaped being permanently maimed or killed. In 1857, against some of the fastest bowlers of the day, on the always lively Lord's wicket, Reginald Hankey for the Gentlemen

68

played an innings which immeditely became famous, and has remained so to this day. He made only 70. W.G. first played for the Gentlemen in 1865, not yet seventeen. Beginning in 1871 he scored against the players, in consecutive innings, 217, 77 and 112, 163, 158 and 70. He put an end to the brute strength which had survived from the previous era. Even in those days bowling was in the hands more of professionals than amateurs. To deal with W.G. the professional bowlers had to develop new skills, new arts. Chiefly they learned from the Australians, but it is ironical that W.G. himself was one of the pioneers of change.

He had been one of the fast slingers and a very successful one. As he grew older and wickets began to get better he bowled slow round the wicket. As late as 1887 A. G. Steel calls him the best change bowler in England 'bar none'. Eight years later, when he is three years short of fifty, he bowls Ranjitsinhji, well set, with the first ball he bowls to him. Ranjitsinhji repeats the 1887 judgment of Steel. The same critic discusses the new phenomenon of balls curling in the air and prophesies that when the practice is perfected it will make batting more difficult than ever. Among those he mentions as being able to do the new trick is W. G. Grace. Steel, Ranjitsinhji, Pelham Warner. They cover a long period in the history of cricket; what between them they do not know is not knowledge. This is Sir Pelham Warner writing many years after, in fact in the memorial biography:

> Of all the feats I witnessed by W.G., the one that most surprised me was a bowling one. It was in 1902 – he was then nearly fifty-four – against the Australians when Trumper was at his very best. The Old Man took the ball and I thought we were in for it. Instead the Australians were – five for 29; marvellously baffling, too, not a pinch of luck to help an analysis of which Tom Richardson would have been proud.

This is the bowling record of the greatest batsman the world has ever known, the creator of modern batting. (He was, by the way, in his younger days, the greatest all-round fieldsman of his time.) His bowling record tells us much about him. His greatest gift was in his head, where resided a genius for the game. He had a general's rapid eye. He saw a boy of eighteen batting at the nets one day at Lord's in 1906 and asked who he was. George Challenor from the West Indies, he was told. 'Take note of him,' said W.G. 'You will hear of him one day.' His marvellous physique was a priceless asset, but it was the lesser half, and later I shall examine this phrase, colossal physique, so glibly used.

W.G.'s batting figures, remarkable as they are, lose all their true significance unless they are seen in close relation with the history of cricket itself and the social history of England. Unless you do this you fall head foremost into the trap of making comparisons with Bradman. Bradman piled up centuries. W.G. built a social organization.

Despite the impression of continuity and expansion which the histories of cricket give, there is little evidence to show that it was widely played or that it was a common public entertainment before the decade in which W.G. first appeared. The histories will say that the University match has been played since 1827. Yet up to 1862 (only 100 years ago) the Oxford University Cricket Club was run by three treasurers, no one knew exactly who was to collect the eleven and, *mirabile dictu,* there was never a definite captain. There were often two captains, both directing the field and changing the bowling; each of the treasurers had some sort of right, *ex officio,* to play in the eleven, even to the exclusion of better players. One conclusion is inescapable – such doings were responsible to no public interest or public opinion. Cricket at Cambridge was not quite so haphazard but only that. Of the counties only Surrey had been long established. W.G.'s own county, Gloucestershire, was formally founded only in 1871. Despite the long and famous record of Hampshire cricketers, the Hampshire County Cricket Club was founded only in 1863 and it was twenty years before the cricket of this county was established on a sound footing. The Lancashire county club came into existence only in 1864. The same decade saw the birth of Middlesex and Yorkshire. Most indicative is the history of so famous a cricketing county as Kent. Late in the century it was once more organised and then had no more than 300 members. There is no need to go through the list. When in 1871 W.G. made 2,739 runs, with an average of 78.9, he played but five matches for Gloucestershire and one of these was against M.C.C. and Ground. His season comprised matches against the Players, for South *v.* North, for Gentlemen of the South *v.* Players of the South. One of the early Australian teams advertised in the papers for fixtures. A county championship was organised only in 1873. The whole imposing structure and organisation of first-class cricket as we know it today we owe to W.G. The crowds flocked to see him play.

Batsmen followed in his footsteps and became great. He swelled the treasuries of the counties and earned thousands of pounds for professionals in benefit matches.

Most dramatically, he had sprung on to the field fully fledged. He blew a note to signal that he had arrived, and no brass band or orchestra could keep up with him. In 1864, brought by his older brother Henry from South Wales to play against Surrey in London and against Gentlemen of Sussex at Hove, he made only 5 and 38 at the Oval, and his captain wanted to drop him. He was saved by the protests of his brother Henry. The boy made 170 and 56 not out, the second score against the clock. The next season he scored five centuries, including a 224. In two years, not yet twenty years old, he was the greatest batsman in England, scoring as no one had ever scored before and batting as no one had ever batted before. He was news, and as he continually broke all precedents (even his own) before he had passed the middle twenties, each amazing new performance told the public, cricketing and otherwise, that here was one of those rare phenomena, something that had never been seen before and was not likely to be seen again.

In 1868 he scored a century in each innings of a match. This had been done once, and as long ago as fifty years past. When he made 2,739 runs in a season no batsman had ever made 2,000. No wonder the record stood unbroken for twenty years. In that year the batsman second to him made about half as many as W.G.'s total. To visualise what he did and the impression it made we must imagine a contemporary batsman making over 5,000 runs in a season, with an average of 200. In 1874 he made 1,000 runs and took 100 wickets, the first man ever known to do so. In 1876 he scored the first 300 ever made in first-class cricket. This was in the East, in Canterbury, on August 11th and 12th. He travelled by train to the West and on the 14th he made 177 for Gloucestershire against Notts. He set off to the North and at Sheffield against Yorkshire made another 300. In seven days, covering ground like some Alexander, he had made 839 runs. In 1880 the first Test match against Australia in England was played. England won by five wickets, Grace 152. He went twice to Australia, where he often faced conditions as bad if not worse than those of the Hambledon men 100 years before. No matter. He was the champion there as well as on the perfect Oval turf. He was only thirty-one when he was the recipient of a national testimonial including a cheque for nearly £1,500. He created the technique of the modern game and he created the arena in which it could thrive. The county clubs and the organisation of cricket as a national institution followed in his wake. Of how many Englishmen in the nineteenth century could anything similar be said?

What manner of man was he? The answer can be given in a single sentence. He was in every respect that mattered a typical representative of the pre-Victorian Age.

The evidence for it abounds. His was a Gloucestershire country father who made a good wicket in the orchard and the whole family rose at dawn to get in a few hours of cricket. Their dogs were trained to act as retrievers. They organised clubs and played matches all over their part of the country. W.G. was taking part from the time he was nine. It is 1857, but one is continually reminded of Tom Brown's childhood thirty years before. The back-swording, running and wrestling have been replaced by a game which provides all that these gave in a more organised manner befitting a new age. But the surroundings are the same, the zest, the concentration, the desire to excel, are the same. The Grace family make their own ground at home. I am only surprised that they did not make their own bats, there must have been much splicing and binding. If they try to play according to established principles, well, the father is a trained man of science. Four sons will become doctors. The wicket the father makes is a good one. The boys are taught to play straight. With characteristically sturdy independence, one brother hits across and keeps on hitting across. They let him alone while W.G. and G.F. are encouraged to stick to first principles. Such live and let live was not the Victorian method with youth.

W.G.'s fabulous stamina was not a gift from the gods. Boys of the Grace clan once walked seven miles to school in the morning, seven miles home for lunch, seven miles back to school and seven miles home in the evenings. Decadence was already creeping in and made this seem excessive. So the midday fourteen miles was cut out. That was the breed, reared in the pre-Victorian days before railways. He was not the only pre-Victorian in the family. His elder brother E.M. was even more so than he. The records show that the family in its West Gloucestershire cricketing encounters queried, disputed and did not shrink from fisticuffs. To the end of their days E.M. and W.G. chattered on the field like magpies. Their talking at and even to the batsman was so notorious that young players were warned against them. They were uninhibited with each other and could be furious at fraternal slights or mistakes. They were uninhibited in general. The stories of W.G. which prove this are among the best about him. There is room here for only one.

W.G. enquired about a new bowler from the opposing captain and was told enigmatically, 'He mixes them up.' The Old Man watched the newcomer carefully for a few overs. Then he hit him far away and as he ran between the wickets shouted to his partner: 'Run up. Run up. We'll mix 'em up for him. We'll mix 'em up for him.' It is quite impossible even to imagine anyone shouting such a remark in a big match today. It was most probably out of place already when W.G. made it.

In his attitude to book-learning he belonged entirely to the school of the pre-Arnold Browns. He rebuked a fellow player who was always reading in the dressing-rooms: 'How do you expect to score if you are always reading?' Then follows this priceless piece of ingenuous self-revelation: 'I am never caught that way.' It would be idle to discount the reputation he gained for trying to diddle umpires, and even on occasions disputing with them. He is credited with inducing a batsman to look up at the sun to see a fictitious flight of birds and then calling on the bowler to send down a fast one while the victim's eyes were still hazy. Yet I think there is evidence to show that his face would have become grave and he would have pulled at his beard if a wicket turned out to be prepared in a way that was unfair to his opponents. Everyone knows such men, whom you can trust with your life, your fortune and your sacred honour, but will peep at your cards when playing bridge at a penny a hundred. His humours, his combativeness, his unashamed wish to have it his own way on the field of play, his manoeuvres to encompass this, his delight when he did, his complaints when he didn't, are the rubs and knots of an oak that was sound through and through. Once only was he known to be flustered, and that was when he approached the last few runs of his hundredth century. All who played with him testify that he had a heart of gold, loyal, generous to the end of his life, ready to place his knowledge, his experience and his time at the disposal of young players, even opponents. He is all of one piece, of the same family as the Browns with whom Thomas Hughes begins his book.

We can sum up. W.G. seems to have been one of those men in whom the characteristics of life as lived by many generations seemed to meet for the last, in a complete and perfectly blended whole. His personality was sufficiently wide and firm to include a strong Victorian streak without being inhibited. That I would say was his greatest strength. He was not in any way inhibited. What he lacked he would not need. All that he had he could use. In tune with his inheritance and his environment, he was not in any way repressed. All his physical and spiritual force was at his disposal to do what he wanted to do. He is said on all sides to have been one of the most typical of Englishmen, to have symbolised John Bull, and so on and so forth. To this, it is claimed, as well as to his deeds, he owed his enormous popularity. I take leave to doubt it. The man usually hailed as representative is never quite typical, is more subtly compounded than the plain up-and-down figure of the stock characteristics. Looking on from outside and at a distance it seems to me that Grace gives a more complex impression than is usually attributed to him. He was English undoubtedly, very much so. But he was typical of an England that was being superseded. He was the yeoman, the country doctor, the squire, the England of yesterday. But he was no relic, nor historical or nostalgic curiosity. He was pre-Victorian in the Victorian Age but a pre-Victorian militant.

There he was using his bat like an axe, building as much of that old world as possible into the new, and fabulously successful at it. The more simple past was battling with the more complex, more dominant present, and the present was being forced to yield ground and make room. In any age he would have been a striking personality and vastly popular. That particular age he hit between wind and water. Yet, as in all such achievements, he could conquer only by adopting methods of the new.

Cricket is an art. Like all arts it has a technical foundation. To enjoy it does not require technical knowledge, but analysis that is not technically based is mere impressionism. That W.G. was a pre-Victorian who made a pre-Victorian game a part of the Victorian era appears nowhere so clearly as in the technique he introduced. It had the good fortune (rare with him) to be beautifully stated.

It is as a batsman that he is best known and surely what he did would take its place in the co-ordination which seeks to plot the process by which the arts develop. Batsmen before him were content to specialise in what suited them best. One great player used the forward style. Another was distinguished for his mastery of back-play. Equally the cut as the leg-hit had its particular exponents. There were aggressive players and players defensive. There were players who were good on good wickets. There were others at their best on bad. Whether on the village green or at Lord's, this was in essence cricket of the age of Browns.

Practically from his very first appearance W.G. put an end to all categorisation. He used all the strokes, he played back or forward, aggressively or defensively, as the circumstances or the occasion required. As he approached forty he confessed to preferring a good slow wicket to a good fast one. In his prime it did not matter to him and in these days when a jumping or turning wicket is regarded as reversal of the order of nature, he shares with Victor Trumper and J. B. Hobbs the distinction of being batsmen who at their best were least concerned about the state of the pitch. The crowd at Lord's once rose at him for stopping four shooters in succession. In 1896 on a wicket at Sheffield Park the Australian fast bowler Jones frightened out a magnificent batting side. The batsmen went in with the obvious intention of getting out as fast as possible. W.G., then forty-eight, shared with F. S. Jackson the only batting honours of the day. This then, in the classic passage from Ranjitsinhji's *Jubilee Book of Cricket*, was his achievement. I give it in full.

Before W.G. batsmen were of two kinds, a batsman played a forward game or he played a back game. Each player, too, seems to have made a specialty of some particular stroke. The criterion of style was, as it were, a certain mixed method of play. It was bad cricket to hit a straight ball; as for pulling a slow long-hop, it was regarded as immoral. What W.G. did was unite in his mighty self all the good points of all the good players, and to make utility the criterion of style. He founded the modern theory of batting by making forward- and back-play of equal importance, relying neither on the one nor on the other, but on both. Any cricketer who thinks for a moment can see the enormous change W.G. introduced into the game. I hold him to be, not only the finest player born or unborn, but the maker of modern batting. He turned the old one-stringed instrument into a many-chorded lyre. And, in addition, he made his execution equal his invention. All of us now have the instrument, but we lack his execution. It is not that we do not know, but that we cannot perform. Before W.G. batsmen did not know what could be made of batting. The development of bowling has been natural and gradual; each great bowler has added his quota. W.G. discovered batting; he turned its many narrow straight channels into one great winding river. Anyone who reads his book will understand this. Those who follow may or may not get within measurable distance of him, but it was he who pioneered and made the road. Where a great man has led, many can go afterwards, but the honour is his who found and cut the path. The theory of modern batting is in all essentials the result of W.G.'s thinking and working on the game.

The age of the Browns is left behind. What they had created is now organised and sublated. Note particularly the words 'thinking and working on the game': remember what he added to bowling. We can be so dazzled by the splendours of his youth that we are apt to forget the mental labours that made him what he was and kept him there.

It is not merely that he cleared the road along which all succeeding batsmen have travelled. He met and conquered such a succession of conditions and bowlers, strategy and tactics, as it has never fallen to the lot of any batsman to face. Late in life he met the googly and was said to be troubled by it. Sir Donald Bradman claims that O'Reilly was a greater bowler than George Lohmann, because O'Reilly bowled the googly and Lohmann did not. All such reasonings and ratings are low tide against the rock of Grace's batsmanship. Trumper used to say that if you got to the pitch of the ball it did not matter which way it was breaking. In his early days W.G. also used to run out of his crease and hit the slow bowlers all over the place. No batsman was more scientific than W.G. and science was his servant, not his master. He was not one who by unusual endowment did stupendously what many others were doing well. He did what no one else had ever done, developed to a degree unprecedented, and till then undreamt of, potentialities inherent in the game. And it was this more than anything else which made possible W.G.'s greatest achievement. It was by modern scientific method that this pre-Victorian lifted cricket from a more or less casual pastime into the national institution which it rapidly became. Like all truly great men, he bestrides two ages. It is at the very least obvious that he was not the rather simple-minded smiter of a cricket ball which is the usual portrayal of him.

So far the best that has been said of W.G. as an historical personage is this, by a bishop:

Had Grace been born in Ancient Greece the *Iliad* would have been a different book. Had he lived in the Middle Ages he would have been a Crusader and would now have been lying with his legs crossed in some ancient abbey, having founded a great family. As he was born when the world was older, he was the best known of all Englishmen and the King of that English game least spoilt by any form of vice.

At least it is not unworthy of its subject. Which is precisely why it does W.G. the greatest injustice of all.

When the bishop implies that W.G.'s gifts would have served him a more distinguished place in another age he did at least put his finger on the heart of the matter. My contention is that no crusader was more suited to his time than was W.G. to his own; none rendered more service to his world. No other age that I know of would have been able to give him the opportunities the Victorian Age gave him. No other age would have been able to profit so much by him. In the end judgment depends not on what you think of Grace but on the role you give to sports and games in the lives of modern people. As usual, it is Mr Neville Cardus, in his vivid darting style, who has got closest to W.G.: 'The plain, lusty humours of his first practices in a Gloucestershire orchard were to be savoured throughout the man's gigantic rise to a national renown.' Only it was not the plain, lusty humours of an orchard, but of a whole way of life. 'He rendered rusticity cosmopolitan whenever he returned to it. And always did he cause to blow over the fashionable pleasances of St. John's. . . .' There they needed it least. It was to bleak Sheffield, to dusty Kennington and to grim Manchester that W.G. brought the life they had left behind. The breezes stirred by his bat had blown in their faces, north, south and east, as well as in the west.

We have peered below the surface at what W.G. did for the people. When we try to find what the people did for him we begin with a blank sheet. They went to see him, they cheered him on the field, they walked behind him in the streets. It is accepted that the athlete, the entertainer, the orator, is spurred to excel himself by the applause and excitement of his audience. We apostrophise his marvellous physique. There was more to it than muscle and sinew.

We have seen the state of cricket when he began, with its first tentative attempts at county, not even national, organisation. He loved the game passionately and always served it. The proof is in the fact that all the success and all the adulation never turned his head. As he made his tremendous scores he could see the game visibly growing and expanding around him. In 1857 the Cricketers' Fund Friendly Society was started. It could not supply the requirements of the ever-growing body of professionals. W.G. was greatly in demand to play in benefit matches. Their success depended on him and in them he was always at his best. In 1871 he played in three and scored 189 not out, 268 and 217. Thus stimulated by a specific need, he obviously mobilised himself specially to satisfy it. When he made his first triple century in Kent, followed it with a century not out in Gloucestershire and took guard in Yorkshire, I do not see him as merely judging the length, driving and cutting, his personal powers supplying the resources. Such records are not built on such limited premises. He was strong with the strength of men who are filling a social need. Every new achievement made a clearing in the forest, drew new layers of the population, wiped off debts, built pavilions. How warmly the county secretaries and treasurers must have met him at the gates; how happy his fellow Gentlemen must have looked in the dressing-room as they prepared to add another victory over the Players to atone for their long list of defeats; how the crowds must have roared as they saw his gigantic figure with the red-and-yellow cap and black beard emerge from the pavilion to start an innings. The point is that whatever his fatigue, he could not take notice of it. The crowds and the people made of every innings a Test innings. Professor Harbage has boldly written that half the credit for Shakespeare's plays must go to the skilled artisans, the apprentices and the law students (the groundlings), who for twenty years supported him and Burbage against all rivals. Anyone who has participated in an electoral campaign or observed closely key figures in it will have noted how a speaker, eyes red with sleeplessness and sagging with fatigue, will rapidly recover all his power at an uproarious welcome from an expectant crowd. If Grace could be so often and so long at his best it was because so much depended on it, so many hundreds of thousands of people, high and low, were expecting him to be at his best, even to exceed it, as he had so often done in the past. Except for commonplaces and pseudo-scientific misuse of terms (father image), we know as yet very little of the nourishment given to the hero by the crowd. Here it must have been very great – Grace's career was exceptionally long. At times he must have been very tired of it all. Once he even thought of retiring. He didn't. Such a decision could not rest on his individual judgment or inclination.

In the spring of 1895 he was nearly forty-seven. He had scored 98 centuries. Not merely he but the whole country was wondering if, how and when he would add the other two. Eighteen-ninety-four had been a miserable year for everybody. He had scored as well as most of the others, with a total of 1293 runs, average 29·38, number of centuries three. Only Brockwell with five had scored more. In fact, except for Robert Abel, no one else had scored as many. The centuries scored in the season were 52, no one had scored over 200, there were only five innings which totalled over 400. There had been years in which the Old Man had scored no century at all. His county, Gloucestershire, formerly at the top, was now often at the bottom of the list. As usual he started to practise in March and ran into form early. A whole season and just two more centuries! He had the habit of rising to the occasion and then shooting far above it.

I do not propose to recapitulate in any detail what he did in May. Those who know it know it by heart. Those who don't could spend time worse than in finding out. What I want to stress is that in the words of H. D. G. Leveson-Gower: 'Nothing W. G. Grace ever did, nothing any other champion at any other game ever achieved such widespread and well deserved enthusiasm as his batting in May, 1895, when he was in his forty-eighth year and so burly in figure.'

Burly as the figure was, it was sustained and lifted higher than ever before by what has been and always will be the most potent of all races in our universe – the spontaneous, unqualified, disinterested enthusiasm and goodwill of a whole community. The spontaneity was only in appearance. Once he had scored the 99th century in the second match of the season, the thirty years of public service and personal achievement gathered themselves together in the generations, willing him to complete the edifice with a crown worthy of it and of them. He did not keep them long. Two modest innings against Yorkshire alone intervened before a magnificent 283. Followed 257 and 73 not out against Kent when he was on the field for every minute of the game, and on the last playing day of May he reached and passed the thousand runs, the first player in the game ever to do so. (It gives us an insight into his mind that in deference to his weight and age he scored heavily by hitting balls on the wicket or outside the off-stump over to the on-side.)

Never since the days of the Olympic champions of Greece has the sporting world known such enthusiasm and never since. That is accepted and it is true and it is important – I am the last to question that. What I take leave to ask even at such a moment is this: On what other occasion, sporting or non-sporting, was there ever such enthusiasm, such an unforced sense of community, of the universal merged in an individual? At the end of a war? A victorious election?

With its fears, its hatreds, its violent passions? Scrutinise the list of popular celebrations, the unofficial ones; that is to say, those not organised from above. I have heard of no other that approached this celebration of W.G.'s hundredth century. If this is not social history what is? It finds no place in the history of the people because the historians do not begin from what people seem to want but from what they think the people ought to want.

He finished as grandly as he had begun. That year of 1895 he made nine centuries. Abel was next with five and all the others made fewer still. Next year he was one of the three who scored over 2,000 runs and he made another triple century. As late as 1902 he was still high on the list of heavy scorers for the season. On his fifty-eighth birthday he played for the Gentlemen at the Oval. He made 74 and hit a ball out of the ground. When he hit a stroke for three he could only run one, and the runs were worth a century. Of all his innings this is the one I would choose to see. He had enriched the depleted lives of two nations and millions yet to be born. He had extended our conception of human capacity and in doing all this he had done no harm to anyone. He is excluded from the history books of his country. No statue of him exists.[1] Yet he continues warm in the hearts of those who never knew him. There he is safe until the whole crumbling edifice of obeisance before Mammon, contempt for Demos and categorising intellectualism finally falls apart.

C. L. R. JAMES, Beyond a Boundary, 1963

As befits an outstanding historian, C. L. R. James understands W. G. Grace as a man of his times and a man who shapes history. But he was also human and he was also known for his duplicity.

A S well as demonstrating his durability and courage, Grace was the beneficiary of further dubious umpiring decisions. When he had made only six, he appeared to be caught and bowled. It seemed so clearly out that, at first, no one bothered to appeal. When W.G., who thought it was a bump ball, stood his ground Mead appealed and the umpire, George Burton, gave him out. W.G. roared, 'What, George?' and Burton changed his mind. In W.G.'s defence, Burton's view was obscured by the bowler and Cyril Sewell, the other batsman, thought W.G. was correct.

[1] The Grace gates at Lord's, with its chaste inscription, 'To William Gilbert Grace, the great cricketer,' is the nearest he has come to a monument.

As angry as the rest of the Essex team, Kortright now bowled as fast as he had ever done. With Gloucestershire on 96–3, he reached within himself for one more lethal salvo. First, he trapped W.G. plumb lbw, but the umpire, presumably totally cowed by now, declined to give it. Grace edged the next one to give a catch behind, but again the umpire was the only other man on the field not to see or hear it. Infuriated, Kortright pounded in and produced an unplayable ball which knocked two of Grace's stumps out of the ground, one of them cartwheeling through the air and landing yards away. W.G. was one short of his half-century. As he slowly turned to leave the crease, the triumphant Kortright approached and remarked: 'Surely you're not going, Doctor – there's still one stump standing.'

ROBERT LOW, *W.G.*, 1997

Next to W.G. in cricket's pantheon stands Sir Donald Bradman. His importance to Australian cricket, and Australia itself as the country struggled with the depression of the twenties, is equal to that of Grace. The Australian writer, Ray Robinson, looks at the legend of Bradman.

Sir Donald Bradman

FULL justice has never been done Don Bradman, outstanding batsman between two World Wars and, maybe, since the Wars of the Roses (we know that Nelson had a good eye and Marlborough was never at a loss in the field, but evidence is lacking whether either of those lesser heroes could hook from outside the off stump).

If the countless columns and chapters published about Bradman were placed end-to-end they would stretch, on a still day, from the pavilion end to Puckapunyal, and would reach beyond the bounds of credibility. To begin with, no writer of schoolboy fiction would have dared to credit his hero with performances so astonishing: a hundred in his opening first-class match; 236 in his first match in England; first visiting batsman to score 1,000 before the end of May;

131 in his first Test match in England; 254 in his first Test at Lord's; 105 before lunch and 309 in one day at Leeds a fortnight later (all before he turned 22); and so on until in his 190th first-class match he scored his 93rd century.

His successes are enough to make a United States Air Force Communiqué seem like an understatement. Around these astonishing deeds is being woven the Bradman legend, the legend of the cricketer who, in the year the war began, was given 21 lines in *Who's Who* – only eight fewer than Hitler, and 17 more than Stalin.

There is much in the contention that no history is so true as the legend, the people's impression of a man or event, which is handed down and survives, unencumbered by precise detail or cold, obscuring fact - some anecdote, fable or even a phrase which, though inexact in itself, is more revealing than whole sheets of verified data. Drake is, rightly, better known for the tale that he finished a game of bowls before tackling the Great Armada than for his outstanding feat of seamanship, circumnavigation of the world. Many who know little of the lives of the great composers, and are more familiar with the *Footlight Serenade* than the *Moonlight Sonata*, have been struck by the wonder of a Beethoven creating music after he could not hear a note.

The legend of W. G. Grace, founder of modern batting and 43 years a first-class cricketer, owes much to a bushy beard, which played no part in adding even a snicked single to his scores, and to his artfulness in fooling umpires – all the more comic because he didn't need to.

The legend of Don Bradman, though it will hinge on his unprecedented run-getting, will not be fashioned from score-sheets, averages and aggregates alone. If that were so, it would be too impersonal – the sort of thing that someone who never saw him could put together. It would lack enough flesh and blood to live. Embalmed with decimal points, it would be entombed between the covers of books, to be exhumed only when some later champion rivalled or surpassed the records. The living legend will be a fusion of reminiscence, a montage from the mass-impressions of those who have watched Bradman, admired his skill, marvelled at him and been puzzled and shocked by him.

What has been written about Bradman will have some influence on this. But most of it leaves an impression wholly preposterous: it leaps from crag to crag, with no more than a passing glance into the valleys and rarely a peep into the ravines. This is partly because of the urgency of the efforts of the Press to serve cricket piping-hot from the pitch. Even reports that are not read until next morning have to be lodged by a deadline that leaves little time for rumination. Another reason is that some newspapers entrust cricket reporting to men with no more qualification than that they write about football in winter, or have become known to the public as boxing or tennis critics, or have proved their flair for sport by beating the news editor at darts.

One of London's largest-selling dailies published a front-page story of Verity's triumph against the Australians on the Monday of the 1934 Test at Lord's, with never a word about the state of the wicket after heavy rain in the night. Unless those who read that account had watched the match or had seen another newspaper, they were left to guess an answer to the seemingly-insoluble riddle of how a bowler who had taken only two Australian wickets for 113 in the preceding Test, a fortnight earlier, had suddenly developed the knack of getting 14 for 80 in one day.

Anyway, regardless of writing against the clock, and blind spots here and there on the Press benches, cricket was not invented merely so that a Bradman, a Hammond or a Hutton could play it. When a great cricketer falls below his customary standard, or is on view only briefly, the spotlight moves on to whoever are the heroes of the day. Few would want it deflected from the action of the play for an autopsy of an innings that died of natural causes.

Then there have been a few Australian lily-gilders who, over-zealously observing the newspaper rule about catering for the public's inclination for hero-worship, have avoided or played down anything about Bradman that they imagined might impair the build-up (which never needed bolstering).

It is the cumulative effect of all this emphasis on success, with so little counterweight, that presents an unreal picture of Bradman as something superhuman, not of this world. Like a trick mirror at a seaside fun park, it distorts him to the point of giving the impression that, unlike mortals, 'tis in him to command success – excepting only the occasional twists and turns of the luck of the game, which are beyond the control of even a batsman above human fallibility.

The future student of cricket history may easily be set wondering why Don ever got out – unless it were from boredom with run-making – and what could have gone astray to prevent his scoring 100, 200, 300 or more every time. Many who have seen him only a few times and know him only as a small, alert figure in flannels or a smiling face in a photograph probably wonder the same way.

Bradman has been over-simplified to the public, like Hitler, Petain, blitzkrieg, non-aggression pacts, and other notabilities and events which superceded him in the headlines. It has all been made to look so easy for him, as if he were a cricketing counterpart of those Hollywood film stars who are never called on to do anything except smile, burst into song and canoodle comely leading ladies.

That is why Bradman has not been done full justice. It has not been a pushover for him. The impression that he is an unemotional gatherer of easily-won triumphs is false. He is far from being like a piece of mass-production machinery, without the hopes and anxieties, the exultations and despairs, that others feel.

To understand him properly, you have to get down from the peaks to the lower levels of his career. Chief result of this mountaineering is to heighten the wonder of his deeds and to discover that he is an even more remarkable batsman than is commonly thought. It has given me a firmer-based esteem for his qualities than could be built on a foundation of blind hero-worship or local patriotism. When isolated happenings, sometimes unexplained, are fitted together they make a pattern which leads to a truer valuation of his unparalleled achievements, too often taken for granted.

RAY ROBINSON, *Between the Wickets*, 1946

Even those whose teams were put to the sword by Bradman could only marvel at his singlemindedness. A. A. Thomson writes of his record at Headingley.

AND now, as the old novelists would say, we approach the incredible. The incredible is Bradman, who for nearly twenty years bestrode our petty world like a Colossus. The records show that he broke records everywhere, but he must have had an especial affection for Leeds. Looking back from 1948 to 1930, when his onslaughts began, he might well have been regarded as Leeds's most eminent citizen of the period, with a statue in City Square beside the Black Prince, and mounted not on a handsome bronze charger, but on a chain-gang of English bowlers, *couchant*. Sir Donald's knighthood was richly deserved on any grounds; it would have been well merited on one ground alone: Headingley, services to entertainment, at.

In 1930, on the first of his Test appearances at Headingley, he scored 334 in 375 minutes. That was Bradman's way. Where most batsmen would be happy with one hundred and elated with two, Bradman could seldom be prevailed on to settle for less than three. The Yorkshire crowd applauded wholeheartedly. This method of not merely defeating but overwhelming the opposition was one of which they approved in theory, though when inflicted on their own side, they may have regarded it a little wryly. This score of 334, though his first at Leeds, was his fourth successive century in Tests. The others had risen in a flamboyant curve from 123 to 131 and from 131 to 254. The holocaust of Headingley had begun.

In 1934 the massacre continued. On the first day of the Leeds Test England made 200. This, heaven knows, was a feeble score, but by six-thirty they appeared to have redressed the balance for Bowes had taken three quick wickets with only 37 on the board. The morning and the evening were the next day and only one wicket fell. It was not Bradman's. By the end of the innings he had made 304, hitting two sixes and forty-three fours. You could describe this second three-hundred at Leeds by many adjectives beginning with an m: magnificent, monumental, monolithic; for the spectator who hoped for one little flaw in infallibility, monotonous; and for the bowler whose figures were round about none for 150, monstrous. In spite of Australia's 584 the game was drawn, and England owed their escape to a cloud-burst and Maurice Leyland, in about equal proportions.

The summer of 1938 was a high-scoring season in which England also seemed to have learned the trick of piling up the score. This, you remember, was Hutton's year, in which a slender young Yorkshireman at the Oval beat Bradman's Test record and everyone else's with that historic 364. But it did not win England the rubber. At Leeds, a month before, Australia had won by five wickets, but it was, curiously enough, a low-scoring game which England might conceivably have won if (a) they had been able to bat *at all* after No. 6 and (b) if two catches had not been dropped in the last vital hour. Bradman did not rise to the 300 mark in this game. In fact, all he made was 103, but this in an innings in which five people failed to make double figures and six made only 35 between them. In the whole of the match only two players, one on each side, made 50 runs and one of the finest innings of the match was B. A. Barnett's 15 not out at the game's most palpitating point. The Leeds spectators knew great batting when they saw it and they knew that Bradman's innings of 103 was probably greater than his earlier gigantic totals of 334 and 304.

Even if 1938 saw a regression in quantity, if not in quality, Bradman came back with a vengeance in his next series, which was delayed until 1948, after the war. Australia trampled on England in their first post-war tour, repeating history as it had happened in 1921, and England's turn for triumph was not to come for another five years. The Australians had built up their cricket sooner and built it up well.

At Leeds in 1948 was played that fantastic game in which 1,723 runs were scored and Australia won by seven wickets fifteen minutes from time after England had declared. On the last day of this game, I was in my London office and listened to snatches of commentary as it came. A colleague of mine, a dour patriot, could scarcely control his emotion. He strode up and down and adjured the portable radio: 'But they can't get 'em; they can't *let* them get 'em.' But nobody could stop them getting 'em. Australia made 404 for three in 345 minutes and Bradman's share was 173 not out.

As he left the crease after this, his last great innings at Headingley, the crowd rose to him, cheering and clapping until throats and palms were sore. The crush was terrific and, as he set out upon his return to the pavilion, a posse of police had to force a way for him through the mob of enthusiastic admirers. Despite legal assistance, the pressure was so violent that for the moment movement was impossible and Bradman found himself standing opposite an old Yorkshireman whose wrinkled features were a study of conflicting emotions. It did not need a psychiatrist to interpret the old man's feelings: here was the greatest batsman in the world who had just swept his side to glorious triumph when, by all the laws of probability, they had no chance whatever. Here was the hated enemy, the man who had battered England's bowlers to a pulp; here was the foe of iron will, the ruthless tyrant who four times had brought England to the proud foot of a conqueror. Bradman was wonderful, Bradman was terrible. He admired him, he loved him, he hated him . . . Tears rained down the old man's cheeks. He stretched out his hand, but he could not speak. ' Ee,' he murmured. His lips moved, but no words came. And then there came forth the word which, without offence, by-passes the mere superlative, to denote the supreme, the infinite, the absolute, ' E,' he exclaimed, ' yer . . . booger!'

A. A. THOMSON, *Pavilioned in Splendour*, 1956

W. G., Bradman, then who? There have been many great batsmen in the post-war era but as a destroyer of bowling, Isaac Vivian Alexander Richards stands out. When on form, no one could contain his measured destruction. His greatest Test innings came at the Oval, the West Indies' home ground in south London, and was witnessed by John Woodcock.

I. V. A. Richards

AS inevitably as if his name was Bradman and the year was 1930 or 1934, Vivian Richards played another long innings against England when the fifth Test match started yesterday. By close of play he had made 200 out of a West Indian score of 373 for three. Fredricks scored 71, Rowe 70, and Lloyd and King, as well as Richards, are still to be dismissed.

If ever there was a day for winning the toss, this was it. England's one real chance seemed to lie in scoring some runs and then hoping to embarrass West Indies on a wearing pitch. Instead, Lloyd called right, for the fourth time out of five, and although England made an early break, they lacked the penetration that only truly fast bowling can provide on a pitch as slow as this and still in good repair. Any self-respecting county side would have expected to make runs against this England attack in yesterday's conditions.

Richards's 100 was his 12th of the year, seven of them in his last 10 Test matches. No one, I think, scored seven Test hundreds in the same year before. Hammond once got six, so did Compton. Walcott scored five in one series, but Richards's seven, against Australia, India and England, is something new. Supremely well he played, too. There is not a shot he lacks, though yesterday, when no bouncers were bowled, he did not hook.

In the first Test match at Trent Bridge, when he was making 232, he played and missed any number of times. This time he was hardly beaten. He gave no chance until he was 166 and needed to take none either. Fredericks, also, did much as he pleased. Rowe, reduced to a skeleton by Thomson and Lillee in Australia last winter, found the English bowling exactly what his psychiatrist would have ordered.

His last seven scores against Australia were 7, 7, 15, 6 and 6. Once, after a particularly nasty ball from Thomson had got him out, he threw his bat across the West Indian dressing room and said: 'Not even God could play those.' Yesterday, he was back to his wristy best. By the evening England gave the impression of feeling as powerless as they looked.

Balderstone, who had held a wonderful catch to dismiss Fredericks, put down a percher from Richards, which was symptomatic of England's plight. Poor Underwood was the bowler. The only members of the England side not to bowl were Knott and Amiss. There is no reason on this evidence why West Indies, if they choose to, should not make 1,000 or why Richards should not beat Gary Sobers's record Test match score of 365. By the end his aggregate for the series of 738 put him in the top 10 for any series at any time.

On the pitch that is sure to take spin later in the match, West Indies have packed their side with speed. To discourage them, in future, from so discounting spin, I only hope that before next Tuesday evening Lloyd feels like giving his kingdom for Padmore. For England, Snow decided against playing, because of a slight strain, which left Selvey to open the bowling with Willis. It was another hot, cloudless day.

In the second over of the match Fredericks was missed at the wicket off Selvey. In the third, Greenidge was leg-before to Willis. The chance off Selvey was going straight to Greig at first slip when Knott dived across him and dropped it. England had a long wait for Frederick's next mistake. The ball that accounted for Greenidge came back at him off the pitch. At five for one, nearly five for two, England were not without hope, though it was soon fading.

Greig made an early change of bowling which took everyone by surprise, not least, I imagine, Willis. After four overs, Underwood was brought on in Willis's place, although Willis, having just taken Greenidge's wicket, had his tail up. Underwood had six overs in this spell and 10 were bowled before Willis came on again in place of Selvey.

The first hour brought 59 runs off 15 overs, the second 64 off 16 overs. By lunch Greig had tried six bowlers, which did not include himself. With his first ball in Test cricket Balderstone surprised Richards by turning one, Miller began with a tidy enough maiden.

Selvey and Willis were comfortably played once the ball had lost its shine. Batting was made to seem absurdly easy almost throughout the partnership between Richards and Fredericks. It was ended, when it was worth 154, by a brilliant catch by Balderstone.

Spying a long hop from Miller, Fredericks picked a gap to the right of Balderstone in the covers. Although not renowned for his agility, Balderstone threw himself at the ball and held it one-handed. Had Knott caught Rowe soon afterwards off Underwood that, too, would have been a fine catch, taken off the under edge. At 215 Knott put another one down, this time off Greig, with Rowe, then 29, again the batsman. It was another nasty chance.

By tea England had used eight bowlers. In spite of these half chances at the wicket, no one posed much of a problem. Greig, bowling offbreaks for the first time since the second Test match, was tolerably accurate, Underwood looked anxious and Miller was not unpromising. During the afternoon England bowled 36 overs and West Indies scored 127 runs.

Greig had been keeping Steele up his sleeve for the evening. When he came on Richards eased him through or over mid-wicket as he had everyone else. Past mid-wicket or through the covers was where Richards scored most of his 24 fours. When fatigue, or boredom, caused him to give mid-off a straight-forward chance, Balderstone dropped it. With Rowe he had added 191 when Rowe went for a walk to Underwood and was stumped by Knott down the leg side.

The day ended with Lloyd and Richards quietly playing it out (Richards reached 200 with five minutes to go) and Knott as the holder of a world record. With the stumping of Rowe he passed Godfrey Evans's bag of 219 Test dismissals. Of Evans's 219, 173 were caught and 46 stumped. Of Knott's 220, 203 have been caught and only 17 stumped. Of the late Bert Oldfield's 132, as many as 52 were stumped. That is how much the game has changed.

When, eventually, England start their innings, they are likely to do so amid noises from the north country to the effect that Boycott is wanting to go to India with MCC – to return to Test cricket, in fact. If so, those who have borne the brunt against Thomson, Lillee, Roberts and Holding for the past two years will have to be careful not to be cynical. So, come to think of it, shall I.

West Indies – First Innings

R. C. Frederick, c Balderstone, b Miller	71
C. G. Greenidge, lbw b Willis	0
I. V. A. Richards, b Greig	291
L. G. Rowe, st Knott, b Underwood	70
C. H. Lloyd, c Knott, b Greig	84
C. L. King, c Selvey, b Balderstone	63
D. L. Murray, c & b Underwood	36
V. A. Holder, not out	13
M. A. Holding, b Underwood	32
Extras (b 1, lb 17, nb 8)	27
Total (8 wkts dec.)	687

A. M. E. Roberts and W. W. Daniel did not bat
Fall of wickets: 1-5, 2-53, 3-350, 4-524, 5-547, 6-640, 7-642, 8-687

England Bowling

	O.	M.	R.	W.
Willis	15	3	73	1
Selvey	15	0	67	0
Underwood	60.5	15	165	3
Woolmer	9	0	44	0
Miller	27	4	106	1
Balderstone	16	0	80	1
Greig	34	5	96	2
Willey	3	0	11	0
Steele	3	0	18	0

JOHN WOODCOCK, *The Times*, 13 August 1976

As the scorecard shows, Richards went on to make 291 and failed to break Sobers' indvidual test record before he was bowled by Tony Greig. Richards was not only the heir to Grace and Bradman's throne, he was also the culmination of a tradition of West Indian batsmanship whose roots are beautifully documented in C. L. R. James's book, Beyond a Boundary *quoted above. James traces the line back to George Challenor. Then came Sir Learie Constantine, the first black West Indian to make his living from the game in the professional leagues of northern England. Next was another knight, Sir Frank Worrell, the first black man to captain the West Indies. Jim Swanton gave the address at his memorial service in Westminster Abbey.*

Sir Frank Worrell

IN this ancient Abbey church, which enshrines so much of the history of England and of the British Empire and Commonwealth, we, gathered here today, are taking part in a unique service. Here, where the most famous have been buried, and the lives of the greatest commemorated, we are assembled to mourn for, and to pray for the soul of Sir Frank Mortimer Maglinne Worrell, a cricketer. It is making history to open the doors of the Abbey for the passing of a sportsman. My privilege and responsibility now is to try and give you such a picture of the man as will explain why in their wisdom the Dean and Chapter of Westminster have allowed us, his friends and admirers, from so many parts of the world, to pay our last respects in this glorious, awesome setting.

Frank Worrell was born at Bank Hall on the outskirts of Bridgetown, Barbados, on August 1st 1924. His father was a sailor, and so it came that when his mother emigrated to America he was brought up by his grandmother. It was from the roof of her small wooden house, adjoining the ground of the Empire club which has produced so many of the best Barbadian players, that he watched his first cricket. It was this environment no doubt that fired his ambition and gave him models of excellence to follow.

While he was learning to be a cricketer he was also growing up as a Christian. There is perhaps scarcely a firmer stronghold of Anglicanism in the whole communion of Canterbury than Barbados – a fact that perhaps adds a little more to the appropriateness of this service. Frank sang as a boy in the choir of St Michael's Cathedral, and ever after had a great love of church music. A pleasant story is told by his brother-in-law of how some years ago in Lancashire they both attended the three hours' service of devotion on Good Friday. After the service Frank complained there had not been enough hymns, and so they went home and played some more on the piano and sang.

The foundations of the Christian philosophy that governed his life were laid then as a boy. As a cricketer he grew up fast. At the age of only nineteen he scored 308 not out against the great rivals across the water, Trinidad. Here in fact was a prodigy, whose succession to the West Indies team when war ended, and Test Matches were

91

played again, seemed an automatic thing. He was soon being hailed, in company with two other young Bajans, Everton Weekes and Clyde Walcott – all three born close to one another and in the space of 18 months – as a great player. This is not the occasion to speak either of his technique or of his achievements on the field, except perhaps to say this – that cricket, like any other art, is an expression of character, and there was always about Frank's play a grace, a dignity, and an unrufflable serenity that reflected the man.

But Frank had set his eyes on horizons beyond the cricket field. He came to Lancashire to earn his living as a professional in the League, at the same time to take his degree at Manchester University. He warmed to Lancashire (and in particular to Radcliffe, where he played), and Lancashire warmed to him. His twelve years there made him the most fervent of Anglophiles, and so he remained. It was a Lancastrian, George Duckworth – that shrewd, humorous, lovable man – who, I think, first saw in Frank the special qualities of leadership. At the early age of twenty-six (ten years before being honoured by his country), he was captaining with much promise a mixed Commonwealth team, mostly of men a good deal older than he, managed by Duckworth in India.

When at last he was named as captain of the West Indies, on the tour to Australia in 1960, the appointment was accepted by the rest of his team, if not by him, as a challenge to his race. Under the subtle knack of his personality difference of colour, island prejudices, seemed to melt away. The tour of Australia was a triumph both on the field and off it, ending, as everyone will remember, with a motorcade through the streets of Melbourne lined with half a million cheering people. Three summers later he brought the West Indies team to England for a tour that enthused the sporting world no less than the one in Australia. He retired from playing after this, and in the New Year of 1964 received the honour of knighthood.

For the last three years of his life he was, of course, a national hero, but in bearing that difficult mantle he lost none of his modesty, none of his warmth. It is, of course, a deep sorrow that by the workings of Providence he has been taken away with such suddenness when it seemed that he had so much more to contribute in areas outside sport: in social fields, and in particular in the life of the University of the West Indies. He had made a deep mark already in Jamaica as University Warden (with a seat also in the Jamaican Senate). Since last year he had been Dean of Students in Trinidad. In both these islands the civic authorities had utilised his influences with young people and his readiness to identify himself with them. He had not worked in Trinidad for long but it was a measure of the affection he attracted that four chartered aeroplanes were needed to fly mourners to the funeral in Barbados.

No doubt, in course of time, he might have served as representative in one or other of the Caribbean territories in the very highest office. He was a Federalist, nearest whose heart was the unity of the West Indian peoples in all their diversity. Myself, I believe he harboured a special ambition to help bring on that branch of the University in his native Barbados which is now building, and on the site on which he is buried.

He had a warm, understanding heart and a sort of sleepy charm that endeared old and young alike.

He was essentially a bringer-together by the sincerity and friendliness of his personality; a sporting catalyst in an era where international rivalries too often grow sour and ugly. In the television age men famous in the world of games have a formidable influence, and strange figures are sometimes magnified into heroes. Frank Worrell was the absolute antithesis of the strident and the bumptious, of, so to speak, the great-sportsman-who-is-not. It is his example – and that of many of his West Indian cricket contemporaries – that has helped so much towards an appreciation and an admiration for his countrymen in England and throughout the Commonwealth. One of his opposing captains in an appreciation of him wrote that however the game ended, 'he made you feel a little better.' Which isn't a bad epitaph. No doubt he made many of us feel a little better, from the youngsters in Boys' Town at Kingston to Sydney hoboes on the Hill.

Have I pictured a paragon? Well, he certainly didn't look the part and would have been horrified at the very thought of a tribute such as this. He was gay and convivial, and though his convictions were deep and sincere they were never paraded. Yet, just as England brought cricket to the West Indies, the West Indies in return, I believe, has given us the ideal cricketer. When His Excellency the High Commissioner was reading those haunting Beatitudes just now the thought came: whom do I know who has fulfilled them better? May God rest his soul and give consolation to his widow and daughter. And may his example live with us.

E. W. SWANTON, 1967

*From Worrell, the baton was passed to a third knight of the Windies,
Sir Garfield Sobers.*

Sir Garfield Sobers

S IR Garfield Sobers, the finest all-round player in the history of
cricket, has announced his retirement from full time county
cricket at the age of thirty-eight. Circumstances seem to suggest he
will not be seen again in Test matches. He was not with West Indies
on their recent tour of India and Pakistan; and they have no other
international commitment until 1976, when their full length tour of
England might well prove too physically trying for a forty-year-old
Sobers, most deservedly given a knighthood in the New Year
Honours.

So it is likely that international cricket has seen the last of its most
versatile performer. For twenty years plus, to be precise, seven days,
he served and graced West Indian cricket in almost every capacity.
To review his career compels so many statistics as might mask the
splendidly exciting quality of his play. Nevertheless, since many of
his figures are, quite literally, unequalled, they must be quoted.
Between 30 March 1954 and 5 April 1974 for West Indies, he
appeared in 93 Tests – more than any other overseas cricketer: he
played the highest Test innings – 365 not out against Pakistan at
Kingston in 1958; scored the highest individual aggregate of runs in
Test matches; and captained his country a record 39 times. His 110
catches and – except for a left-hander – his 235 wickets are not
unique: but his talents in those directions alone justified a Test
place.

Garfield Sobers was seventeen when he first played for West
Indies – primarily as an orthodox slow left-arm bowler (four for 81),
though he scored 40 runs for once out in a losing side. His batting
developed more rapidly than his bowling and, in the 1957–58 series
with Pakistan in West Indies, he played six consecutive innings of
over fifty – the last three of them centuries. Through the sixties he
developed left-arm wrist-spin, turning the ball sharply and conceal-
ing his googly well. Outstanding, however, at the need of his
perceptive captain, Sir Frank Worrell, he made himself a Test-class

fast-medium bowler. Out of his instinctive athleticism he evolved an ideally economic action, coupling life from the pitch with late movement through the air and, frequently, off the seam. Nothing in all his cricket was more impressive than his ability to switch from one bowling style to another with instant control.

He was always capable of bowling orthodox left arm accurately, with a surprising faster ball and as much turn as the pitch would allow a finger-spinner. He had, though, an innate urge to attack, which was his fundamental reason for taking up the less economical but often more penetrative 'chinaman', and the pace bowling which enabled him to make such hostile use of the new ball.

As a fieldsman he is remembered chiefly for his work at slip – where he made catching look absurdly simple – or at short leg where he splendidly reinforced the off-spin of Lance Gibbs. Few recall that as a young man he was extremely fast – and had a fine 'arm' – in the deep, and that he could look like a specialist at cover-point.

Everything he did was marked by a natural grace, apparent at first sight. As he walked out to bat, six feet tall, lithe but with adequately wide shoulders, he moved with long strides which, even when he was hurrying, had an air of laziness, the hip joints rippling like those of a great cat. He was, it seems, born with basic orthodoxy in batting; the fundamental reason for his high scoring lay in the correctness of his defence. Once he was established (and he did not always settle in quickly), his sharp eye, early assessment, and inborn gift of timing, enabled him to play almost any stroke. Neither a back foot nor a front foot player, he was either as the ball and conditions demanded. When he stepped out and drove it was with a full flow of the bat and a complete follow through, in the classical manner. When he could not get to the pitch of the ball, he would go back, wait - as it sometimes seemed, impossibly long – until he identified it and then, at the slightest opportunity, with an explosive whip of the wrists, hit it with immense power. His quick reactions and natural ability linked with his attacking instinct made him a brilliant improviser of strokes. When he was on the kill it was all but impossible to bowl to him – and he was one of the most thrilling of all batsmen to watch.

Crucially, Garfield Sobers was not merely extremely gifted, but a highly combative player. That was apparent on his first tour of England, under John Goddard in 1957. Too many members of that team lost appetite for the fight as England took the five-match rubber by three to none. Sobers, however, remained resistant to the end.

He was a junior member of the side – his twenty-first birthday fell during the tour – but he batted with immense concentration and determination. He was only twice out cheaply in Tests: in two Worrell took him in to open the batting and, convincingly, in the rout at The Oval, he was top scorer in each West Indies innings. He was third in the Test batting averages of that series which marked his accession to technical and temperamental maturity.

The classic example of his competitive quality was the Lord's Test of 1966 when West Indies, with five second-innings wickets left, were only nine in front and Holford – a raw cricketer but their last remaining batting hope – came in to join his cousin Sobers. From the edge of defeat, they set a new West Indies Test record of 274 for the sixth wicket and, so far from losing, made a strong attempt to win the match.

Again, at Kingston in 1967-68, West Indies followed on against England and, with five second-innings wickets down, still needed 29 to avoid an innings defeat. Sobers – who fell for a duck in the first innings – was left with only tailenders for support yet, on an unreliable pitch, he made 113 – the highest score of the match – and then, taking the first two English wickets for no runs, almost carried West Indies to a win.

For many years, despite the presence of some other handsome stroke-makers in the side, West Indies placed heavy reliance on his batting, especially when a game was running against them. Against England 1959-60 and Australia 1964-65, West Indies lost the one Test in each series when Sobers failed. His effectiveness can be measured by the fact that in his 93 Tests for West Indies he scored 26 centuries, and fifties in 30 other innings; four times – twice against England – averaged over one hundred for a complete series; and had an overall average of 57.78. There is a case, too, that he played a crucial part as a bowler in winning at least a dozen Tests.

To add captaincy to his batting, different styles of bowling and close fielding may have been the final burden that brought his Test career to an early end. He was a generally sound, if orthodox, tactician but, after thirty-nine matches as skipper, the strain undoubtedly proved wearing. In everyday life he enjoys gambling and, as a Test captain, he is still remembered for taking a chance which failed. It occurred in the 1967-68 series against England, when he made more runs at a higher average and bowled more overs than anyone else except Gibbs – on either side. After high scores by England the first three Tests were drawn, but in the fourth, after

Butcher surprisingly had bowled out England in their first innings
with leg-spin, Sobers made a challenging declaration. Butcher could
not repeat his performance and Boycott and Cowdrey skilfully paced
England to a win. Thereupon the very critics who constantly
bemoaned the fact that Test match captains were afraid to take a
chance castigated Sobers for doing so – and losing. The epilogue to
that 'failure' was memorable. With characteristic confidence in his
own ability, he set out to win the Fifth Test and square the rubber.
He scored 152 and 95 not out, took three for 72 in the first England
innings and three for 53 in the second only to fall short of winning
by one wicket.

Students of sporting psychology will long ponder the causes
of Sobers's retirement. Why did this admirably equipped, well
rewarded and single-minded cricketer limp out of the top level game
which had brought him such eminence and success? He was only
thirty-eight: some great players of the past continued appreciably
longer. Simply enough, mentally and physically tired, he had lost his
zest for the sport which had been his life – and was still his only
observable means of earning a living. Ostensibly he had a damaged
knee; in truth he was the victim of his unique range of talents – and
the jet age. Because he was capable of doing so much, he was asked
to do it too frequently. He did more than any other cricketer, and did
it more concentratedly because high speed aircraft enabled him to
travel half across the world in a day or two. Perhaps the long sea
voyages between seasons of old had a restorative effect.

In a historically sapping career, Sobers has played for Barbados
for twenty-one seasons; in English league cricket for eight, for South
Australia in the Sheffield Shield for three, and Nottinghamshire for
seven; he turned out regularly for the Cavaliers on Sundays for
several years before there was a Sunday League in England; made
nine tours for West Indies, two with Rest of the World sides and
several in lesser teams; 85 of his 93 Tests for the West Indies were
consecutive and he averaged more than four a year for twenty years.
There is no doubt, also, that his car accident in which Collie Smith
was killed affected him more profoundly and for longer than most
people realised.

The wonder was not that the spark grew dim but that it endured
so bright for so long. Though it happened so frequently and for so
many years, it was always thrilling even to see Sobers come to the
wicket. As lately as 1968 he hit six sixes from a six-ball over. In 1974
on his 'farewell' circuit of England he still, from time to time, recap-

tured his former glory, playing a lordly stroke or making the ball leave the pitch faster than the batsman believed possible. As he walked away afterwards, though, his step dragged. He was a weary man – as his unparalleled results do not merely justify, but demand. Anyone who ever matches Garfield Sobers's performances will have to be an extremely strong man – and he, too, will be weary.

An amazing man, he still insists, 'As long as I am fit and the West Indies need me, I will be willing to play for them.' Only time will tell if we shall see him in the Test arena again. In October last he joined the executive staff of National Continental Corporation to promote the company's products in the Caribbean and United Kingdom.

And now he has joined his lamented compatriots Sir Learie Constantine and Sir Frank Worrell with the title Sir Garfield Sobers.

JOHN ARLOTT, *Wisden Cricketers' Almanack,* 1975

He, too, could touch humility.

IT is easy to give one's wicket away, but it takes an artist to do this as well as Gary did to me in a Benefit game in the 1960s. He decided he had provided sufficient entertainment and had scored enough runs, so he got out. Nothing unusual about that. It was the way he did it which typified both the man and his craft. He waited until I sent down a ball of good length which pitched on his leg stump and hit the middle as he played a full forward defensive stroke, deliberately and fractionally down the wrong line. He made it look a very good delivery – it wasn't a bad one! But he played his shot so well that the wicket-keeper and first slip – though both county professionals – came up to congratulate me. I knew instinctively what Gary had done. But no spectator realised it was an act of charity; only Gary and myself.

TREVOR BAILEY, *Sir Gary,* 1976

A 20-year-old country boy showed little charity to the bowlers when he made the most sensational debut in county cricket history. Perhaps it is the Somerset air that encourages swashbucklers, for both Viv Richards and Ian Botham, an all-time great if ever there was one, plied their trade down in the West Country. But not even those two legends burst onto the Somerset scene with such a resounding thump as did the tortured genius of Gimblett. David Foot recounts what happened.

Harold Gimblett

Tortured Genius

WEST Country schoolboys came to recite the facts and circumstances of Gimblett's magnificent and impudent century of 18th May 1935 with a vocal vigour never remotely matched in the ritual of the twice-times table. It almost became part of the required curriculum.

The century belonged to fiction. The plot was altogether too thrillingly fashioned: a confectioned scenario that mocked credulity. It came from the genre of sporting stories of excessive heroism on the field, written by Victorian and Edwardian clergy, warmed by their imagination as they sat in draughty rectories. Young readers enjoyed but did not need to believe. It was all part of the romance of cricket.

Yet it did happen, at Frome. A village lad from the Quantocks, turned down by his county, was suddenly asked to play because no one else could be found to make up the eleven. For once, not even an extra from Somerset's intermittent band of strolling players, amateurs who appeared from abroad or the pages of Debrett for a jolly game or two between country house parties, could be spirited up at such short notice. So there was John Daniell saying, without too much conviction: 'Do you know where Frome is, young Gimblett? Can you get there on your own?'

Harold was not too sure that he could. He stammered that perhaps he could catch one very early bus to Bridgwater, and then another to Frome. The secretary pondered the geographical complications. 'You'll never arrive on time that way. Get to Bridgwater by nine o'clock and I'll ask Luckes to pick you up in his car.'

Few centuries have been documented with more detail and loving labour. There have been embellishments at a few thousand cricket dinners since then. The commas and the colour of Harold's pocket handkerchief may have varied slightly, but never the joyful spirit of the day's theatre.

It was a dynamic piece of fledgeling cricket by a player so unknown that the scorecard could give no initials for him. Yet his reputation was to be established forever, by what happened on that bitterly cold May afternoon at Frome, where the tents billowed noisily as they do at an early Spring point-to-point. White railings circled the small playing area, adding to the hint of a rural racing scene.

Frome was proud of its one county match a season. The town had a small population but a lively and loyal support for Somerset cricket. Facilities on the ground were modest, with plenty of functional corrugated iron, and wooden benches transported in for the occasion. There was no room on the scoreboard for individual innings. The voices around the boundary were pure, throaty Somerset: but different from Taunton, Weston or Yeovil. And different from Bicknoller.

On his cassettes, Gimblett talked ramblingly of many things. He chose to give only a brief, factual account of his century at Frome. It occupied just a minute of reminiscence. The dismissive attitude was part of him and we shall return to it. Mrs Gimblett told me: 'I kept the cuttings. Harold would have destroyed them.'

It would be quite wrong for me also to dismiss his maiden innings for Somerset, although in the ways of folklore, everyone will know that he was up well before 6 a.m. on that Saturday morning and narrowly missed the bus to Bridgwater. The next bus was in two hours' time.

He had a little all-purpose bag within which – you would never have guessed – was his own bruised and discoloured bat and a few sandwiches considerately dropped in by his mother. Maternal kindness had also ensured freshly creased flannels and a clean shirt. He stood, a forlorn figure, on the narrow country road and wondered what he should do now. He started walking, vaguely in the direction of Bridgwater, and then heard a lorry from behind. Harold thumbed it down, something he had never done before. The dialogue that followed had an endearing quality to it.

'Sorry, I've just missed the bus.'
'OK, jump in. Where are you going?'
'To Frome.'
'Why?'
'To play cricket.'
'Who for?'
'Somerset.'
'Oh, ah!'

The lorry driver did not believe Gimblett. How could he have? On his own admission, Harold looked like a wide-eyed innocent, in trouble because he was late for work.

Wally Luckes was waiting for him at Bridgwater and they reached the ground in good time. Some supporters were already in their place. They recognised the little wicket-keeper and offered a cheery greeting. No one recognised Gimblett.

Then I met the Essex players. Jack O'Connor . . . Laurie Eastman . . . Maurice Nichols . . . Ray and Peter Smith . . . Tommy Wade, Tom Pearce . . . I realised I was scared stiff. Wally Luckes gave me the only bit of advice. 'Peter Smith will always bowl you a googlie so be ready for it.' I didn't even know what a googlie was - I'd never seen one. Wally patiently explained that it looked like a leg spinner but went the other way.

Reggie Ingle was the Somerset captain and he put Gimblett at No. 8. He won the toss and was soon regretting it. Nichols was using all his natural speed, as well as a biting wind that was sweeping across the ground. Jack Lee, Ingle and White were all caught at slip and Somerset were 35 for 3. You could hear the groans around the boundary. By lunch, Frank Lee and C. C. C. (Box) Case were also out and the score was 105 for 5.

The Bath amateur, H. D. Burrough quickly followed. At 2.20 p.m. twenty-year-old Harold Gimblett, head down and already pessimistic about what he imagined was a token appearance in county cricket, meandered to the wicket to join Wellard. Someone in the crowd shouted: 'Leave it to Arthur, son.'

During the lunch interval, Wellard had put a friendly hand on Gimblett's shoulder. 'Don't think much of your bat, cock. Why don't you borrow my spare one?' And so he did.

Peter Smith sniffed a novice. His third ball to Gimblett was a googlie. The young batsman had not spotted it but he pushed it away to mid wicket and was off the mark. In his second over from Smith, Gimblett straight-drove to the boundary. That felt good. The Frome supporters rather approved of the way he did that. Who was this lad? Gimb-Gimblett or something? Wasn't he the lad who was always whacking sixes in village matches?

The likeable Peter Smith chuckled silently to himself. He summoned up additional wiles. But so much for cunning. His fourth over after lunch cost 15 runs, all of them to Gimblett. When the leg break was fractionally over-pitched, the young batsman put his left foot down and heaved the spinning ball over mid-off for six. It landed on the top of the beer tent, a marquee temporarily deserted as the rubicund drinkers moved outside to savour this jaunty newcomer.

Gimblett suddenly realised he was enjoying himself. Nichols was by far the fastest bowler he had ever met but the young batsman had the clear eyes and nimble feet to keep him out of trouble. In nine overs, Somerset added 69 runs; 48 of them came from Gimblett. He was actually outscoring Wellard, and not many managed that. The ever-bronzed Arthur, jangling the loose change in his flannel trousers, ready for the next poker school, only smiled.

The half-century came with a six. It had taken 28 minutes and he had received 33 balls. By now the spectators had shed their reserve: they were cheering every shot. The beer was left undrunk.

Wellard miscalculated an off break from Vic Evans and was stumped. But then came his look-alike and inseparable mate, Andrews. In between, Luckes had been bowled by Nichols, back with the new ball.

New ball? You couldn't afford such niceties around the village greens of West Somerset. Gimblett threshed his way on, swinging and sweeping and driving whenever he could. There was hardly a false shot. Essex fielders rued the short boundary; they were generous enough to applaud some of the sixes.

Nichols dug one in short and the Somerset No. 8, with ludicrous time to spare, hooked it for four. Then, oblivious to pace, Gimblett took two more runs through the covers.

He had no idea how many he had scored; the scoreboard gave the minimum of information. But the spectators soon told him. The cover drive had brought him his century. It had been scored out of 130 and had taken 63 minutes. As the fastest hundred of the season it earned him the Lawrence Trophy.

It was, I suppose, one of those days you dream of. I can't work it out. I took all the praise but Bill Andrews, who got 71, was even faster in his scoring. I savoured the moment – but loathed the publicity that followed.

Gimblett gave a simple return catch when he had scored 123 in 79 minutes. Nichols still returned a splendid 6–87 in 23 overs. Peter Smith finished with 1–89 in 13 overs and must have been particularly wary when bowling to low-order newcomers after that. Essex never recovered from such an unceremonious mauling. They were bowled out for 141 and 147. The late Jack Lee took four wickets in their first innings and five in their second.

DAVID FOOT, *Tortured Genius*, 1982

If great batsmanship is marked by the grace with which a bat is wielded, bowling is often stamped by hostility, especially great fast bowling. Bowlers can be elegant but more often than not they are explosive, driven by a hatred of the batsman qua batsman and a desire to rid the world of the breed. This animosity is expressed in many ways: the scowl, the imprecations, muttered or otherwise, the ice-cold glare. A quickie is not satisfied with just getting a batsman out, he wants to humiliate him, hurt him and then get him out. Legend has it that the greatest over ever bowled by a fast bowler was that sent down to Geoffrey Boycott by Michael Holding in Barbados.

Michael Holding

IN the Barbados Test match nine years ago, Gooch was Boycott's junior opening partner. Gooch made a valiant 116 out of an England total of 224. Geoffrey made one of Test cricket's most famous ducks. I will never forget it. Bridgetown's rickety, crickety stadium was full to every corrugated rooftop, and the jabbering din only died into an expectant quiet as Boycott took guard and Michael Holding paced out his menacing run. He was almost using the sight-screen at the pavilion end as a catapulting starting-block.

First ball snortingly tore a strip off the knuckle of Boycott's left-hand batting glove and dropped just in front of third slip as the batsman wrung his hand in pain. The second was shorter and even more spiteful, and Boycott jack-knifed his forehead out of the way with a millimetre between his life and a coroner's verdict of misadventure due to the whiplash effect.

Next ball was off a fuller length, but no less wicked, and it licked back cruelly to splatter the inside of Geoffrey's unguarded left thigh. The infinitely courageous Englishman stuck to his middle-stump scratch-mark, and the fourth ball had him in all sorts of ungainly contortions as he endeavoured to keep down the missile again with his already wounded left hand; the thing squirmed away to gully. The fifth delivery again had you fearing for the stubbornly gallant knight's life as it reared angrily at his throat like a buzzsaw looking to at least peel his Adam's Apple. Still Boycott stood his ground.

As if the hateful half-dozen had been orchestrated into one gigantic, discordant crescendo, the sixth and last ball of the over was a snaking yorker which fiercely ripped Boycott's off-stump out of the ground and had it spearing fully 20 yards as if, for a moment we thought, it would impale itself in the very heart of the wicket-keeper, Murray. It missed him by a whisker.

The vast throng was silent, stunned, for a split second. Boycott jerked round to watch the flight of the stump then, as the great crazed noise erupted all around his ears, his mouth gaped and he tottered in his crease as if he'd seen the very Devil himself. Then, agonised and tremulous, he walked away, tearing his batting gloves off with his nervously juddering teeth. By the time he got to the pavilion step he was erect again; beaten this time, sure, but already determined on his counter.

FRANK KEATING, *Punch Magazine*, 1990

If Michael Holding's forte was pure pace, the Pakistani duo of Wasim Akram and Waqar Younis had added an extra menace by the early nineties.

Wasim and Waqar

THIS time it's not the early eighties, it is the here and now. A Test match against Pakistan at Trent Bridge. You're an older and wiser head now, one of the senior batsmen in the England team. You've been in the side over ten years and you've seen a few things in your time. You've not faced Pakistan in a Test match before though. Your captain wins the toss, the pitch is excellent for batting – so flat and true that it occurs to you that even West Indies would have a job to bowl you out on it – and you are sent out to create the platform for a big total. Don't want to see you until the lunch interval, that sort of thing. Your opening partner is Graham Gooch, who is, incredibly, still playing. He seems to have been around for ever, ever since the mid-seventies. The era of Lillee and Thomson and all that. The age of the dinosaurs.

Rather impressively, you and Gooch do the job. You bat through to lunch unbeaten. You even pick up runs quite quickly, for the score at the interval is 98 for no wicket. These are untold riches. It's not at all like when you bat against West Indies.

It is not all plain sailing, however. Waqar Younis and Wasim Akram, Pakistan's opening bowlers, have given you some uncomfortable moments. The most striking thing about them is that they're always trying something different. They're not content just to bowl fast, or ping the ball around your head: they try to swing the ball and are capable of doing so both ways. Fortunately, neither has been able to settle during the morning session, otherwise they might have been a real handful. Waqar, remarkably, began by bowling at his top pace. He seemed to have no need to loosen up at all, he just started bowling fast from the outset. And he is capable of a distinctly lively pace: he had not been playing Test cricket a year, and was reportedly still in his teens, when Martin Crowe, the New Zealand captain, said late in 1990 that Waqar was the fastest bowler he had ever faced. Mercifully, here he has struggled to find his line and several times strayed down the leg side, giving away either byes or easy runs when either you or Gooch could get a bat to the ball. His methods seem touchingly naive: he charges in to bowl and hurls himself through his delivery with all the gung-ho enthusiasm of a new boy in the nets, and it seems what he would really like to do is to bowl fast, swinging yorkers every ball. What he often ends up doing though is serving up half volleys and full tosses that do not swing very much at all. Many of these you and Gooch have despatched to the boundary with scarcely disguised glee. He has really been quite expensive. Even so, he has resorted to surprisingly few bouncers. It's amazing, he seems to regard them as a waste of time.

Wasim is different. For one thing he is a left-armer. He is also 6 foot 3 inches, three inches taller than Waqar, and is five years older. He began in the Pakistan team in 1985, early enough to see at first hand Imran bowling at something like his best. Wasim has potentially more variety than Waqar, as he demonstrated by going round the wicket as well as over, of swinging the ball in as well as moving it away, of pitching it up as well as dropping it short, but he seemed preoccupied with trying to bounce you and Gooch out and spent a lot of deliveries to no great effect. He is always doing this. In his second Test match he put Lance Cairns, the New Zealand tailender, into hospital for several days with blurred vision, and he has had several run-ins with umpires over his fondness for the short pitched ball. It's fairly obvious he doesn't like it when things don't go his way because he got very upset when neither you nor Gooch fell for his bouncer trap, but he'll have to try harder than that because both of you have been around long enough, and played West Indies enough times, not to succumb to that old trick. Perhaps he is so fond of the bouncer because he spent so much time under Imran's wing.

When the pair of them take a breather, they are succeeded by two bowlers of similar style, Ata-ur-Rehman and Aamir Nasir. They are relatively inexperienced and not too difficult to handle but they are clearly being moulded along the same lines. They too, like Wasim and Waqar, are from Imran's part of Pakistan, the hardier northern reaches around Lahore. To think that the country took so long to produce a fast bowler worthy of the name!

So what's the difference? What's the difference between this means of attack and that so beloved of the West Indies? OK, so these guys are always looking for wickets, but one of them keeps over-pitching and giving away easy runs and the other overdoes the bouncer. Whatever you say about West Indies, at least they don't give runs away. So what's new?

Well, the difference comes after the lunch interval, in this case about half an hour into the afternoon session. The ball is about forty overs old and Wasim and Waqar have come back. It all happens very quickly, like a great wave washing over you. You have made sure you are up at the non-striker's end for Wasim's first over back – you have not been around all these years for nothing – so you are able to watch him start by going round the wicket to Gooch. He starts by drilling a series of short-pitched balls into his ribs; they're not full-blown bouncers but they're enough to get Gooch firmly on to the back foot. Then, with the final ball of the over, he brings his arm over much faster – it's a sort of round-arm action, funnily enough, much rounder than when he goes over the wicket – and delivers a ball of fuller length which screams back in from outside off stump, following the line of his arm, and takes Gooch, who is far too late with his bat, plumb on the back pad right in front of the stumps. Salim Yousuf is already tearing up to congratulate Wasim before the umpire has even raised his finger.

You don't know how you survive the next over from Waqar. It may be his first of the spell but he again starts by bowling at his top pace and this time the ball, which is polished on one side and rough on the other, is really starting to swing. Two or three times Waqar beats you all ends up. The first time you are trying to remain positive after the loss of Gooch's wicket and you look to drive what appears to be another of his over-pitched wannabe yorkers, but it dips and swings late and would undoubtedly have taken your middle stump had you not got half a bat and half a pad to it (the audible snick does not stop the wicket-keeper and all the close fielders going up for the earth-shattering shout). Another late inswinger, fortunately one that was this time going well down the leg side, crunches you a painful blow – sorry, forgot about that one – on the side of the foot, and the outswinger with which Waqar finishes the over practically turns you inside out. By now, the atmosphere has definitely changed.

Wasim immediately decides to go over the wicket to Ramprakash. He gets in close to the stumps and starts bowling him a series of big inswingers and keeps committing him to playing a shot. Then he goes wider and sends down a yorker that looks for most of its flight – from where you're standing – like it's heading for first slip, before it swerves in over its last few yards of travel to neatly pluck out the off-stump. Ramprakash, who did not move his feet one inch, has gone without scoring.

For the next few overs you and Smith hang on. Smith even plunders a few boundaries off Waqar's more wayward deliveries and feels confident enough to come down the pitch and tell you that he's liking the way the ball is coming on to his bat. You don't feel so sanguine, however, and your fears are soon justified when Smith thrusts his front leg down the pitch in an attempt to pad away a wide ball from Waqar only for it to swing later than he expects and take him on the back pad in front of off-stump. Hick is in next. He survives his first two balls and looks like he is going to survive his third before it nips back and takes his glove on its way through to the wicket-keeper. Hussain does not even last that long. His first ball is another fast inswinging yorker – Waqar has really got this delivery going by now – which spreadeagles his stumps. In the space of eight overs you have gone from 114 for no wicket to 138 for five: two wickets for Wasim, three in five balls for Waqar, and not a bouncer in sight.

This sort of collapse against this pair of bowlers is not in fact anything new, particularly when they are operating with the old ball, which they swing far more readily than the new one. They have been accused by more than one set of opponents of using illegal means to achieve this movement – fingernails, bottle-tops and nails have all been suggested as implements with which one side of the ball is roughened – and some have even confessed to having tampered with the ball themselves in an attempt to show that the practice is wide-spread within the game. But what many people forget – even those who testified in defence of Allan Lamb when Sarfraz Nawaz took him to court in 1993 for alleging in a newpaper article that Sarfraz had shown him how to tamper with the ball – is that the ability to swing an old ball is neither new nor the preserve of Pakistan cricketers. Do you not remember the likes of Procter, Lillee, Botham (in his early days), Marshall and Hadlee all being capable of swinging the old ball?

What is different about Wasim and Waqar is their ability to swing the ball late in its flight. Geoff Arnold, Surrey's coach when Waqar first arrived at Surrey in 1990, identified this as Waqar's special gift when he said that year: 'He has greater ability to swing the ball late, and at a faster pace, than anyone I've seen.' But even this was not a new technique; as long ago as 1977 Lillee was writing in his *Art of Fast Bowling* that, 'Tests have shown that a cricket ball will not swing when it is travelling above a certain critical velocity and this may be why some fast bowlers have the ability to swing the ball very late in its trajectory.' It just depends on the precise speed of your bowling and how full a length you bowl – and, let's face it, how many fast bowlers of the past twenty years have pitched the ball up enough to

see it swing late? What Wasim and Waqar have done is to demonstrate that Hadlee was right: there is not much science in banging in
the ball halfway down the pitch.

It's still 133 for five and you're on strike. Wasim's bowling and
you take the whole over from him. He's going round the wicket
again now, trying to swing one into you late and beat you for pace in
the way he did with Gooch; he's also varying his pace by adjusting
the speed of his arm, which is often, in any case, so fast that it's
difficult to pick up the ball's flight. You know he's doing it, but it's
one thing knowing it and another coping with it. Luckily, he hasn't
quite got his line right and although he beats your bat a couple of
times it only happens outside off-stump. By the end of his next over,
though, which you also take, you think you've started to work out a
way of playing him. The way he ambles up it's easy to think that he's
not very fast when in fact he is, so what you start to do is get
yourself ready two seconds before he delivers the ball. This helps
your timing, you play a couple confidently out of the middle of the
bat, and when Wasim attempts to ruffle you by dropping one short
you pull him with certainty through mid-wicket for four.

You start to feel more comfortable. You go down the pitch to offer
some words of encouragement to Russell, who has still not stopped
looking ashen-faced. For goodness' sake . . . anyone would think
they were going to hurt you. They're not going to take your head off,
you know. This is the nineties!

Russell manages to squirt one wide of the slips for a single. This
leaves you the rest of the over to face Waqar. The trouble is, you've
got into a rhythm watching Wasim's delivery arm and that's no
use against Waqar: he gets his variety in a more surreptitious way
still, through minor adjustments of his grip. His first ball is a big
swinging yorker into the block-hole: you're late on to it and only
just manage to keep it out. You actually trap the ball between the
base of your bat and the ground. Waqar, thinking at first he
had bowled you, has to cut short his celebrations and you are so
relieved at your escape that you have still not settled properly when
he starts to charge in for his next delivery. What's he going to
try next? What's the last thing you'd expect him to do? A
bouncer. That's what he'll bowl now. A bouncer. But it isn't. It's
another yorker, only this time it swings even later and more extrav-
agantly. In your urgency to get your legs out of the way and make
room for your bat, you virtually swing off your feet: when the ball
thumps you on the right shin your legs are indeed knocked from

under you. As the ball rebounds into the stumps, you stumble, drop your bat and finish scrabbling on your hands in the popping crease.

Your first feeling, as you pick up your bat, dust yourself down and troop off for the pavilion, is one of humiliation. You've never before been made to look so stupid! No wonder people harbour dark suspicions about these guys: you want to do the same. But almost immediately you forget your hurt pride and marvel at what has just happened. You're so astonished, you're not as disappointed at being out as you normally would be. This is the finest bowling you've ever faced. More destructive than West Indies, more devastating than any new-fangled leg-spinner. This is the real revolution! You shake your head in disbelief: half an hour ago the score was 114 for no wicket, now it is 145 for six. And the pitch is still perfect! West Indies may be more relentless and more disciplined, but these Pakistanis are unquestionably more sophisticated. A touch more steel and they might soon be the ones no one else can beat. Put it this way, if Ambrose could bowl like this, he would!

As you reach the pavilion gate, you still can't believe it. Wasim and Waqar have beaten you, all of you, through the air. Gooch leg-before, Ramprakash bowled, Smith leg-before, Hick caught behind, Hussain bowled . . . you bowled . . . they scarcely need any help from the fielders and none at all from pitch. The pitch they just by-pass altogether. They maroon you on the back foot. How ironic. Just when you all thought how good you were getting on the back foot . . .

Then, as you sit down in the corner of the dressing-room, a thought strikes you. Maybe that's it, maybe that's where you're now going wrong.

Maybe it's time to start getting back on the front foot again . . .

SIMON WILDE, *Letting Rip*, 1994

Reverse swing, the bumper, the yorker, new-fangled inventions all. For great fast bowling, pure and simple, some argue that, one has to go back to grass roots.

David Harris

WHILE waiting, I inspected the famous pavilion. It was antiquated, and, despite periodic renovations, the authorities evidently found it unusable. There was little to show it had been requisitioned, for tables and chairs had accumulated much dust, and faded photographs still lined the walls.

Examining these, I recognised many celebrated cricketers, while two individual portraits hung apart. One was of F. R. Spofforth, the other of Sydney Barnes.

I was peering at them in the uncertain light, when I heard some-one sniff and turned to discover an old gentleman at my elbow. He had white hair, side-whiskers, and sunken cheeks, and wore a frock coat over tight-fitting trousers. He seemed to have emerged from the Committee Room, whose door stood ajar.

I wished him good morning, and explained that I was just having a look round. 'I'm waiting for a friend,' I added, 'but he can't see me for another half-hour.'

The old fellow gave an asthmatic chuckle, while his brown, bird-like eyes flitted from me to the photographs and back again. He shook his head smilingly, and I wondered whether he was deaf.

'Great bowlers,' I remarked, nodding at Spofforth and Barnes. 'I suppose nobody will ever know who was the greater.'

He shook his head and smiled again before answering in precise tones:

'Very fine in their way no doubt. Able enough. But not to be compared with David Harris.'

David Harris! This was going back to antiquity. Had he said Alfred Shaw or Tom Emmett, I would not have been surprised. But the eighteenth century seemed rather too remote.

'An underarm bowler,' I protested, 'could hardly challenge comparison with modern speed and swing.' 'My dear young man,' came the amused voice, 'forgive my bluntness, but your logic will not bear an instant's examination. By similar reasoning, present-day military commanders are superior to Bonaparte, because they have the advantage in weapons. A man's genius must surely be judged by the manner in which he employs the powers actually at his disposal.'

He paused to indulge in the wheezing chuckle and head-shake which regularly punctuated his remarks.

111

'I have watched cricket from this pavilion for many years. Much longer than you suspect' – he gave a cryptic smile – 'and, in my judgement, the fact that Harris bowled underarm, and in his earlier days at two stumps, is an added proof of his superiority.'

Obviously he was riding a pet hobby-horse, and it was only charitable to humour him.

'That's an interesting point of view,' I observed politely.

The brown eyes twinkled. 'Of course,' he mused, 'he had frequently the advantage of choosing where the wickets should be pitched. But that again was a test of skill, judgement, and character. Compare him with his contemporaries – Lumpy, for instance, who ignored the needs of his fellow-bowlers – and you see the difference. Harris never forgot his partner at the other end, though his own delivery was best suited by an upward slope, to help the rise of the ball.'

'It must have come awkwardly off the pitch,' I hazarded.

'Awkwardly! Heh! Why, Harris *invented* the real length ball that got batsmen caught! It came from just under his arm, pitched near the bat, spun away – and rose. But his action was superb, sir. He would raise his right arm, draw back the right foot, and then advance with the left – no stooping or side-stepping – before he let loose that ball which beat the batsman by its sharp lift.'

'This would be about 1780, wouldn't it?' I felt rather proud of knowing this, but an amused head-shake quelled my complacence.

'1778, sir, was Harris's first big match. He didn't only show bowlers how to bowl. He compelled batsmen to *go forward in defence*. There was nothing like it before.'

'How do you suppose he acquired his art? Wasn't he a potter or something?'

'By practice, sir. That's what modern bowlers don't understand – the need for practice. Why, David Harris practised during his dinnertime - aye, and in a barn all the winter. He'd wear away a patch of grass by his accuracy – you could see it turning brown!'

'Did anyone ever master him?'

'Beldham was the nearest. There was a lad called Crawte too. But they couldn't be sure. No, sir, David Harris was the greatest bowler ever known, and *nobody* really mastered him.'

I became somewhat exasperated with this ancient's extremism. Every age has its champions, but after all he was eulogising someone he had only read about, for, despite his years, he could hardly even have met anyone who had seen David Harris.

'All this is hearsay,' I commented firmly. 'There's nothing to show that Harris, however successful in the eighteenth century, would have triumphed in the twentieth. Consider the strain of modern Test Matches . . .' That asthmatic chuckle interrupted me.

'Strain!' he scoffed. 'Yes, I've watched your moderns strain themselves – come off the field with hurt muscles! Why, David Harris was afflicted with gout - crippled, sir! D'ye think he gave in? Not he! When he couldn't stand up, they brought an armchair on to the field, and, as soon as he'd delivered a ball, he sat down in it! Strain of modern matches! Tell me another, young man!'

I was so irritated by his derisive chuckle and headshaking that I turned away in annoyance, and, when I looked round again, he had gone – back to the Committee Room, I imagined, to brood over the dim past.

G. D. MARTINEAU, *The Field is Full of Shades*, 1946

Despite the hatred and the divide, batsmen cannot live without bowlers, nor bowlers without batsmen. Only against the ability of one can the prowess of the other be measured. That struggle is best exhibited by the war between a batsmen and a spinner, particularly a leg-break bowler, and captured by Alan Ross.

Richie Benaud

WATCHING BENAUD BOWL

Leg-spinners pose problems much like love,
Requiring commitment, the taking of a chance.
Half-way deludes; the bold advance.

Right back, there's time to watch
Developments, though maybe too late.
It's not spectacular, but can conciliate.

Instinctively romantics move towards,
Preventing complexities by their embrace,
Batsman and lover embarked as overlords.

ALAN ROSS

113

The leg-break bowler, Arthur Mailey, fleshes out the bones of this struggle in his description of the battle of wits he enjoyed with Victor Trumper, another who made an art of the craft of batsmanship around the turn of the century.

Victor Trumper

IT is difficult to realise that a relatively minor event in one's life can still remain the most important through the years. I was chosen to play for Redfern against Paddington, and Paddington was Victor Trumper's club. This was unbelievable, fantastic. It could never happen – something was sure to go wrong. A war – an earthquake – Trumper might fall sick. A million things could crop up in the two or three days before the match.

I sat on my bed and looked at Trumper's picture still pinned on the canvas wall. It seemed to be breathing with the movement of the draught between the skirting. I just couldn't believe that this, to me, ethereal and godlike figure could step off the wall, pick up the bat and say: 'Two legs, please, umpire,' in my presence. My family, usually undemonstrative and self-possessed, found it difficult to maintain that reserve which, strange as it may seem, was characteristic of my father's Northern Irish heritage. 'H'm,' said Father, 'Playing against Trumper on Saturday? By Jove, you'll cop old harry if you're put on to bowl to him.' 'Why should he?' protested Mother. 'You never know what you can do until you try.'

I had nothing to say. I was little concerned with what should happen to me in the match. What worried me was that something would happen to Trumper which would prevent his playing. Although at that time I had never seen Trumper play, on occasions I had trudged from Waterloo across the sandhills to the Sydney Cricket Ground and waited at the gate to see the players come out. Once I had climbed on to a tram and actually sat opposite my hero for three stops. I would have gone farther, but having no money I did not want to take the chance of being kicked in the pants by the conductor. Even so I had gone half a mile out of my way.

In my wildest dreams I never thought I would even speak to Trumper – let alone play against him. I am fairly phlegmatic by nature but between the period of my selection and the match I must have behaved like a half-wit. Right up to my first Test match, I always washed and pressed my own flannels, but before this match I pressed them not once but several times. On the Saturday I was up with the sparrows looking anxiously at the sky. It was a lovely morning but it still might rain. Come to that, lots of things could happen in two hours – there was still a chance that Vic be taken ill or knocked down by a tram or twist his ankle or break his arm . . .

My thoughts were interrupted by a vigorous thumping on the back gate. I looked out of the washhouse-bathroom-woodshed-workshop window and saw that it was the milkman who was kicking up the row. 'Hey,' he roared, 'yer didn't leave the can out. I can't wait round here all day. A man should pour it in the garbage tin – that'd make yer wake up a bit.' On that morning I wouldn't have cared whether he poured the milk in the garbage tin or all over me. I was playing against the great Victor Trumper. Let the milk take care of itself.

I kept looking at the clock. It might be slow – or it might have stopped. I'd better whip down to the Zetland hotel and check up. Anyway, I mightn't bowl at Trumper at all. He might get out before I come on. Or I mightn't get a bowl at all – I can't put myself on. Wonder what Trumper is doing this very minute . . . bet he's not ironing his flannels. Sends them to the laundry, I suppose. He's probably got two sets of flannels anyway. Perhaps he's at breakfast, eating bacon and eggs. Wonder if he knows I'm playing against him? Don't suppose he's ever heard of me. Wouldn't worry him anyhow, I shouldn't think. Gosh, what a long morning. Think I'll dig the garden. No, I won't. I want to keep fresh. Think I'll lie down for a bit . . . better not, I might fall off to sleep and be late.

The morning did not pass in this way. Time just stopped. I couldn't bring myself to do anything in particular and yet I couldn't settle to the thought of not doing anything. I was bowling to Trumper and I was not bowling to Trumper. I was early and I was late. In fact, I think I was partly out of my mind. I didn't get to the ground so very early after all, mainly because it would have been impossible for me to wait around so near the scene of Trumper's appearance – and yet for it to rain or news to come that something had prevented Vic from playing.

'Is he here?' I asked Harry Goddard, our captain, the moment I did arrive at the ground. 'Is who here?' he countered. My answer was probably a scornful and disgusted look. I remember that it occurred to me to say, 'Julius Caesar, of course,' but that I stopped myself being cheeky because this was one occasion when I couldn't afford to be.

Paddington won the toss and took first knock. When Trumper walked out to bat Harry Goddard said to me: 'I'd better keep you away from Vic. If he starts on you he'll probably knock you out of grade cricket.'

I was inclined to agree with him, yet at the same time I didn't fear punishment from the master batsman. All I wanted to do was just bowl at him. I suppose in their time other ambitious youngsters have wanted to play on the same stage with Henry Irving, or sing with Caruso or Melba, to fight with Napoleon or sail with Columbus. It wasn't conquest I desired. I simply wanted to meet my hero on common ground. Vic, beautifully clad in creamy, loose-fitting but well-tailored flannels, left the pavilion with his bat tucked under his left arm and in the act of donning his gloves. Although slightly pigeon-toed in the left foot he had a springy athletic walk and a tendency to shrug his shoulders every few minutes, a habit I understand he developed through trying to loosen his shirt off his shoulders when it became soaked with sweat during his innings.

Arriving at the wicket, he bent his bat handle almost to a right angle, walked up the pitch, prodded about six yards of it, returned to the crease and asked the umpire for 'two legs'; then he took a quick glance in the direction of fine leg, shrugged again and took up his stance.

I was called to bowl sooner than I expected. I suspect now that Harry Goddard changed his mind and decided to put me out of my misery early in the piece. Did I ever bowl that first ball? I don't remember. My mind was in a whirl. I really think I fainted and the secret of that mythical first ball has been kept over all these years to save me embarrassment. If ball was sent down it must have been hit for six, or at least four, because I was awakened from my trance by that thunderous barracker Yabba booming, 'O for a strong arm and a walking stick!'

I do remember the next ball. It was, I imagined, a perfect leg-break. When it left my hand it was singing sweetly like a humming-top. The trajectory could not have been more graceful if designed by a professor of ballistics. The tremendous leg-spin caused the ball to swing and curve from the off and move in line with the middle and leg stump. Had I bowled this particular ball at any other batsman I would have turned my back early in its flight and listened for the death rattle. However, consistent with my idolatry of the champion, I watched his every movement. He stood poised like a panther ready to spring. Down came his left foot to within a foot of the ball. The bat, swung from well over his shoulders, met the ball just as it fizzed off the pitch and the next sound I heard was a rapping on the off-side fence. It was the most beautiful shot I have ever seen.

The immortal Yabba made some attempt to say something but his voice faded away to the soft gurgle one hears at the end of the kook-aburra's song. The only person on the ground who didn't watch the course of the ball was Victor Trumper. The moment he played it he turned his back, smacked down a few tufts of grass and prodded his way back to the batting crease. He knew where the ball was going.

What were my reactions? Well, I never expected that ball or any other I could produce to get Trumper's wicket. But that being the best ball a bowler of my type could spin into being, I thought that at least Trumper might have been forced to play a defensive stroke, partic-ularly as I was almost a stranger, too, and it might have been to his advantage to use discretion rather than valour. After I had bowled one or two other reasonably good balls without success I found fresh hope in the thought that Trumper had found Bosanquet, creator of the 'wrong-un' or 'bosie' (the latter, I think, a better name) rather puzzling. This left me with one shot in my locker, but if I didn't use it quickly I would be taken out of the firing line. I therefore decided to try this most undisciplined and cantankerous creation of the great Bosanquet - not, as many might think, as a compliment to the inven-tor but as the gallant farewell, so to speak, of a warrior who refused to surrender until all his ammunition was spent.

Again fortune was on my side in that I bowled the ball I had often dreamed of bowling. As with the leg-break, it had sufficient spin to curve in the air and break considerably after making contact with the pitch. If anything it might have had a little more top-spin, which would cause it to drop rather suddenly. The sensitivity of a spinning ball against the breeze is governed by the amount of spin imparted, and if a ball bowled at a certain pace drops on a certain spot, one bowled with identical pace but with more top-spin should drop eighteen inches or two feet shorter. For this reason I thought the difference in the trajectory and ultimate landing of the ball might provide a measure of uncertainty in Trumper's mind. While the ball was in flight this reasoning appeared to be vindicated by Trumper's initial movement. As at the beginning of my over, he sprang in to attack but did not realise that the ball, being an off-break, was floating away from him and dropping a little quicker.

In a split second Vic grasped this and tried to make up the deficiency with a wider swing of the bat. It was then I could see a passage-way to the stumps with our 'keeper, Con Hayes, ready to claim his victim. Vic's bat came through like a flash but the ball passed between his bat and legs, missed the stumps by a fraction, and the bails were whipped off with the great batsman at least two yards out of his ground.

Vic had made no attempt to scramble back. He knew the ball had beaten him and was prepared to pay the penalty, and although he had little chance of regaining his crease on this occasion I think he would have acted similarly if his back foot had been only an inch from safety.

As he walked past me he smiled, patted the back of his bat and said: 'It was too good for me.' There was no triumph in me as I watched the receding figure. I felt like a boy who had killed a dove.

ARTHUR MAILEY, *10 for 66 and All That*, 1958

'*Davidson is roughing up the wicket for Benaud's leg-breaks. Instructions, please!*'

EARLY DAYS

'Archaeological'

T HE instinct to throw and to hit is the basis of man's primitive armoury. Nature, of her bounty, has supplied him with an endless variety of missiles, of means of striking, and of targets, and, in her wisdom, has provided that what the man must do for life, the boy should attempt for fun. That is the genesis of cricket.

From time immemorial a ball has exercised an irresistible attraction on man. Five thousand years ago the Egyptian played ninepins; Nausicaa and her maidens were having fielding practice when Odysseus discovered himself to them; the Athenian boys, in the famous relief, are obviously 'bullying off' at hockey; only pinkeye stayed Horace and indigestion Virgil from joining Maecenas in a ball game on the famous journey to Brundisium, and in AD 150 Fronto could write to Marcus Aurelius, with reference to an argument between them, *'Malitiosam pilam mihi dedisti'* – you have bowled me a pretty dirty ball!

Hurley was played in Ireland before St Patrick came; St Cuthbert as a boy is said to have excelled his fellows in playing at ball. Specialisation in ball games seems to have set in from a very early date. The Eastern peoples took to hitting the ball with their familiar mall, or mallet, and it was from the East, and following on the Crusades, that polo reached Europe; from the Roman 'fives' *(pila palmaris)* developed all the varieties of racquet games with royal tennis, *jeu de paume,* at their head.

As early as 1292 Phillip le Bel had to issue an edict discouraging the nobility of France from playing tennis to the neglect of the profession of arms: there are, of course, the famous references to 'chases' and 'hazard' in Shakespeare's *Henry V* and Henry VIII in his youth was a famous player of the game.

But the northern branch of the Nordic family had their own preference. They liked to kick a ball, and, even if the line in *King Lear* 'nor tripped neither, you base football player' may be historically anticipatory, we read how early in the fourteenth century the peasants on a Monastic estate rose in revolt, cut off the head of the Abbott's bailiff, and played football with it down the village street. But most of all did our own forefathers enjoy hitting a ball with that which it was second nature for them to carry, a staff or club, be it straight or 'crooked'.

From this parent tree of what we may call 'club ball' sprang in different branches the hockey group in which the ball is driven to and fro between two 'goals', the golf group in which it is hit towards a mark, and the cricket group in which it is aimed at a mark and driven away from it. A good deal has been written, and to no great end, as to the possible and primitive relationship between cricket, as we understand that word, and other early variations of club ball such as stool-ball, cat and dog, trap-ball and rounders. It is unlikely that this maze can ever be unravelled: let us concentrate then on reviewing the earliest evidence for cricket itself.

By a striking coincidence the first two references are almost exactly contemporary. One is visual, and available as a postcard (No. 11 of set 58) at the British Museum. It represents part of the illumination to a Decretal of Pope Gregory IX, embellished in England somewhere about the beginning of the fourteenth century. On it we see two figures, the one a boy with a straight club and a ball, and the other, his tutor, demonstrating, left-handed and with convincing technique, a stroke played with what, except for its length, is indistinguishable from a modern cricket stump.

The second was unearthed from their library in 1787 by the Society of Antiquaries and consists of an entry in the Wardrobe accounts of the Royal Household for the twenty-eighth year of the reign of Edward I – 1300. It reads as follows:

Domino Johanni de Leek, capellano Domini Edwardi fil' Regis, pro den' per ipsum liberat' eidem Domino suo ad ludendum ad *creag*',

et alios ludos per vices, per manus proprias apud Westm' 10 die
Marcii 100s.

Et per manus Hugonis camerani sui apud Newenton mense
Marcii 20s. Summa . . . 6 . 0 . 0.

Translated:

To Master John de Leek, chaplain of Prince Edward, the King's son,
for monies which he has paid out, personally and by the hands of
others, for the said Prince's playing at Cr – and other sports – at
Westminster March 10-100s.

And by the hands of Hugo, his Chamberlain, at Newenton in the
month of March – 20s. Total . . . £6 . 0 . 0.

Now, what was this 'creag' at which the Black Prince's grandfather
was playing, when a boy of sixteen, possibly in the company of the
notorious Piers Gaveston, whose evil influence was to contribute so
much to his tragic end, and, surely not without significance, at
Newenton, (or Newendon), on the edge of the Weald where we
know beyond argument that 'cricket' started? The learning of
philologists has debated it in vain, but from their contentions
certain conclusions can now safely be drawn. There is no known
Latin word corresponding to 'creag', and capable of any satisfactory
interpretation in a sporting sense. But if we regard it as an attempt
to 'low-Latinise' a native word, we may find ourselves on a hotter
scent.

In the mother tongue of the northern branch of the Aryan race
there was a syllable beginning with *cr*, ending with a hard *c*, having
for its middle letter every variety of the vowels according to tribal
predilection, and meaning a staff or stick. Witness the earliest
English version of the Twenty-third Psalm, 'Thy rod and Thy staff
comfort me', which reads, 'Gird thin and *cricc* thin me frefredon'.
Furthermore, the termination 'et', though it sounds French, need
not be anything of the sort: it may really be of good old English
stock, a variant form of the diminutive terminal 'el'. Hence,
'cricket' is simply a small 'crick' or staff, cricket-bat a redundancy
exactly paralleled by golf-club, hockey-stick, or billiard-cue; and Dr
Johnson was right when he derived cricket from *'cryce*, Saxon, a
stick', though less happy when he defined it as a sport 'in which
contenders drive a ball with sticks in opposition to each other'!

Reverting then, for a moment, to Prince Edward, let us now see

121

what can be made of the puzzle. With the hard terminal 'c' of *cric*, a 'g' was virtually interchangeable; now suppose Piers, or some other French playfellow of Edward's, attempted to pronounce the word, he would sound the 'i' as 'ee', or 'ea', and straightway we have 'creaget', which the clerk of accounts, following his consistent practice, shortened down to *'creag'*.

The next possible reference to the game would seem to be in a statement made by a certain John Combe of Quidhampton in Wilts when, testifying to the miracles of St Osmund, he quoted his own experience of miraculous cure after having his head broken when engaged with his neighbours *'ludentes ad pilam cum magnis baculis'*.

But whether or not we accept this evidence for cricket being played under the Plantagenets, there is no doubt about it when we come to the Tudors.

In 1598 John Derrick, gentleman and Queen's Coroner for the county, bore written testimony (still preserved at Guildford) as to a parcel of land in the parish of Holy Trinity in that town, which, originally waste, had been appropriated and enclosed by one John Parvish to serve as a timber yard. This land, says Derrick, he had known for fifty years past, and, when a scholar of the Free Schoole of Guildeford (founded 1509), 'he and diverse of his fellowes did runne and play there at creckett and other plaies'. Now at the time of writing John Derrick was fifty-nine years old, so that we may safely date that definite testimony as not later than 1550.

About the same time we hear that when, consequent on the Reformation, Stoney Hurst School migrated to Rouen, they took their game of 'Stoney Hurst Cricket' with them.

In 1598 Giovanni Florio, tutor to the children of Shakespeare's patron, the Earl of Southampton, translated in his English–Italian dictionary the word *sgrittare* as 'to make a noise like a cricket; to play cricket-a-wicket and be merry'. A few years later John Bullokar in his *English Expositor* is defining cricket as 'a kind of game with a ball', and Randle le Cotgrave's French and English Dictionary identifies 'Crosse', inter-alia , 'the crooked staff wherewith boys play at cricket'.

The next piece of evidence is of more general interest. Sir William Dugdale, a Royalist writer, refers to Oliver Cromwell, then a boy of eighteen, going up to London in 1617, indulging there in football, cricket, cudgelling and wrestling and 'gaining for himself the name of royster'. Cricket then had spread beyond its Wealden home and that it was no longer just a game for boys is proved by a 'Bill of Presentment' dated 1622, against six parishioners of Boxgrove for playing cricket in the Churchyard on a Sunday.

Ten years or so later a Puritan Divine, The Rev Thomas Wilson, is converting the inhabitants of Maidstone from the same profanation of the Sabbath: about the same time the park at West Horsley is being ploughed and sown for a cricket field, and in 1653 Sir Thomas Urquhart, translating Rabelais, is describing Gargantua as playing cricket. Despite what we have just read about the Lord Protector's boyhood we would not expect the Major-Generals to have had much sympathy with any profane sport and sure enough we read of them issuing orders that all bats and balls in Ireland should be surrendered and burnt by the common hangman!

Again, during the Commonwealth, Edward Phillips, a nephew of Milton's, makes one of the ladies in his *Mysteries of Love and Eloquence* torture herself with the doubt whether one day her beloved may not say, 'Would my eyes had been beat out of my head with a cricket-ball the day before I saw thee!'

By 1676 the missionary process had begun in earnest, for in that year we find a naval chaplain, Henry Teonge, recording how he and a party from three of His Majesty's ships in the Levant rode up from Antioch to Aleppo, and there, on May 6th, 'did in a fine valley pitch a princely tent and divert themselves with various sports, including "krickett".' Eight years earlier, at home, the proprietor of 'The Ram' in Smithfield was rated for a cricket field, and before the end of the century we find the Jeremiah who wrote *The World Bewitch'd*, complaining that cricket, among other sports, 'will be very much in fashion and more tradesmen may be seen playing in the fields than working in their shops'. Chamberlayne's *State of England* mentions cricket among the people's recreations for the first time in its 1707 edition, and by 1720 the Rev John Strype, editing Stow's *Survey of London*, has been forced to add cricket to the list of amusements popular with the citizens of the metropolis.

The truth seems to be that the last half of the seventeenth century was really the critical stage in the game's evolution, the era in which it developed from the pastime of boys, or, at best, of the yeomen of the exclusive Weald into a game with a national appeal, enjoying in ever-increasing measure the patronage of the leaders of Society. To this, it would seem, political history may have decisively contributed. With the temporary eclipse of the Royalist cause, it is probable that many of the nobility and gentry would retire to their country seats, and here some at least of them, such as the Sackvilles of Knole Park and the Richmond family of Goodwood, would find themselves watching the Wealden game as played by their gardeners, huntsmen, foresters and farm hands and from sheer *ennui* would try their own hand at it and find that it was good.

With the Restoration, back they came to London with their new discovery, bringing with them, perhaps, in their service some of the local experts. In a year or two it became the thing in London society to make matches and to form clubs – a club at St. Albans is said to date from 1666 – and thus was inaugurated the regime of feudal patronage which was to control the destinies of the game for the next century and more.

In 1677 we hear of Thomas Dacre, the Earl of Sussex, borrowing three pounds from his steward 'to take to the cricket match at the Dicker', a ground near Hurstmonceux, and of his wife, a daughter of Charles II and Lady Castlemaine, growing tired of the prevailing amusements there, of which one was cricket.

The increasing interest in and status of the game is soon reflected in the contemporary Press. In 1697 the Foreign Post announces 'a great cricket match' in Sussex, eleven a side and for fifty guineas. In March 1700 – the season seems to have started earlier then – the Post Boy refers to a 'match at cricket', the best of five games, the first to be played 'on Clapham Common near Foxhall on Easter Monday next, for £10 a head each game and £20 the odd one'. In 1705 an XI of Chatham are meeting an XI of the West of Kent; two years later London meets Croydon at Lamb's Conduit Fields near Holborn, and in 1709 Kent and Surrey face each other at Dartford in what would seem to be the first recorded county match.

H. S. ALTHAM, *History of Cricket*, 1926

Judge for yourselves whether, at the top of the above piece, H. S. Altham has correctly interpreted the scene from the opening chapter of Homer's Odyssey. Surely this is more than an afternoon's fielding practice.

BEACH CRICKET

. . . Having dined, Nausicaa
With other virgins did at stool-ball play,
Their shoulder-reaching head-tires laying by.
Nausicaa, with the wrists of ivory,
The liking stroke strook, singing first a song,
As custom order'd, and amidst the throng
Made such a shew, and so past all was seen.
. . . Then Minerva thought
What means to wake Ulysses might be wrought,
That he might see this lovely-sighted maid,
Whom she intended should become his aid,
Bring him to town, and his return advance.
Her means was this, though thought a stool-ball chance:
The queen now, for the upstroke, strook the ball
Quite wide off th' other maids, and made it fall
Amidst the whirlpools. At which out shriek'd all,
And with the shriek did wise Ulysses wake.

GEORGE CHAPMAN,
translation of Homer's *The Odyssey*

Maybe the Middle East was the cradle of cricket for, as Altham also notes, they were playing at Aleppo back in 1675. Altham's archaeology ends in 1709. Reports of cricket matches were being carried in newspapers shortly after that date, although according to some of the reports the games were played on far from level terms and ill-feeling and skulduggery were never far from the surface. The Saturday Post *of 1718 gives this review of a match between the White Conduit Club, a precursor of the Marylebone Club, and the Rochester Punch Club.*

Cricket in the Raw

O N Monday the first inst. was played a famous game of Cricket in the White Conduit Fields at Islington by eleven London gamesters against eleven Kentish gamesters, who call themselves the Punch Club Society, for half a guinea a man. After a trial of their skill, which lasted about four hours, the Kentish men, whether it was for want of their celestial liquor (punch) to cheer up their exhausted spirits, I cannot determine; but be that as it will, they thought they should be worsted and therefore to the surprise of a numerous crowd of spectators, three of their men made an elopement, and got off the ground without going in, and made the best of their [way] home, hoping thereby to save their money; but we hear the London gamesters are resolved not to be bubbled in that manner, and are therefore determined to commence a suit at law against them to oblige them to pay their money. (6 Sept.)

The Rochester Punch Club Society are very much surprised that men who call themselves the London Gamesters should risk the little reputation they have upon a forgery, since it would have been a much greater wonder to the numerous crowd of spectators if the Rochester men had not beat all those bragging hectors, but no gamesters, than that three of their men should not be able to bear the violence of the rains, which fell so heavy it was impossible to continue the game. To convince them that the Rochester men do not think they had the worst of the match, they are willing to meet eleven of the best of them whenever they please, at Dartford in Kent, where they will play them for a guinea a head; but they think proper to give them this advice, that if they cannot choose better men than they did the last encounter, it will be but throwing away their money and they had much better stay at home. If in spite of this caution they dare venture, the Rochester men don't doubt but sprightly Punch will easily overcome foggy Ale. (20 Sept.)

Saturday Post, 1718

Humours and gamesmanship had not much improved by 1772, when Sheffield took on Nottingham, Sheffield showing characteristic Yorkshire guile.

Monday the first instant at six in the evening, the cricket match, eleven on a side, between the Sheffield club, and the Nottinghamshire Sherwood youths, was finally determined at Sheffield, in favour of the former. The Nottingham party laboured under great disadvantages; fatigued with their journey, they went in first, on a very wet piece of ground, and played in such a slippery soil, that they could neither run, strike or catch without danger of falling, by which unlucky situation, they gained only fourteen notches on their first inning, but thereby prepared the ground for their adversaries, who coming in fresh, and in top spirits, gained near seventy notches, which gave them such a superiority as could not be recovered. But here it is to be observed, that before the Sheffield club went in, they ordered a large quantity of coal sack to be laid on the ground, and thereby secured their running, etc.

Derby Mercury, 1772

It would appear that early cricket was every bit as perilous as a series in the Caribbean or a visit to a Sydney nightclub, but the rude vigour of this early game must have been an exceptionally fine way of working off one's frustrations. That is one possible interpretation of G. M. Trevelyan's famous passage.

Vive le Cricket, Vive la Révolution

IN Stuart times cricket had grown up obscurely and locally, in Hampshire and Kent, as a game of the common people. The original method of scoring, by 'notches' on a stick, argues illiteracy. But in the early eighteenth century cricket enlarged both its geographic and its social boundaries. In 1743 it was observed that 'noblemen, gentlemen and clergy', were 'making butchers, cobblers or tinkers their companions' in the game. Three years later, when

Kent scored 111 notches against All England's 110, Lord John Sackville was a member of the winning team of which the gardener at Knole was captain. Village cricket spread fast through the land. In those days, before it became scientific, cricket was the best game in the world to watch, with its rapid sequence of amusing incidents, each ball a potential crisis! Squire, farmer, blacksmith and labourer, with their women and children come to see the fun, were at ease together and happy all the summer afternoon. If the French *noblesse* had been capable of playing cricket with their peasants, their châteaux would never have been burnt.

G. M. TREVELYAN, *English Social History*, 1944

Julian Barnes puts flesh on Trevelyan's bones in the short story Melon *from which this extract is taken.*

Melon

S IR Hamilton Lindsay departed for Chertsey on Thursday, 6th August. Samuel Dobson travelled on top with the groom, Sir Hamilton inside with the cricket bats. This was, he knew without reflection, the correct priority: Dobson would only be toughened by rain and rough weather, whereas the bats were more sensitive to the displeasure of the elements and must be treated with care. In tedious moments of the journey, Hamilton would take out a soft cloth and gently rub a little butter into the blade of his bat. Others preferred oil, but he felt a certain local pride in this particularity of his. The instrument itself was carved from a branch of willow on his own estate; now it was being swabbed with butter made from the milk of cows which had grazed in the very water-meadow at whose edge the willows grew.

He finished soothing his bat and wound around it the yard of muslin within which it always travelled. Dobson's bat was a cruder engine, and Dobson no doubt had his own secrets for making it as strong and supple as he required. Some men rubbed ale into their bats; others the fat of a ham; others again were said to warm their

128

bats before the fire and then make water upon them. No doubt the moon had to be in a certain quarter at the same time, thought Sir Hamilton with a sceptical jerk of the head. The only thing that counted was how you smote the ball; and Dobson could smite with the best of them. But it was the persistency and valour of the man's right arm that had persuaded Sir Hamilton to bring him to Nesfield.

Dobson was the second under-gardener at the Hall. It was not, however, to Dobson that a man would readily turn for the implementation of a landscape by the late Mr Brown. The fellow could scarce tell a lupin from a turnip, and his duties were confined to the physical and the general rather than to the skilled and the particular. In short, he was not permitted to handle a spade without the presence of an overseer. But Sir Hamilton had not offered him employment – or played the poacher, to use the description of Dobson's previous employer – with the intention of procuring a lady-fingered turf-trimmer. Dobson's expertise was with another kind of turf. To witness the man's unflinchingness when standing at bat's end was sure compensation for his failure of wit in the kitchen garden.

They would arrive at Chertsey the next day, and then proceed for Dover on the Saturday. Five of the Duke's cricketers lived hard by Chertsey: Fry, Edmeads, Attfield, Etheridge and Wood. Then there was to be himself, Dobson, the Earl of Tankerville, William Bedster and Lumpy Stevens. The Duke was naturally in Paris; Tankerville and Bedster were coming separately to Dover; so eight of them would meet at Mr Yalden's inn at Chertsey. It was here, some years back, that Lumpy Stevens had won Tankerville his famous bet. The Earl had wagered that his man could in practice-bowling hit a feather placed on the ground one time in four. Mr Stevens had obliged his employer, who, it was rumoured, profited by several hundred pounds in the business. Lumpy Stevens was one of Tankerville's gardeners, and Sir Hamilton had often set himself musing over the prospect of separate wager with the Earl: as to which of their two men knew the less about horticulture.

He admitted to a gloomy and irritable mood as he ignored the passing countryside. Mr Hawkins had declined the invitation to accompany him on the journey. Hamilton had urged his former tutor to cast his eyes upon the Continent of Europe one last time. More than that, he thought it a damned generous offer on his behalf to cart the old fellow across to Paris and back, no doubt enduring many gross and whining episodes of vomit on the packet, if the past were any indicator of the present. But Mr Hawkins had answered that he preferred his memories of tranquillity to a vision of present troubles. He saw no prospect of excitement in the matter, grateful as he was to Sir Hamilton. Grateful and pusillanimous, Sir Hamilton reflected as he took his leave of the broken-kneed old man. As pusillanimous as Evelina, who had poured thunderstorms from her eyes in an attempt to thwart his departure. Twice he had discovered her in hugger-mugger with Dobson, and had been unable to obtain from either the matter of their discussions. Dobson claimed that trying to lighten Milady's burden of apprehension and fear regarding the voyage, but Sir Hamilton did not entirely believe him. What did they have to fear anyway? The two nations were not at war, their mission was peaceful, and no Frenchman, however untutored, would ever mistake Sir Hamilton for one of his own race. And besides, there would be eleven of them, all stout fellows armed with pieces of English willow. What possible harm could befall them?

At Chertsey they put up at The Cricketers, where Mr Yalden gave them good hospitality and regretted that his cricketing days were now in the past. Others regretted this less than Mr Yalden, since their host had not always shown himself scrupulous when the laws of the game impeded him from winning. He was, however, scrupulous in launching his Chertsey men and their compatriots off to war with his strongest hogshead. Hamilton lay in bed with an image of the beefsteak in his stomach tossing on a sea of ale like the Dover packet in a Channel storm.

His emotions were scarcely less turbulent. Evelina's water-spouts had affected him the more because she had never, in their ten years of marriage, sought to deter him from any of his cricketing ventures. She was not like Jack Heythrop's wife, or Sir James Tinker's: ladies who shrank from the notion of their husbands consorting on the turf with blacksmiths and gamekeepers, chimney-sweeps and shoeboys. Mrs Jack Heythrop, her nose pointing to Heaven, would ask how you might expect to exert your authority over the coachman and the gardener when the previous afternoon the coachman had caught you out and the gardener had shown such disrespect to your bowling? It did not make for social harmony, and the sporting universe should be a reflection of the social universe. Hence, according to Mrs Heythrop, the manifest superiority and virtue of racing: owner, trainer, jockey and groom all knew their places, and such places were of themselves fixed by their self-evident importance. How different from the foolish commingling of cricket, which was besides, as everyone knew, little more than a vulgar excuse for gambling.

Of course there was gambling. What was the point of sport if a man did not gamble? What was the point of a glass of soda if it did not have brandy in it? Wagering, as Tankerville had once put it, was the salt which brought out the savour of the dish. Nowadays Hamilton himself wagered modestly, just as he had promised Evelina and his mother before his marriage. In his present mood, however, and having regard to the money he had saved by Mr Hawkins' absence, he was damned inclined to wager a little above the normal on the outcome of the match between Dorset's XI and the Gentlemen of France. To be sure, some of the Chertsey fellows were becoming a little dull of eye and plump of shank. But if Dorset's men could not have the beating of Monsieur, then they should turn their bats into winter kindling.

They left Chertsey by post-coach on the morning of Sunday, 9th August. Approaching Dover, they encountered several carriages of French making towards London.

'Running away from the bowling of Mr Stevens, I wouldn't doubt,' observed Sir Hamilton.

'Best not to bowl full tilt, Lumpy,' said Dobson, 'or they'll be filling their breeches.'

'So will you, Dobson, if you dine French-style too often,' replied Stevens.

Sir Hamilton had a sudden memory, and recited to the occupants of the post-coach the lines:

> She sent her priest in wooden shoes
> From haughty Gaul to make ragoos.

Inchoate murmurings greeted the verse, and Sir Hamilton caught Dobson's eyes upon him, their expression more that of an anxious tutor than of a second under-gardener.

At Dover they met the Earl of Tankerville and William Bedster at an inn already over-crowded with emigrant French. Bedster had formerly been the Earl's butler and the most celebrated bat in Surrey; now he was a publican in Chelsea, and his retirement had helped increase his circumference. He and the Chertsey men taunted one another over their last English dinner with the contentious happenings of forgotten seasons, and noisily argued the merits of two-stump cricket over its modern replacement. In another corner of the inn sat Tankerville and Sir Hamilton Lindsay, ruminating upon the general situation in France and the particular position of their friend John Sackville, third Duke of Dorset and His Majesty's Ambassador, these six years past, to the Court of Versailles. Such matters were not for the ears of Lumpy Stevens and the Chertsey men.

Dorset's embassy had from the beginning been conducted in a manner to make Mrs Jack Heythrop tip her nose in disapproval. His hospitality in Paris was of the most generous kind, embracing under its roof gamesters and card-sharps, wh—s and parasites. His intimacy with many of the finest ladies of French society extended, it was said, even as far as Mrs Bourbon herself. It was whispered – yet especially not before the likes of either Mrs Jack Heythrop or Mr Lumpy Stevens – that Dorset even lived *en famille* at Versailles. The mundane business of mere diplomacy he left to his friend Mr Hailes.

Ever since his appointment in 1783, the Duke had thought nothing of returning to England annually for the cricketing months. But this summer he had failed to appear. From such absence, rather than from the ubiquitous presence of French refugees in London, Tankerville and Lindsay had judged the current disturbances across the Channel to be of proper gravity. As the summer had proceeded and public order deteriorated in the French capital, scoundrels began issuing libels on the British nation, and rumours were started of the Royal Navy blockading French ports. In these darkening circumstances Dorset had proposed, towards the end of July, as a gesture of conciliation and friendship between the two countries, that a team of English cricketers be sent to play a team of Frenchmen in the Champs-Elysées. The Duke, who during his six years had done much to foment interest in the game, was to organise the eleven Parisians; Tankerville was enjoined to arrange transport of the English players with all despatch.

Sir Hamilton lay in bed that night recalling his tour with Mr Hawkins a dozen, no, nearer fifteen years ago. He himself was now becoming almost as plump of shank as many of the Chertsey fellows. He remembered the ratty horses and the lank pigtail queues trailing down like an eel; the stinking macquerel and the voluptuous melon; the coachman and his horse, kneeling in whipped equality; the blood running from the roast thrushes when the knife was inserted. He imagined himself smiting the French bowling to all parts of the Champs-Elysées, and Frenchmen carrying barbered dogs applauding him from beneath their umbrellas. He imagined seeing the French coast approach; he remembered being happy.

Sir Hamilton Lindsay was never put to the test on the Elysian Fields, nor did Lumpy Stevens ever make Frenchmen fill their breeches as they received his demon bowling. Instead, Lumpy Stevens played at Bishopsbourne in the match between Kent and Surrey, watched by several Chertsey men and Sir Hamilton Lindsay. Their *rendez-vous* with Dorset had not taken place, as originally intended, at the Duke's *hôtel* in Paris, but on the quayside of Dover in the morning of Monday, 10th August 1789. The Duke had relinquished his embassy two days previously, and had travelled the 90 miles to Boulogne on roads even more infested with bandits than was usual. It was presumed that Dorset's *hôtel* had been plundered by the mob within hours of his departure; but in spite of this he was in remarkably cheerful spirits. He was, he said, much looking forward to spending the late summer and autumn in England as he normally did. The French capital would not seem so far away, since many of his Parisian friends had now come to England. He would discover whether there were enough among their number for the match which had been intended for the Champs-Elysées to be played instead at Sevenoaks.

JULIAN BARNES, *Cross Channel*, 1992

So what would have been England's first overseas touring party was turned back. As has become customary, the tourists were setting out full of optimism, convinced of the merits of their squad. A contemporary, certainly flattering, study of the prowess of the Duke suggests he was an all-rounder of the calibre of an Ian Botham or Wasim Akram.

Equalled by few he plays with glee.
Nor peevish seeks for victory.
His Grace for bowling cannot yield.
To none but Lumpy in the field.
And far unlike the modern way.
Of blocking every ball at play.
He firmly stands with bat upright.
And strikes with his athletic might.
Sends forth the ball across the mead.
And scores six notches for the deed.

Gentleman's Magazine, 1773

Wherever and however the game started, cricket grew to maturity in the villages of southern England, foremost among them Hambledon in Hampshire. One of the more celebrated natives of that village, John Nyren, gives the following biographies of the great Hambledon team of the eighteenth century.

A Hambledon XI

I WAS born at Hambledon, in Hampshire – the *Attica* of the scientific art I am celebrating. No eleven in England could compare with the Hambledon which met on the first Tuesday in May on Broad-Halfpenny. So renowned a set were the men of Hambledon, that the whole country round would flock to see one of their trial matches. 'Great men,' indeed, 'have been among us – better, none'; and in the course of my recollections I shall have occasion to instance so many within the knowledge of persons now living, as will, I doubt not, warrant me in giving the palm to my native place.

The two principal bowlers in my early days were Thomas Brett and Richard Nyren, of Hambledon; the *corps de reserve*, or change-bowlers, were Barber and Hogsflesh. Brett was, beyond all comparison, the fastest as well as straightest bowler that was ever known: he was neither a thrower nor a jerker, but a legitimate downright *bowler*, delivering his ball fairly, high, and very quickly, quite as strongly as the jerkers, and with the force of a point blank shot. He was a well-grown, dark-looking man, remarkably strong, and with rather a short arm. As a batter, he was comparatively an inferior player – a slashing hitter, but he had little guard of his wicket, and his judgement of the game was held in no great estimation. Brett, whose occupation was that of a farmer, bore the universal character of a strictly honourable man in all his transactions, whether in business or in amusement.

Richard Nyren was left-handed. He had a high delivery, always to the length, and his balls were provokingly deceitful. He was the chosen General of all the matches, ordering and directing the whole. In such esteem did the brotherhood hold his experience and judgement, that he was uniformly consulted on all questions of law or precedent; and I never knew an exception to be taken against his opinion, or his decision to be reversed. I never saw a finer specimen of the thoroughbred old English yeoman than Richard Nyren. He was a good face-to-face, unflinching, uncompromising, independent man. He placed a full and just value upon the station he held in society, and he maintained it without insolence or assumption. He could differ with a superior, without trenching upon his dignity, or losing his own. I have known him maintain an opinion with great firmness against the Duke of Dorset and Sir Horace Mann; and when, in consequence of his being proved to be in the right, the latter has afterwards crossed the ground and shaken him heartily by the hand. Nyren had immense advantage over Brett; for, independently of his general knowledge of the game, he was practically a better cricketer, being a safe batsman and an excellent hitter. Although a very stout man (standing about five feet nine) he was uncommonly active. He owed all the skill and judgement he possessed to an old uncle, Richard Newland, of Slindon, in Sussex, under whom he was brought up – a man so famous in his time, that when a song was written in honour of the Sussex cricketers, Richard Newland was especially and honourably signalised. No one man ever dared to play him. When Richard Nyren left Hambledon, the club broke up, and never resumed from that day. The head and right arm were gone.

Barber and Hogsflesh were both good hands; they had a high delivery, and a generally good length; not very strong, however, at least for those days of playing, when the bowling was all fast. These four were our tip-top men, and I think such another stud was not to be matched in the whole kingdom, either before or since. They were choice fellows, staunch and thoroughgoing. No thought of treachery ever seemed to have entered their heads. The modern politics of trickery and '*crossing*' were (so far as my own experience and judgement of their actions extended) as yet 'a sealed book' to the Hambledonians; what they did, they did for the love of honour and victory; and when one (who shall be nameless) sold the birthright of his good name for a mess of pottage, he paid dearly for his bargain. It cost him the trouble of being a knave - (no trifle!); the esteem of his old friends, and, what was worst of all, the respect of him who could have been his *best* friend – himself.

Upon coming to the old batters of our club, the name of JOHN SMALL, the elder, shines among them in all the lustre of a star of the first magnitude. His merits have already been recorded in a separate publication, which every zealous brother of the pastime has probably read. I need, therefore, only subscribe my testimony to his uncommon talent, shortly summing up his chief excellencies. He was the best short runner of his day, and indeed I believe him to have been the first who turned the short hits to account. His decision was as prompt as his eye was accurate in calculating a short run. Add to the value of his accomplishment as a batter, he was an admirable fieldsman, always playing middle wicket; and so correct was his judgement of the game, that old Nyren would appeal to him when a point of law was being debated. Small was a remarkably well-made and well-knit man, of honest expression, and as active as a hare.

He was a good fiddler, and taught himself the double bass. The Duke of Dorset, having been informed of his musical talent, sent him as a present a handsome violin, and paid the carriage. Small, like a true and simple-hearted Englishman, returned the compliment, by sending his Grace two bats and balls, also *paying the carriage*. We may be sure that on both hands the presents were choice of their kind. Upon one occasion he turned his Orphean accomplishment to good account. Having to cross two or three fields on his way to a musical party, a vicious bull made at him; when our hero, with the characteristic coolness and presence of a good cricketer, began playing upon his bass, to the admiration and perfect satisfaction of the mischievous beast.

About this time, 1778, I became a sort of farmer's pony to my native club of Hambledon, and I never had cause to repent the work I was put to; I gained by it that various knowledge of the game, which I leave in the hands of those who knew me in my 'high and palmy state' to speak to and appreciate. This trifling preliminary being settled, the name and figure of TOM SUETER first comes across me – a Hambledon man, and of the club. What a handful of steel-hearted soldiers are in an important pass, such was Tom in keeping the wicket. Nothing went by him; and for coolness and nerve in this trying and responsible post, I never saw his equal. As a proof of his quickness and skill, I have numberless times seen him stump a man out with Brett's tremendous bowling. Add to this valuable accomplishment, he was one of the manliest and most graceful of hitters. Few would cut a ball harder at the point of the bat, and he was, moreover, an excellent short runner. He had an eye like an eagle – rapid and comprehensive. He was the first who departed from the custom of the old players before him, who deemed it a heresy to leave the crease for the ball; he would get in at it, and hit it straight off and straight on; and, egad! it went as if it had been fired. As by the rules of our club, at the trial-matches no man was allowed to get more than thirty runs, he generally gained his number earlier than any of them. I have seldom seen a handsomer man than Tom Sueter, who measured about five feet ten. As if, too, Dame Nature wished to show at his birth a specimen of her prodigality, she gave him so amiable a disposition, that he was the pet of all the neighbourhood: so honourable a heart, that his word was never questioned by the gentlemen who associated with him: and a voice, which for sweetness, power, purity of tone (a tenor) would, with proper cultivation, have made him a handsome fortune. With what rapture have I hung upon his notes when he has given us a hunting song in the club room after the day's practice was over!

GEORGE LEAR, of Hambledon, who always answered to the title among us of 'Little George', was our best long-stop. So firm and steady was he, that I have known him stand through a whole match against Brett's bowling, and not lose more than two runs. The ball seemed to go into him, and he was as sure of it as if he had been a sand bank. His activity was so great, and, besides, he had so good a judgement in running to cover the ball, that he would stop many that were hit in the slip, and this, be it remembered, from the swiftest bowling ever known. The portion of ground that man would cover was quite extraordinary. He was a good batsman, and a tolerably sure guard of his wicket; he averaged from fifteen to twenty runs, but I never remember his having a long innings. What he did not bring to the stock by his bat, however, he amply made up with his perfect fielding. Lear was a short man, of a fair complexion, well-looking, and of a pleasing aspect. He had a sweet counter tenor voice. Many a treat have I had in hearing him and Sueter join in a glee at the 'Bat and Ball' on Broad-Halfpenny:

> I have been there, and still would go;
> 'Twas like a little Heaven below!

EDWARD ABURROW, a native of Hambledon, was one of our best long fields. He always went by the name of Curry; why, I cannot remember, neither is it of the utmost importance to inquire. He was well calculated for the post he always occupied, being a sure and strong thrower, and able to cover a great space of the field. He was a steady and safe batter, averaging the same number of runs as Lear. We reckoned him a tolerably good change for bowling. Aburrow was a strong and well made man, standing about five feet nine; he had a plain, honest-looking face, and was beloved by all his acquaintance.

BUCK, whose real name was PETER STEWARD, is the next Hambledon man that occurs to my recollection. He, too, played long field, and was a steady man at his post; his batting, too, reached the same pitch of excellence; he could cut the balls very hard at the point of the bat – nothing like Sueter, however – very few could have equalled *him*. Buck was a dark-looking man, a shoemaker by trade, in height about five feet eight, rather slimly built, and very active. He had an ambition to be thought a humorist. The following anecdote may serve both as a specimen of his talent and of the unfastidious taste of the men of Hambledon. When a match was to be played at a distance, the whole eleven, with the umpire and scorer, were conveyed in one caravan, built for their accommodation. Upon one occasion, the vehicle having been overturned, and the whole cargo unshipped, Buck remained at his post, and refused to come out, desiring that they would right the vessel with him in it; for that 'one good turn deserved another'. This repartee was admired for a week.

The tenth knight of our round table (of which old Richard Nyren was the King Arthur) was a man we always called 'The Little Farmer'; his name was LAMBERT. He was a bowler – right-handed, and he had the most extraordinary delivery I ever saw. The ball was delivered quite low, and with a twist; not like that of the generality of right-handed bowlers, but just the reverse way: that is, if bowling to a right-handed hitter, his ball would twist from the off stump into the leg. He was the first I remember who introduced this deceitful and teasing style of delivering the ball. When All England played the Hambledon Club, the Little Farmer was appointed one of our bowlers; and, egad! this new trick of his so bothered the Kent and Surrey men, that they tumbled out one after another, as if they had been picked off by a rifle corps. For a long time they could not tell what to make of that cursed twist of his. This, however, was the only virtue he possessed, as a cricketer. He was no batter, and had no judgement of the game. The perfection he had attained in this one department, and his otherwise general deficiency, are at once accounted for by the circumstance that, when he was tending his father's sheep, he would set up a hurdle or two, and bowl away for hours together. Our General, old Nyren, after a great deal of trouble (for the Farmer's comprehension did not equal the speed of lightning), got him to pitch the ball a little to the offside of the wicket, when it would twist full in upon the stumps. Before he had got into this knack, he was once bowling against the Duke of Dorset, and, delivering his ball straight to the wicket, it curled in, and missed the Duke's leg-stump by a hair's breadth. The plainspoken little bumpkin, in his eagerness and delight, and forgetting the style in which we were always accustomed to impress our aristocratical playmates with our acknowledgment of their rank and station, bawled out – 'Ah! it was *tedious* near you, Sir!' The familiarity of his tone, and the genuine Hampshire dialect in which it was spoken, set the whole ground laughing. I have never seen but one *bowler* who delivered his balls in the same way as our Little Farmer; with the *jerkers* the practice is not uncommon. He was a very civil and inoffensive young fellow, and remained in the club perhaps two or three seasons.

With TOM TAYLOR the old *eleven* was completed. There were, of course, several changes of other players, but these were the established picked set – the *élite*. Tom was an admirable field – certainly one of the very finest I ever saw. His station was between the point of the bat and the middle wicket, to save the two runs; but Tom had a lucky knack of gathering in to the wicket, for Tom had a license from our old General; so that, if the ball was hit to him, he had so quick a way of meeting it, and with such a rapid return (for no sooner was it in his hand than with the quickness of thought it was returned to the top of the wicket), that I have seen many put out by this manoeuvre in a single run, and when the hit might be safely calculated upon for a prosperous one. He had an excellent general knowledge of the game; but of fielding, in particular, he was perfect both in judgement and practice. Tom was also a most brilliant hitter, but his great fault lay in not sufficiently guarding his wicket: he was too fond of cutting, at the point of the bat, balls that were delivered straight; although, therefore, he would frequently get many runs, yet, from this habit, he could not be securely depended on; and, indeed, it was commonly the cause of his being out. I have known Lord Frederick Beauclerc (certainly the finest batter of his day) throw away the chance of a capital innings by the same incaution – that of cutting at *straight* balls – and he has been bowled out in consequence. Taylor was a short, well-made man, strong, and as watchful and active as a cat; but in no other instance will the comparison hold good, for he was without guile, and was an attached friend.

There was high feasting held on Broad-Halfpenny during the solemnity of one of our grand matches. Oh! it was a heart-stirring sight to witness the multitude forming a complete and dense circle round that noble green. Half the county would be present, and all their hearts with us. Little Hambledon pitted against All England was a proud thought for the Hampshire men. Defeat was glory in such a struggle -- Victory, indeed, made us only 'a little lower than angels'. How those fine brawn-faced fellows of farmers would drink to our success! And then, what stuff they had to drink! – Punch! – not your new *Ponche à la Romaine*, or *Ponche à la Groseille*, or your modern cat-lap milk punch – punch be-deviled; but good, unsophisticated John Bull stuff – stark! – that would stand on end – punch that would make a cat speak! Sixpence a bottle! We had not sixty millions of interest to pay in those days. The ale too! – not the modern horror under the same name, that drives as many men melancholy-mad as the hypocrites do; – not the beastliness of these days, that will make a fellow's inside like a shaking bog – and as rotten; but barleycorn, such as would put the souls of three butchers into one weaver. Ale that would flare like turpentine – genuine Boniface! – This immortal viand (for it was more than liquor) was vended at twopence per pint. The immeasurable villany of our vintners would, with their march of intellect (if ever they could get such a brewing), drive a pint of it out into a gallon. Then the quantity the fellows would eat! Two or three of them would strike dismay into a round of beef. They could no more have pecked in that style than they could have flown, had the infernal black stream (that type of Acheron!) which soddens the carcass of a Londoner, been the fertilizer of their clay. There would this company, consisting most likely of some thousands, remain patiently and anxiously watching every turn of fate in the game, as if the event had been the meeting of two armies to decide their liberty. And whenever a Hambledon man made a good hit, worth four or five runs, you would hear the deep mouths of the whole multitude baying away in pure Hampshire – 'Go hard! – go hard! – *Tich* and turn! – *tich* and turn!' To the honour of my countrymen, let me bear testimony upon this occasion also, as I have already done upon others. Although their provinciality in general, and personal partialities individually, were naturally interested in behalf of the Hambledon men, I cannot call to recollection an instance of their wilfully stopping a ball that had been hit out among them by one of our opponents. Like *true* Englishmen, they would give an enemy fair play. How strongly are all those scenes, of fifty years bygone, painted in my memory! – and the smell of that ale comes upon me as freshly as the new May flowers.

JOHN NYREN, *The Hambledon Men*, 1833

Hambledon and Broadhalfpenny Down still provide a romantic backdrop for an afternoon's cricket. Little has changed on the Down since the late eighteenth century and William Wordsworth would recognise the sward as being as comely as those of Kent he praises in the following sonnet.

SONNET

Dear fellow Traveller! here we are once more.
The cock that crows, the smoke that curls, that sound
Of Bells, those boys that in yon meadow ground
In white sleev'd shirts are playing by the score,
And even this little River's gentle roar,
All, all are English. Oft I have looked round
With joy in Kent's green vales; but never found
Myself so satisfied in heart before.
Europe is yet in bounds; but let that pass,
Thought for another moment. Thou art free,
My Country! and 'tis joy enough and pride
For one hour's perfect bliss, to tread the grass
Of England once again, and hear and see,
With such a dear Companion at my side.

WILLIAM WORDSWORTH

Charles Dickens, too, saw the game as one of pastoral innocence, albeit Dickens being Dickens, a game not untouched by tragedy and he gives us an interesting insight into the pre-history of cricket in the West Indies.

Dingley Dell *v.* All-Muggleton

THE wickets were pitched, and so were a couple of marquees for the rest and refreshment of the contending parties. The game had not yet commenced. Two or three Dingley Dellers, and All-Muggletonians, were amusing themselves with a majestic air by throwing the ball carelessly from hand to hand; and several other gentlemen dressed like them, in straw hats, flannel jackets, and white trousers – a costume in which they looked very much like amateur stone-masons – were sprinkled about the tents, towards one of which Mr Wardle conducted the party.

Several dozen of 'How-are-you's?' hailed the old gentleman's arrival; and a general raising of the straw hats, and bending forward of the flannel jackets, followed his introduction of his guests as gentlemen from London, who were extremely anxious to witness the proceedings of the day, with which, he had no doubt, they would be greatly delighted.

'You had better step into the marquee, I think, sir,' said one very stout gentleman, whose body and legs looked like half a gigantic roll of flannel, elevated on a couple of inflated pillow-cases.

'You'll find it much pleasanter, sir,'- urged another stout gentleman, who strongly resembled the other half of the roll of flannel aforesaid.

'You're very good,' said Mr Pickwick.

'This way,' said the first speaker; 'they notch in here -it's the best place in the whole field;' and the cricketer, panting on before, preceded them to the tent.

'Capital game – smart sport – fine exercise – very,' were the words which fell upon Mr Pickwick's ear as he entered the tent: and the first object that met his eyes was his green-coated friend of the Rochester coach, holding forth, to the no small delight and edification of a select circle of the chosen of All-Muggleton. His dress was slightly improved, and he wore boots; but there was no mistaking him.

The stranger recognised his friends immediately: and, darting forward and seizing Mr Pickwick by the hand, dragged him to a seat with his usual impetuosity, talking all the while as if the whole of the arrangements were under his especial patronage and direction.

'This way – this way – capital fun – lots of beer – hogsheads; rounds of beef – bullocks; mustard – cart loads; glorious day – down with you – make yourself at home – glad to see you – very.'

Mr Pickwick sat down as he was bid, and Mr Winkle and Mr Snodgrass also complied with the directions of their mysterious friend. Mr Wardle looked on, in silent wonder.

Mr Wardle – a friend of mine,' said Mr Pickwick.

'Friend of yours! – My dear sir, how are you? – Friend of *my* friend's – give me your hand, sir' – and the stranger grasped Mr Wardle's hand with all the fervour of a close intimacy of many years, and then stepped back a pace or two as if to take a full survey of his face and figure, and then shook hands with him again, if possible, more warmly than before.

'Well; and how came you here?' said Mr Pickwick, with a smile in which benevolence struggled with surprise.

'Come,' replied the stranger – 'stopping at Crown – Crown at Muggleton – met a party – flannel jackets – white trousers – anchovy sandwiches – devilled kidneys – splendid fellows – glorious.'

Mr Pickwick was sufficiently versed in the stranger's system of stenography to infer from this rapid and disjointed communication that he had, somehow or other, contracted an acquaintance with the All-Muggletons, which he had converted, by a process peculiar to himself, into that extent of good fellowship on which a general invitation may be easily founded. His curiosity was therefore satisfied, and putting on his spectacles he prepared himself to watch the play which was just commencing.

All-Muggleton had the first innings: and the interest became intense when Mr Dumkins and Mr Podder, two of the most renowned members of that most distinguished club, walked, bat in hand, to their respective wickets. Mr Luffey, the highest ornament of Dingley Dell, was pitched to bowl against the redoubtable Dumkins, and Mr Struggles was selected to do the same kind office for the hitherto unconquered Podder. Several players were stationed, to 'look out,' in different parts of the field, and each fixed himself into the proper attitude by placing one hand on each knee, and stooping very much as if he were 'making a back' for some

143

beginner at leap-frog. All the regular players do this sort of thing; – indeed it's generally supposed that it is quite impossible to look out properly in any other position.

The umpires were stationed behind the wickets; the scorers were prepared to notch the runs; a breathless silence ensued. Mr Luffey retired a few paces behind the wicket of the passive Podder, and applied the ball to his right eye for several seconds. Dumkins confidently awaited its coming with his eyes fixed on the motions of Luffey.

'Play!' suddenly cried the bowler. The ball flew from his hand straight and swift towards the centre stump of the wicket. The wary Dumkins was on the alert: it fell upon the tip of the bat, and bounded far away over the heads of the scouts, who had just stooped low enough to let it fly over them.

'Run – run – another. – Now, then, throw her up – up with her – stop there – another – no – yes – no – throw her up, throw her up!' – Such were the shouts which followed the stroke; and, at the conclusion of which All-Muggleton had scored two. Nor was Podder behindhand in earning laurels wherewith to garnish himself and Muggleton. He blocked the doubtful balls, missed the bad ones, took the good ones, and sent them flying to all parts of the field. The scouts were hot and tired; the bowlers were changed and bowled till their arms ached; but Dumkins and Podder remained unconquered. Did an elderly gentleman essay to stop the progress of the ball, it rolled between his legs or slipped between his fingers. Did a slim gentleman try to catch it, it struck him on the nose, and bounded pleasantly off with redoubled violence, while the slim gentleman's eye filled with water, and his form writhed with anguish. Was it thrown straight up to the wicket, Dumkins had reached it before the ball. In short, when Dumkins was caught out, and Podder stumped out, All-Muggleton had notched some fifty-four, while the score of the Dingley Dellers was as blank as their faces. The advantage was too great to be recovered. In vain did the eager Luffey, and the enthusiastic Struggles, do all that skill and experience could suggest, to regain the ground Dingley Dell had lost in the contest; – it was of no avail; and in an early period of the winning game Dingley Dell gave in, and allowed the superior prowess of All-Muggleton.

The stranger, meanwhile, had been eating, drinking, and talking, without cessation. At every good stroke he expressed his satisfaction and approval of the player in a most condescending and patronising manner, which could not fail to have been highly gratifying to the party concerned; while at every bad attempt at a catch, and every failure to stop the ball, he launched his personal displeasure at the head of the devoted individual in such denunciations – as 'Ah, ah! – stupid' – 'Now, butter-fingers' – 'Muff' – 'Humbug' – and so forth – ejaculations which seemed to establish him in the opinion of all around, as a most excellent and undeniable judge of the whole art and mystery of the noble game of cricket.

'Capital game – well played – some strokes admirable,' said the stranger, as both sides crowded into the tent, at the conclusion of the game.

'You have played it, sir?' inquired Mr Wardle, who had been much amused by his loquacity.

'Played it! Think I have – thousands of times – not here – West Indies – exciting thing – hot work – very.'

'It must be rather a warm pursuit in such a climate,' observed Mr Pickwick.

'Warm! – red hot – scorching – glowing. Played a match once – single wicket – friend the Colonel – Sir Thomas Blazo – who should get the greatest number of runs. – Won the toss – first innings – seven o'clock a.m. – six natives to look out – went in; kept in – heat intense – natives all fainted – taken away – fresh half-dozen ordered – fainted also – Blazo bowling – supported by two natives – couldn't bowl me out – fainted too – cleared away the Colonel – wouldn't give in – faithful attendant – Quanko Samba – last man left – sun so hot, bat in blisters, ball scorched brown – five hundred and seventy runs – rather exhausted – Quanko mustered up last remaining strength – bowled me out – had a bath, and went out to dinner.'

'And what became of what's-his-name, sir?' inquired an old gentleman.

'Blazo?'

'No – the other gentleman.'

'Quanko Samba?'

'Yes, sir.'

'Poor Quanko – never recovered it – bowled on, on my account – bowled off, on his own – died, sir.' Here the stranger buried his countenance in a brown jug, but whether to hide his emotion or imbibe its contents, we cannot distinctly affirm.

CHARLES DICKENS, *The Pickwick Papers*, 1836

Shortly before Dickens was writing The Pickwick Papers, *Mary Russell Mitford had composed one of the most beautiful accounts of village cricket.*

Our Village

I DOUBT if there be any scene in the world more animating or delightful than a cricket-match – I do not mean a set match at Lord's Ground, for money, hard money, between a certain number of gentlemen and players, as they are called – people who make a trade of that noble sport, and degrade it into an affair of bettings, and hedgings and cheatings, it may be, like boxing or horse-racing; nor do I mean a pretty fête in a gentleman's park, where one club of cricketing dandies encounter another such club, and where they show off in graceful costume to a gay marquee of admiring belles, who condescend so to purchase admiration, and while away a long summer morning in partaking cold collations, conversing occasionally, and seeming to understand the game – the whole being conducted according to ball-room etiquette, so as to be exceedingly elegant and exceedingly dull. No! the cricket that I mean is a real solid old-fashioned match between neighbouring parishes, where each attacks the other for honour and a supper, glory and half-a-crown a man. If there be any gentlemen amongst them, it is well – if not, it is so much the better. Your gentleman cricketer is in general rather an anomalous character. Elderly gentlemen are obviously good for nothing; and your beaux are, for the most part, hampered and trammelled by dress and habit; the stiff cravat, the pinched-in-waist, the dandy-walk – oh, they will never do for cricket! Now, our country lads, accustomed to the flail or the hammer (your blacksmiths are capital hitters) have the free use of their arms; they know how to move their shoulders; and they can move their feet too - they can run; then they are so much better made; so much more athletic, and yet so much lissimer – to use a Hampshire phrase, which deserves at least to be good English. Here and there, indeed, one meets with an old Etonian, who retains his boyish love for that game which formed so considerable a branch of his education; some even preserve their boyish proficiency, but in general it wears away like the Greek, quite as certainly, and almost as fast; a few years of Oxford, or Cambridge, or the Continent, are sufficient to annihilate both the power and the inclination. No! a village match is the thing - where our highest officer – our conductor (to borrow a musical term) is but a little farmer's second son; where a day-labourer is our bowler, and a blacksmith our long-stop; where the spectators consist of the retired cricketers, the veterans of the green, the careful mothers, the girls, and all the boys of two parishes, together with a few amateurs, little above them in rank, and not at all in pretension; where laughing and shouting, and the very ecstasy of merriment and good-humour prevail: such a match, in short, as I attended yesterday, at the expense of getting twice wet through, and as I would attend tomorrow, at the certainty of having that ducking doubled.

For the last three weeks our village has been in a state of great excitement, occasioned by a challenge from our north-western neighbours, the men of B., to contend with us at cricket. Now, we have not been much in the habit of playing matches. Three or four years ago, indeed, we encountered the men of S., our neighbours south-by-east, with a sort of doubtful success, beating them on our own ground, whilst they in the second match returned the compliment on theirs. This discouraged us. Then an unnatural coalition between a high-church curate and an evangelical gentleman-farmer drove our lads from the Sunday-even practice, which, as it did not begin before both services were concluded, and as it tended to keep the young men from the ale-house, our magistrates had winked at if not encouraged. The sport, therefore, had languished until the present season, when under another change of circumstances the spirit began to revive. Half-a-dozen fine active lads, of influence amongst their comrades, grew into men and yearned for cricket; an enterprising publican gave a set of ribands: his rival, mine host of the Rose, and out-doer by profession, gave two; and the clergyman and his lay ally, both well-disposed and good-natured men, gratified by the submission to their authority, and finding, perhaps, that no great good resulted from the substitution of public houses for out-of-doors diversions, relaxed. In short, the practice re-commenced, and the hill was again alive with men and boys, and innocent merriment; but farther than the riband matches amongst ourselves nobody dreamed of going, till this challenge – we were modest, and doubted our own strength. The B. people, on the other hand, must have been braggers born, a whole parish of gasconaders. Never was such boasting! such crowing! such ostentatious display of practice! such mutual compliments from man to man – bowler to batter, batter to bowler! It was a wonder they did not challenge all England. It must be confessed that we were a little astounded; yet we firmly resolved not to decline the combat; and one of the most spirited of the new growth, William Grey by name, took up the glove in a style of manly courtesy, that would have done honour to a knight in the days of chivalry – 'We were not professed players,' he said, 'being little better than school-boys, and scarcely older; but, since they have done us the honour to challenge us, we would try our strength. It would be no discredit to be beaten by such a field.'

Having accepted the wager of battle, our champion began forthwith to collect his forces. William Grey is himself one of the finest youths that one shall see – tall, active, slender and yet strong, with a piercing eye full of sagacity, and a smile full of good honour – a farmer's son by station, and used to hard work as farmers' sons are now, liked by everybody, and admitted to be an excellent cricketer. He immediately set forth to muster his men, remembering with great complacency that Samuel Long, a bowler *comme il y en a peu*, the very man who had knocked down nine wickets, had beaten us, bowled us out at the fatal return match some years ago at S., had luckily, in a remove of a quarter of a mile last Ladyday, crossed the boundaries of his old parish, and actually belonged to us. Here was a stroke of good fortune! Our captain applied to him instantly; and he agreed at a word. Indeed, Samuel Long is a very civilised person. He is a middle-aged man, who looks rather old amongst our young lads, and whose thickness and breadth gave no token of remarkable activity, but he is very active, and so steady a player! so safe! We had half gained the match when we had secured him. He is a man of substance, too, in every way; owns one cow, two donkeys, six pigs, and geese and ducks beyond count – dresses like a farmer, and owes no man a shilling and all this from pure industry, sheer day-labour. Note that your good cricketer is commonly the most industrious man in the parish; the habits that make him such are precisely those which make a good workman – steadiness, sobriety, and activity – Samuel Long might pass for the beau ideal of the two characters. Happy were we to possess him! Then we had another piece of good luck. James Brown, a journeyman blacksmith and a native, who, being of a rambling disposition, had roamed from place to place for half-a-dozen years, had just returned to settle with his brother at another corner of our village, bringing with him a prodigious reputation in cricket and in gallantry – the gay Lothario of the neighbourhood. He is said to have made more conquests in love and in cricket than any blacksmith in the county. To him also went the indefatigable William Grey, and he also consented to play. No end to our good fortune! Another celebrated batter, called Joseph Hearne, had likewise recently married into the parish. He worked, it is true at the A. mills, but slept at the house of his wife's father in our territories. He also was sought and found by our leader. But he was grand and shy; made an immense favour of the thing; courted court-ing and then hung back – 'Did not know that he could be spared; had partly resolved not to play again – at least not this season; thought it rash to accept the challenge; thought they might do with-out him –' 'Truly I think so too,' said our spirited champion; 'we will not trouble you, Mr Hearne.'

Having thus secured two powerful auxiliaries and rejected a third, we began to reckon and select the regular native forces. Thus ran our list: William Grey, 1 – Samuel Long, 2 – James Brown, 3 – George and John Simmons, one capital the other so-so – an uncertain hitter, but a good fieldsman, 5 – Joel Brent, excellent, 6 – Ben Appleton – here was a little pause – Ben's abilities at cricket were not completely ascertained; but then he was so good a fellow, so full of fun and waggery! no doing without Ben. So he figured in the list, 7 – George Harris – a short halt there too! Slowish – slow but sure. I think the proverb brought him in, 8 – Tom Coper – Oh, beyond the world, Tom Coper! the red-headed gardening lad, whose left-handed strokes send *her* (a cricket-ball, like that other moving thing, a ship, is always of the feminine gender), send her spinning a mile, 9 – Harry Willis, another blacksmith, 10.

We had now ten of our eleven, but the choice of the last occasioned some demur. Three young Martins, rich farmers of the

149

neighbourhood, successively presented themselves, and were all rejected by our independent and impartial general for want of merit – cricketal merit. 'Not good enough,' was his pithy answer. Then our worthy neighbour, the half-pay lieutenant, offered his services – he, too, though with some hesitation and modesty, was refused – 'Not quite young enough' was his sentence. John Strong, the exceeding long son of our dwarfish mason, was the next candidate – a nice youth – everybody likes John Strong – and a willing, but so tall and so limp, bent in the middle – a threadpaper, six feet high! We were all afraid that, in spite of his name, his strength would never hold out. 'Wait till next year, John,' quoth William Grey, with all the dignified seniority of twenty speaking to eighteen. 'Coper's a year younger,' said John. 'Coper's a foot shorter,' replied William: so John retired: and the eleventh man remained unchosen, almost to the eleventh hour. The eve of the match arrived, and the post was still vacant, when a little boy of fifteen, David Willis, brother to Harry, admitted by accident to the last practice, saw eight of them out, and was voted in by acclamation.

That Sunday evening's practice (for Monday was the important day) was a period of great anxiety, and, to say the truth, of great pleasure. There is something strangely delightful in the innocent spirit of party. To be one of a numerous body, to be authorised to say *we*, to have a rightful interest in triumph or defeat, is gratifying at once to social feeling and to personal pride. There was not a ten-year-old urchin, or a septuagenary woman in the parish who did not feel an additional importance, a reflected consequence, in speaking of 'our side'. An election interests in the same way; but that feeling is less pure. Money is there, and hatred, and politics, and lies. Oh, to be a voter, or a voter's wife, comes nothing near the genuine and hearty sympathy of belonging to a parish, breathing the same air, looking on the same trees, listening to the same nightingales! Talk of a patriotic elector! Give me a parochial patriot, a man who loves his parish. Even we, the female partisans, may partake the common ardour. I am sure I did. I never, though tolerably eager and enthusiastic at all times, remember being in a more delicious state of excitement than on the eve of that battle. Our hopes waxed stronger and stronger. Those of our players who were present were excellent. William Grey got forty notches off his own bat, and that brilliant hitter, Tom Coper, gained eight from two successive balls. As the evening advanced, too, we had encouragement of another sort. A spy, who had been despatched to reconnoitre the enemy's quarters, returned from their practising ground with a most consolatory report. 'Really,' said Charles Grover, our intelligence – a fine old steady judge, one who had played well in his day – 'they are no better than so many old women. Any five of ours would beat their eleven.' This sent us to bed in high spirits.

Morning dawned less favourably. The sky promised a series of deluging showers, and kept its word as English skies are wont to do on such occasions; and a lamentable message arrived at the head-quarters from our trusty comrade Joel Brent. His master, a great farmer, had begun the hay-harvest that very morning, and Joel, being as eminent in one field as in another, could not be spared. Imagine Joel's plight! the most ardent of all our eleven! a knight held back from the tourney! a soldier from the battle! The poor swain was inconsolable. At last, one who is always ready to do a good-natured action, great or little, set forth to back his petition; and, by dint of appealing to the public spirit of our worthy neighbour and the state of the barometer, talking alternately of the parish honour and thunder showers, of last matches and sopped hay, he carried his point, and returned triumphantly with the delighted Joel.

In the meantime, we became sensible of another defalcation. On calling over our roll, Brown was missing; and the spy of the preced-ing night, Charles Grover – the universal scout and messenger of the village, a man who will run half-a-dozen miles for a pint of beer, who does errands for the very love of the trade, who, if he had been a lord, would have been an ambassador – was instantly despatched to summon the truant. His report spread general consternation. Brown had set off at four o'clock in the morning to play in a cricket-match at M., a little town twelve miles off, which had been his last residence. Here was desertion! Here was treachery! Here was treachery against that goodly state, our parish! To send James Brown to Coventry was the immediate resolution; but even that seemed too light a punishment for such delinquency! Then how we cried him down! At ten on Sunday night (for the rascal had actually practised with us, and never said a word of his intended disloyalty) he was our faithful mate, and the best player (take him all in all) of the eleven. At ten in the morning he had run away, and we were well rid of him; he was no batter compared with William Grey or Tom Coper; not fit to wipe the shoes of Samuel Long, as a bowler; nothing of a scout to John Simmons; the boy David Willis was worth fifty of him –

I trust we have within our realm
Five hundred good as he

was the universal sentiment. So we took tall John Strong, who, with an incurable hankering after the honour of being admitted had kept constantly with the players, to take the chance of some such accident - we took John for our *pis aller*. I never saw anyone prouder than the good-humoured lad was of this not very flattering piece of preferment.

John Strong was elected, and Brown sent to Coventry; and when I first heard of his delinquency, I thought the punishment only too mild for the crime. But I have since learned the secret history of the offence (if we could know the secret histories of all offences, how much better the world would seem than it does now!) and really my wrath is much abated. It was a piece of gallantry, of devotion to the sex, or rather a chivalrous obedience to one chosen fair. I must tell my readers the story. Mary Allen, the prettiest girl of M., had, it seems, revenged upon our blacksmith the numberless inconsistencies of which he stood accused. He was in love over head and ears, but the nymph was cruel. She said no, and no, and no, and poor Brown, three times rejected, at last resolved to leave the place, partly in despair, and partly in the hope which often mingles strangely with a lover's despair, the hope that when he was gone he should be missed. He came home to his brother's accordingly, but for five weeks he heard nothing from or of the inexorable Mary, and was glad to beguile his own 'vexing thoughts' by endeavouring to create in his mind an artificial and factitious interest in our cricket-match – all unimportant as such a trifle must have seemed to a man in love. Poor James, however, is a social and warm-hearted person, not likely to resist a contagious sympathy. As the time for the play advanced, the interest which he had at first affected became genuine and sincere: and he was really, when he left the ground on Sunday night, almost as enthusiastically absorbed in the event of the next day, as Joel Brent himself. He little foresaw the new and delightful interest which awaited him at home, where on the moment of his arrival, his sister-in-law and confidante presented him with a billet from the lady of his heart. It had, with the usual delay of letters sent by private hands in that rank of life, loitered on the road, in a degree inconceivable to those who are accustomed to the punctual speed of the post, and had taken ten days for its twelve miles' journey. Have my readers any wish to see this *billet-doux*? I can show them (but in strict confidence) a literal copy. It was addressed,

> For mistur jem browne
> 'blaxmith by
> 'S'.

The inside ran thus:

> Mistur browne this is to Inform you that oure parish plays bramley men next monty is a week, i think we shall lose without yew, from your humbell servant to command
> 'Mary Allen.'

Was there ever a prettier relenting? a summons more flattering, more delicate, more irresistible? The precious epistle was undated; but, having ascertained who brought it, and found, by cross-examining the messenger, that the Monday in question was the very next day, we were not surprised to find that Mistur browne forgot his engagement to us, forgot all but Mary and Mary's letter, and set off at four o'clock the next morning to walk twelve miles, and to play for her parish, and in her sight. Really we must not send James Brown to Coventry – must we? Though if, as his sister-in-law tells our damsel Harriet he hopes to do, he should bring the fair Mary home as his bride, he will not greatly care how little we say to him. But he must not be sent to Coventry – True-love forbid!

At last we were all assembled, and marched down to H. common, the appointed ground, which, though in our dominions according to the maps, was the constant practising place of our opponents, and *terra incognita* to us. We found our adversaries on the ground as we expected, for our various delays had hindered us from taking the field so early as we wished; and as soon as we had settled all preliminaries, the match began.

But, alas! I have been so long settling my preliminaries, that I have left myself no room for the detail of our victory, and must squeeze the account of our grand achievements into as little compass as Cowley, when he crammed the names of eleven of his mistresses into the narrow space of four eight-syllable lines. *They* began the warfare – those boastful men of B. And what think you, gentle reader, was the amount of their innings? These challengers – the famous eleven – how many did they get? Think! imagine! guess! – You cannot? – Well! – they got twenty-two, or rather, they got twenty; for two of theirs were short notches, and would never have been allowed, only that, seeing what they were made of, we and our umpires were not particular – They should have had twenty more if they had chosen to claim them. Oh, how well we fielded! and how well we bowled! our good play had quite as much to do with their miserable failure as their bad. Samuel Long is a slow bowler, George Simmons a fast one, and the change from Long's lobbing to Simmons's fast balls posed them completed. Poor simpletons! they were always wrong, expecting the slow for the quick, and the quick for the slow. Well, we went in. And what were our innings? Guess again! – guess! A hundred and sixty-nine! in spite of soaking showers, and wretched ground, where the ball would not run a yard, we headed them by a hundred and forty-seven; and then they gave in, as well they might. William Grey pressed them much to try another innings. 'There was so much chance,' as he courteously observed, 'in cricket, that advantageous as our position seemed, we might, very possibly, be overtaken. The B. men had better try.' But they were beaten sulky and would not move – to my great disappointment; I wanted to prolong the pleasure of success. What a glorious sensation it is to be for five hours together – winning – winning! always feeling what a whist-player feels when he takes up four honours, seven trumps! Who would think that a little bit of leather and two pieces of wood, had such a delightful and delighting power!

The only drawback on my enjoyment was the failure of the pretty boy, David Willis, who, injudiciously put in first, and playing for the first time in a match amongst men and strangers, who talked to him, and stared at him, was seized with such a fit of shamefaced shyness, that he could scarcely hold his bat, and was bowled out without a stroke, from actual nervousness. 'He will come off that,' Tom Coper says – I am afraid he will. I wonder whether Tom had ever any modesty to lose. Our other modest lad, John Strong, did very well; his length told in fielding and he got good fame. He ran out his mate, Samuel Long; who, I do believe, but for the excess of Joel's eagerness, would have stayed in till this time, by which exploit he got into sad disgrace; and then he himself got thirty-seven runs, which redeemed his reputation. William Grey made a hit which actually lost the cricket-ball. We think she lodged in a hedge, a quarter of a mile off, but nobody could find her. And George Simmons had nearly lost his shoe, which he tossed away in a passion, for having been caught out, owing to the ball glancing against it. These, together with a very complete somerset of Ben Appleton, our long-stop, who floundered about in the mud, making faces and attitudes as laughable as Grimaldi, none could tell whether by accident or design, were the chief incidents of the scene of action. Amongst the spectators nothing remarkable occurred, beyond the general calamity of two or three drenchings, except that a form, placed by the side of a hedge, under a very insufficient shelter, was knocked into the ditch in a sudden rush of the cricketers to escape a pelting shower, by which means all parties shared the fate of Ben Appleton, some on land and some by water; and that, amidst the scramble, a saucy gipsy of a girl contrived to steal from the knee of the demure and well-apparelled Samuel Long, a smart handkerchief which his careful dame had tied round it to preserve his new (what is the mincing feminine word?) – his new – inexpressibles, thus reversing the story of Desdemona, and causing the new Othello to call aloud for his handkerchief, to the great diversion of the company. And so we parted; the players retired to their supper, and we to our homes; all wet through, all good-humoured and happy – except the losers.

Today we are happy too. Hats, with ribands in them, go glancing up and down; and William Grey says, with a proud humility, 'We do not challenge any parish; but if we be challenged we are ready.'

MARY RUSSELL MITFORD, *Our Village*, 1832

Mitford refers to Lord's, the spiritual home of the modern game. As the nineteenth century began, the era of village cricket's pre-eminence was fast drawing to a close. The depopulation of the countryside and the growth of the cities was soon to mean the creation of county teams based in urban areas. The great arenas of the modern game were in the process of being built. Lord's was the first and its early history is traced by Sir Pelham Warner.

The Birth of Lord's

MANY who are not familiar with cricket believe that the name Lord's has some connexion with the peerage: nothing could be further from the truth. The name comes from Thomas Lord, the pivot round whom the formation of the Marylebone Club turned. Lord was born at Thirsk, in Yorkshire, on November 23, 1755, and his father, who was a substantial yeoman of Roman Catholic stock, had his lands sequestrated when he espoused the Stuart cause in the rising of 1745, so that he had to work as a labourer on the very farm that once belonged to him. The Lord family moved south to Diss, in Norfolk, where Thomas Lord was brought up, and from here, on reaching manhood, he migrated to London and found employment at the White Conduit Club as a bowler and sort of general attendant.

This club, only a few of whose scores are extant, deserves always to be remembered affectionately by cricketers as 'the acorn that blossomed into the gigantic oak known as the Marylebone Club'. Formed in 1782, it was an offshoot of a West End convivial club called the 'Je-ne-sais-quoi', some of whose members took to frequenting the White Conduit House and playing their matches in adjoining fields near Islington.

In 1786 the members were tiring of this site, and the Earl of Winchilsea, a great patron of cricket, and Charles Lennox, later fourth Duke of Richmond, offered to Lord their guarantee against loss if he would start a new private ground. White Conduit played several matches at Marylebone in 1787, but it seems almost certain that at the end of the season the old club was merged into the newly formed Marylebone Cricket Club. The M.C.C. had been born.

Lord, being assured of support, quickly got to work, with the result that in May 1787 he opened his first ground on what is now Dorset Square, on the Portman Estate. In the Portman Estate Office is a map of 1780 which shows the site of the field of seven acres which Lord secured for his ground. It was at the time leased to one Samuel Adams: whether Lord obtained a sub-lease from him or a new lease cannot be said, as the Portman Estate records all went to salvage during the Second German War.

The first great match at Dorset Square was on May 31 and June 1, 1787, when Middlesex beat Essex by 93 runs in a game played for 200 guineas, and the earliest recorded M.C.C. match was against the White Conduit Club on June 27, 1788, the M.C.C. winning by 83 runs. The first thing Lord did was to put a fence round the ground, thereby ensuring privacy for the Club. It is possible also that no gate money was charged at Islington, and Lord instituted an entrance-fee of sixpence to the public. Lord's quickly became popular, and the matches were well attended, but during its early existence the

M.C.C. played very few games. However, all went well with the ground until 1810, when the last game was played on August 17 of that year, the Old (over thirty-eight) beating the Young by 90 runs.

In that year whatever lease there was apparently ended, and the site was let on building leases, with ground rents of over £600 a year, its value during the twenty-one years' tenancy of Lord having reached a figure far beyond his resources.

Lord had foreseen that he would have to leave his original ground, so as early as October 15, 1808, he rented two fields – the Brick Field and the Great Field, at North Bank, on the St John's Wood Estate – for a term of eighty years, free of land-tax and tithe, at £54 a year. The new ground was ready in 1809, and therefore for two seasons Lord had two grounds on his hands, the St John's Wood C.C. using the new enclosure. This club was afterwards incorporated in the M.C.C.

The new Lord's was officially taken over on May 8, 1811, the turf having been removed from the original ground in Dorset Square, so that 'the noblemen and Gentlemen of the M.C.C.' should be able 'to play on the same footing as before'. The move was not popular with many of the members of the M.C.C., and the Club did not play a single match there in 1811 or 1812 – and only three during the following year.

In that year another move became necessary, as Parliament had decreed that the Regent's Canal should be cut through the centre of the ground. The Eyre family, on whose estate the second ground was situated, were willing to grant Lord another plot, which enabled the Club to make its headquarters on the site it has ever since occupied. And so Lord once again transferred his turf to his third ground (at a rent of £100), in time for the opening of the 1814 season. He was now a person of some importance in the parish of Marylebone, for he was made a member of the Marylebone Vestry in 1807 and also conducted a wine-and-spirit business.

Four days before the ground was due to be opened there was a big explosion in the 'Cricket-ground public-house', which did considerable damage. Despite this inauspicious start the third Lord's soon began to attract the public, and appropriately enough in the first great match recorded on the new site the M.C.C. beat Hertfordshire by an innings and 27 runs.

P. F. WARNER, Lord's 1789–1945, 1946

So closes the early game's chapter. W. G. Grace is about to be born, Lord's is in place and the cricketers of the Weald and Broadhalfpenny Down can continue to practise their art with bucolic delight. As this era closes, Britain begins its widespread colonisation of the world. Where the explorers went, cricket was certain to follow.

'The bowling is utter tripe and the batsman at the other end has a lethal straight drive'

ROUND THE WORLD

Showing the Flag

WHEN the British left home to colonise the world they took with them certain items of baggage whose usefulness would have commended itself to no other imperial adventurers in history. Venturing out on to the deep and perilous waters of tropical speculation, comically eager to get under way and yet utterly convinced of the ineffable superiority of their own civilisation over any other they might encounter on their travels, they clasped to themselves, in an endearing blend of messianic jingo frenzy and respect for creature comforts, as many of the artefacts of their own idiosyncratic culture as they could contrive to stow into the baggage holds:

> The specialist outfitters of London offered all kinds of ingenious devices for defeating the equatorial climates - patent ice machines, spine pads, thornproof linen, the Shikaree Tropical Hat . . . the Union Jack Patent Field Boot Container, the Up-Country Mosquito Net, the Unique Anti-Termite Matting . . . puttees (against snakes) and neckpads (against heatstroke).

Included in this clutter of the practicalities of daily life, among the portable writing desks and the canvas camp baths, the shoe-trees and the diamond shirt studs, the sauceboats and the chandeliers, the grand pianos, ukeleles, monogrammed kerchieves, embossed cutlery, soda siphons and bars of Pear's soap, there were some items of a subtly differing nature without which few itineraries would have been considered complete: Billeness and Weeks' Automatic Wicket, 'adapted for ship's deck cricket'; F. H. Ayres' Billiard Tables, 'specially designed for hotels and clubs'; the William Curtis Scoring Tent; Szaley's Pneumatic-Grip Dumb-bells; Vigon's Home Horse Exerciser and the tennis shirts, croquet hoops, shin guards, hockey sticks, lawn boots, sand boxes, jumping sacks, scoring books, badminton nets, fives gloves, squash rackets, club ties, coloured caps, medals, badges, cups, shields, bowls and vases which distinguished the English from all the other predatory Europeans wandering the surface of the planet in search either of God's work or increased dividends or a happy combination of both.

They sailed down the sealanes of the world, out from Liverpool, down the Bristol Channel, into Southampton Water, away from Tilbury: the brevet colonels flushed with the proud apoplexy of a recent mention in despatches; horse-faced captains whose toothy sibilances would soon be whistling across the remote and dusty townships of the Sudan; staff majors grimly pursuing the succulent carrot of a K.C.I.E.; ruddy adjutants whose leaden gallantries would in a month or two be rattling the bone china teacups of some remote hill station; missionaries dedicated to the export of their religion to areas which had known their own faiths when the English were still daubing their rumps with berry juice; and smooth-cheeked young men who had prepared themselves to serve as Collectors and dispense justice over tracts of land half as big as Wales in the manner of school prefects or house captains. All of them were resolved somehow to reconcile the opposing ideals of playing the game and playing it on someone else's territory, and miraculously they succeeded, at least in part. Off they ventured, across the spacious and still unpolluted plains of the nineteenth century, carrying with them not only the Gatling gun but the polo mallet, not only prayer books but scorebooks, not only cartridge belts but belts to keep up the cricket whites.

Inside the baggage train as it bounced and rattled its way down the dusty imperial road, jostling the Bibles and the bayonets, were cricket bats bearing the imprint of Mr Dark: 'I have always found your bats as good as anyone would wish to play with, Yours truly, W. G. Grace'; tucked away inside the handstitched termite-proof luggage were the handstitched termite-proof cricket balls, perhaps John Wisden's 'Special Crown Brand; London County C.C., Crystal Palace, Oct 27th, 1900; Dear Sirs, Your cricket balls again gave great satisfaction. Please send me half a gross for next season at your earliest convenience, I am, Yours truly, W. G. Grace.' Cricket had now become a kind of recreational paraphrase of the ability to act like a Christian gentleman and a good empire-builder, a sentiment espoused by Sir Henry Newbolt in that bathetic pearl, 'Vitai Lampada', where he solemnly fuses the images of fast bowling in a poor light, jammed guns and the chance of laying down's one life for the honour of the flag.

It would be foolish to assume that to the gentleman-cricketers of the late Victorian age all this was no more than a game. Had it been no more than what the imperceptive Kipling said it was, an elaborate device for these flannelled fools who preferred to fritter away precious energies better spent on imperial pursuits, then W. G. Grace would have been no more than a gifted athlete, instead of what he undeniably was, the Eminent Victorian Lytton Strachey mercifully forgot. But if cricket was not just a game, exactly what else was it? It seems to have been a typically English compromise between a religious manifestation and an instrument of policy, occupying a misty hinterland in which ethics and biceps merged into a third entity, an exquisite refinement of that other imperial concept, the White Man's Burden. And if the mystical pole of this odd and starkly original hybrid is ideally represented by Lord Harris' solemn invocations to God in his grassy classroom, then the political pole is just as precisely defined by Trevelyan, observing, with a censorious glance across the English Channel, that cricket had saved the English from bloody revolution.

The case for cricket as an instrument of imperial policy has been well proven, but the difficulty still facing a baffled post-imperial age is to decide how far the use of team games as a political expedient was calculated and how far fortuitous. If only we knew the solution to that conundrum, it would tell us a great deal more about our great-grandfathers than we already know. But the question remains unanswered, and perhaps always will. Certainly team games have proved to be by far the most durable of all Victorian inventions. It is one of the richest jokes we can enjoy at the expense of the empire-builders that while all the mighty monuments they erected collapsed decades ago, sport still stands. Not the vice-regal lodges, nor the plumed tricorns, nor the standing armies nor the dreadnoughts nor the sewage systems nor the statuary nor the constitutions nor the cathedrals, but the bats and balls. The far-flung battle-line has marched deep into the recesses of history, leaving the flannelled fool in possession of the field. As the Oxford History of England puts it:

'Organised games may on any reckoning rank among England's leading contributions to world culture.'

But the triumph of team games is no proof that this was what the English intended, or hoped for. 'Sport was their chief spiritual export, and was to prove among their more resilient memorials. They took cricket to Samoa and the Indians took it up with enthusiasm.' This begs several questions: why did the English take cricket with them to the South Seas, and to what extent were they gratified by the reactions of the natives? Was the pacifying, colonising, proselytising potential of team games a lucky stroke or a gambit of diabolical cunning, sheer good fortune or political acumen, happy accident or grand design? There is evidence to support both arguments, which is not surprising as both appear to be half-truths. The most relevant fact of all is that the ruling classes of Harris's day acknowledged no limits to their jurisdiction. As they stare glassily at us down the vista of a hundred years, they seem to be telling us that as their knowledge is infallible and their good taste unquestioned, there is no good reason why they should not exercise their authority over the whole of life.

The rulers of Britain had always had great difficulty in controlling their own countrymen; how much more difficult might it not be to control those foreign subjects who were not inhibited, as the British were, by a common stock of religious fear and superstition? To put it another way, how could you hope to cow into conformity a native so barbarous that he didn't even have enough education to be frightened of General Wolseley? It is true that the imperialist first exported cricket in an attempt to beguile the long summers and to simulate the landscapes of home, but they must soon have realised that cricket presented their own culture in a highly flattering light. Its very illogicalities were endearing, and as for the tight formalism of its rules and regulations, what better engine to train subject races in the etiquette of polite submission? The empire-builders had no sooner run up the flag than they started rolling out a pitch, confident in the knowledge that before long the natives gawping at them from the boundary would soon be responding to instruction in the execution of the cover drive. Arthur Grimble, who went out to the Gilbert Islands in the palmy days of the Edwardians and rose to be Resident, inculcated the right spirit into the natives with such success that it was from them that he received one of the most accurate and affecting definitions of the charm of the game:

162

I like best of all the dictum of an old man of the Sun clan, who once said to me, 'We old men take joy in watching the kirikiti of our grandsons, because it is a fighting between factions which makes the fighters love each other.' His remark meant that cricket stood for all the fun of fighting, and all the discipline needed for unity in battle, plus a broad fellowship in the field more valuable than anything the old faction wars had ever given his people. I doubt if anyone of more sophisticated culture has ever summed up the spiritual value of cricket in more telling words.

And Grimble, who wrote those words in 1952, adds ' "Spiritual" may sound over-sentimental to a modern generation, but I stand by it, as everyone else will who has witnessed the moral teaching-force of the game in malarial jungle, or sandy desolation, or the uttermost islands of the sea.'

There are indeed worse concepts to instil into a savage than that there should be rules and that a gentleman is someone who never fails to observe them. And so playing the Game acquired a mystical significance transcending the technicalities of the game to which it referred.

As the cricketing major-generals criss-crossed the globe, scattering the earth with the seeds of imperial mission disguised as assorted sporting goods, it could hardly have occurred to them that there was one threat against which they had not provided. Fearful of the consequences of a second Indian Mutiny, aware of the unsporting envy of France and Germany, haunted for a century by nightmares about the Russian Bear, and conscious that the whole vast edifice of imperial glory was balanced precariously on a tightrope pegged down at one end at Gibraltar and at the other on the Suez Canal, they prepared their defences accordingly. They knew that if insurrection were to rear its ugly head at two or three outposts simultaneously, then their resources, already stretched to the limit, might snap altogether. There were only so many Major Poores available. The answer, they felt, lay in a combination of psychological warfare, discipline and decorum, good manners and plenty of churches, propaganda by polite pretext – a campaign in which one quarter of the earth might be transformed into a vast public school where sweet reason and the prefect system prevailed, and the crackle of the firing squad was superseded by the thwack of leather on willow, all of which might explain why so many England cricket captains were born on the outposts: Harris and Warner in the

West Indies, G. O. Allen in Australia, Jardine, Cowdrey and E. R. T. Holmes in India. History knows of no more extraordinary strategy, conceived in a bumbling idealism compromised from birth by rapacious commercial intent, and excited with a typically English blend of audacity and feeble-mindedness, of determination and indecision, of gentility and ruthlessness, of disgusting greed and heroic altruism, of Disraelian cynicism and Arthurian idealism, a monumental contradiction which Santayana was smiling over when he suggested that perhaps the English would one day be found guilty of being the sweetest conquerors of all. Thus, if you were a patriotic and well-off young man, you joined the ranks of the major-generals, and, armed with the poisoned darts of loyalty, honour and fair play, sailed away to distant shores, prepared to trek to the interior and bring to any Africans, Polynesians, Caribs and Indians you might happen to meet on the way the astonishing news that a gentleman always plays the game, that it is better to compete than to win, that the Empire was embodied in the Umpire. But there was something which nobody anticipated. Suppose the natives believed you?

BENNY GREEN, *A History of Cricket*, 1988

And they did. So fervently have the natives taken to the game that they now eclipse the talents of the mother country. India and Pakistan, South Africa and the West Indies, Australia and New Zealand, even Sri Lanka and Zimbabwe all take on England with equanimity and, for the most part, success. It may have taken them some time to get there, but they have arrived. One country that failed to last the distance was the United States, probably because it said goodbye to the Union flag before cricket had had a proper chance to establish itself. In cricket's place, the Yanks have baseball, a game dismissed by the

playwright Tom Stoppard cuttingly: 'I don't think I can be expected to take seriously any game which takes less than three days to reach its conclusion.' Obviously not a fan of one-day cricket, Mr Stoppard.

But cricket did linger for a while in North America. The first international match was played between the United States and Canada, played for 1,000 dollars worth of stakes. The States was also one of the stops on cricket's first international tour by a British team, that led by Fred Lillywhite in 1859. Then, one of the truly great fast bowlers came from Philadelphia, the bastion of cricket in the United States.

The Great American

NOR should the period be passed without mention of John Barton King, the Philadelphian, who holds an unchallengeable place as the finest of American-born cricketers. He was a superb batsman (still holding the North American record with 344 in a Halifax Cup match in 1906) but is best remembered for his bowling, which was very fast and based upon swerve which he cultivated as a baseball pitcher. He toured England with the Philadelphians in 1897, 1903, and 1908, taking 72 wickets at 24.20, 93 at 14.91, and 87 at 11.01 (the best in England that season). On the first tour he took 7 for 13 against Sussex, bowling Ranjitsinhji for nought first ball; on the second tour he took 5 for 46 and 9 for 62 (eight bowled) against Lancashire. So often he was the star of the annual USA *v.* Canada match.

'Bart' King learned much from a succession of visiting teams to America during the 1890s, and had command of both the late inswinger and outswinger, the former being affectionately referred to as his 'angler' - a ball he could deliver at will preferably with a new ball but quite dependably and almost as deadly with a used ball. 'I liked best a following wind just strong enough to flutter the left corner of my shirt collar,' he wrote in *A Century of Philadelphia Cricket*. 'The fundamental essential I found to be complete relaxation and co-ordination – an absence of any tension in arms, legs, or shoulders. This was necessary because my angler required a whole-souled follow-through of body and arm that would carry me well on down the wicket. When conditions were favourable I had the feeling that I was hurling myself after the ball toward the wicket.'

He must have been one of the most intellectual of fast bowlers, analysing the techniques of himself and others, incorporating this, discarding that. He knew that the 'roundhouse' ('banana ball') was of limited potency since it announced itself early in flight; he was aware that baseball pitchers had refined it many years previously to the 'hook'. i.e. a ball which stores up its swing until the final few feet. Even with his ability to swing the ball either way – and fatefully late – he knew the wisdom of interspersing a straight ball. He made a batsman's life a succession of problems, and the imagination seethes at the thought of what he might have achieved had he played regular county and Test cricket.

John A. Lester vividly described the balding King's appearance: 'Nature endowed this man completely with the physical equipment that a fast bowler covets. He stood six feet one inch, weighed 178 pounds, and never in his life has carried superfluous flesh. The physical characteristic that impressed Bart's friends most deeply, however, was not his powerful shoulders or the long and loosely hung arms and lean hips. It was rather the power in the wrists and fingers. This hand power had been developed and was maintained by special exercises of his own. With his wrist held tight Barr could send a new cricket ball to the second storey window with a snip of two fingers and a thumb.'

King was the subject of many an anecdote, the best known being his humiliation of the Trenton captain. King's club, Belmont, had decimated Trenton when the captain, who had arrived late, came to the crease muttering that his team would not be in such a mess if he had not been delayed. King promptly sent all his fieldsmen from the field, followed by the wicket-keeper. Then as an afterthought he called one fieldsman back and placed him precisely twenty yards behind the stumps and four yards to leg. He bowled his 'angler', hit the leg stump, and the lone fieldsman collected the ball as it ran through without having to move a pace.

On board ship returning from England he once responded to an amateur hypnotist's boast that he could lay anyone low if he chose by swaying, collapsing, and frothing at the mouth. After a doctor, who was in on the act, had declared King dead, the frenzied little hypnotist was clapped in irons, and was rescued only by King himself, who, joke over, went below and exposed the ruse.

At Haverford in 1909 he bowled all eleven of the Irish Gentlemen in an innings – G. A. Morrow, who ended up as the not-out batsman, with a no-ball. This, like the man himself, remains distinctly unique. Bart King died in a Philadelphia nursing home, at the grand age of 92, in 1965, by which time the inswinger was commonplace, even if rarely bowled with the skill and shocking suddenness of King, the other 'Demon'.

DAVID FRITH, *The Fast Men*, 1982

King played his cricket towards the end of the history of the Gentlemen of Philadelphia, no mean team in its time. Now, the game has withered on the vine and is only played in the States by expatriates from England and the Caribbean. It was in the longer-lasting colonies that cricket became fully established. Australia first, then South Africa, and then onwards. One of the more fertile fields in which the game's seed was planted is the West Indies. Though they say the game is now dying in the islands, or at least has been severely stunted by the television images of American sports, cricket was once a religion in the Caribbean and a sport to which the disparate islands rallied in unity. The foremost preacher of cricket's cause has been C. L. R. James.

The West Indies' Tradition

O N June 28th, 1900, in a match against Gloucestershire on the Bristol cricket ground, a West Indies bowler went to his captain and asked permission to take off his boots. West Indies captain Aucher Warner, a brother of Sir Pelham, asked him why; he replied that he could bowl properly only when barefooted. Woods was making the best response he knew to a truly desperate situation.

Gloucestershire had won the toss and batted. Three wickets fell rapidly. Then Wrathall, followed by C. L. Townsend, followed by G. L. Jessop, all made centuries. Jessop hit 157 in an hour. The bowling averages make curious reading. Burton took five wickets for 68 runs in 25 overs. On the figures he was not hit. If Mignon's 33.3 overs cost 162 runs he had the satisfaction of getting five wickets, including those of the three centurymakers. One Hinds bowled three overs which cost 72 runs and if these figures from *Wisden* are correct I would dearly like to know exactly how that happened. The men who really got it were Ollivierre with 137 runs for 23 overs, and Woods with 141 runs for 33 overs. Ollivierre, however, was a batsman who headed the batting averages for the tour. Woods was a bowler and nothing else, so that his emotion prompting a return to nature can be understood. Aucher Warner promptly refused his request. Woods returned to the bowling crease. Jessop despatched his first balls over the boundary, out of the ground, on to roof-tops. Woods made a last attempt. 'Mr. Warner,' he pleaded, 'let me take off one – just one and I could get him – just one, sir.' 'Out of the question. You can't do that here, Woods.' Dragging his feet, Woods had to endure this martyrdom, to the end encumbered by full armour.

The story is true, though perhaps of that higher order of truth which good fiction is. To West Indians it recalls the origin of many a fine bowler of sixty years ago. He came to the nets, often without shoes. He picked up the ball and bowled. In his *Cricket in Many Climes* Pelham Warner relates that he and his fellow Englishmen practised to these boys at the nets and found some of them definitely difficult. The Warners, the Austins, the Goodmans and the Sprostons took over the best of them, shod them and clothed them, and brought them to England. Woods was one of these. His nickname was Float, after a local delicacy, as an Englishman might be called Chips from fish-and-chips. Woods was a very fine fast bowler, and it is to be hoped that he did not take his misadventure with Jessop too hard. Most of the greatest bowlers of the day were wrung through the same mill, not once but many times.

The next generation of black men bowling fast was more sure of itself. In actual fact it produced the greatest of them all, George John. World War I interrupted his international career as it interrupted George Challenor's. These two, the gentleman and the player, the white batsman and the black bowler, were the two finest cricketers the West Indies had produced up to this time, and the most characteristic. John was a man of the people, and an emigrant from one of the most backward of the smaller islands. It is only recent political events in the West Indies which taught me that John incarnated the plebs of his time, their complete independence from the values and aspirations that competed in the spheres above.

The English public who saw him in 1923 and those Englishmen who played against him in 1926 do not know the real John. In 1923 he was already thirty-eight (some say over forty) and, despite his magnificent physique, he was already past his best. His greatest years were, I would say, between 1914 and 1920. He could bowl finely for years afterwards, but three-day cricket was, by 1923, too much for him. I was on the field with him and played against him many times, and the difference between his early years and the later ones was marked.

He was just the right height, about five foot ten, with a chest, shoulders and legs on him all power and proportion. With his fine features he was as handsome a man as you would meet in a day's journey. He was one of those rare ones, a fast bowler who proposed to defeat you first of all by pace and sheer pace. He ran about fifteen yards, a quick step or two first, a long loping stride that increased until near the crease he leapt into the air and delivered, his arm high. Unlike Lindwall, for instance, who seemed to need his arm low to get his thunderbolts. Thunderbolts they were. Read or talk to anybody who knew John and the opinion is always the same: 'One of the most formidable fast bowlers who ever handled a ball.' Even of the 1923 John and Francis, Mr Pelham Warner wrote that he wished England had them to bowl against Australia, and in those days there were great fast bowlers in the land. I believe England in 1923 saw him only once as his real self – in the Scarborough match when he and Francis reduced a powerful England Xl to six for 19 on a good wicket and (it is the considered opinion of too many to be ignored) would have bowled them out for less than the thirty-one they had to make but for some atrocious umpiring. That was the John we knew: pace and body-action off-break, and many a poor batsman hit on the inside of the knee collapsed like a felled ox.

I played against him for the first time in a competition match some time around 1921. It was an experience. After the first ball whizzed past me, I, a confirmed advocate of back-play, played forward, right forward at the ball in the air, with faith in the straight bat and the genius who presides over the universe. I caught sight of one ball outside the off-stump and let loose a drive to mid-off – it

169

flew to the boundary behind point. Next over (it was five minutes before the end of play) I danced down the pitch to a slow left-hander, pushed out at him and was stumped by feet. I was congratulated for having 'stood up' to John. And I certainly didn't flinch. But my head was in a whirl and that was why I made the stupid stroke at the slow bowler. Statham is a splendid bowler and Trueman is a very fine one. But a fast bowler in the sense that John was a fast bowler I have seen only one – Tyson in 1954 – and that is the type I will plump for every time, especially against modern batsmen. How I revelled in the accounts of Tyson's doings in Australia in 1954–5! I don't say John was the best fast bowler I have ever seen; that would be silly. But when I read of Tyson hitting the wicket with balls that did not touch the ground I recognised my John. If Spenser is the poet's poet, John was the fast bowler's bowler.

Bowler John had to be seen to be believed. The whole of a powerful physique and a still more powerful temperament had been educated and moulded by the discipline required to hurl a batsman out and the result was a rare if not unique human being. Other bowlers can be qualified as hostile. John was not hostile, he was hostility itself. If he had been an Italian of the Middle Ages he would have been called Furioso. He had an intimidating habit of following down after the delivery if the ball was played behind the wicket. When his blood was really up he would be waiting to receive it only a few yards from you. A more striking feature of his routine was his walk back to his starting point. At the end of the day he strode back like a man just beginning. Almost every ball he was rolling up his sleeves like a man out to commit some long-premeditated act of violence. He was not the captain of his side, but never saw his captain take him off. John always took himself off. If two batsmen made a stand against him John bowled until he broke it. Then he would take a rest, never before. The only sign of pressure was his taking a few deep breaths as he walked to his place at the end of an over. In between he did not seem to need air. Like the whale doing its business in great waters, he came up to breathe periodically. In a North v. South match during the middle twenties he had been over-bowled all one day and it had become obvious that the man to get out the South was young Ellis Achong. This was agreed upon before the second day's play began. When the team walked on to the field John went up to the umpire, took the ball and measured out his run. Though the North captain was a member of the Queen's Park Club, one of John's employers and a famous cricketer besides, neither he nor anyone else dared to say a word to John, who was bowling the match away. So can a strong man's dedication subdue all around him. He was head groundsman of the Queen's Park Oval and he ruled there like a dictator. Once they actually had to fire him. But I believe they took him back again. He belonged to the Oval and the Oval belonged to him.

In the 1923 tour he was for one reason or another left out of some matches, in his opinion unjustly. He went and sat in a remote corner of the pavilion, ostentatiously avoiding his fellow West Indians, gloomily resentful, like Achilles in his tent. After a day or two of this Austin sent one of the senior members of the team to him. 'John, you don't seem very pleased with things.' John (he told me this himself) replied: 'What you complainin' about? I haven't said nothin' to nobody.' 'Yes – but your face' – John cut him short. 'My face is my own and I'll do what I like with it.'

When John was routed everybody talked of it, as people must have talked of Napoleon's defeats. He got into an argument with another intercolonial fast bowler named Lucas, at that time a man who had not played cricket for ten years. John's only argument was that Lucas was a has-been. Lucas therefore challenged him to a single-wicket match. Money was staked and ten of us agreed to field. John won the toss and batted first. He was not a bad batsman, he could hit hard and straight and he could cut, but he batted only because otherwise he would not have been able to bowl. This day the creaking Lucas bowled him a medium-paced off-break. John played and missed, the ball hit his pads and cannoned into the wicket. John had been dismissed for a duck. He rolled up his sleeves and sent down a terrible ball at Lucas. Lucas pushed out blindly, edged it for a single and John was beaten. The whole thing took two minutes. At moments like this you looked at John in a sort of terror, as if he were going to do something dreadful. He never did. I have seen him scowl at umpires, and grumble to himself, never anything else. I have never known him to get into any fights either on or off the field. Strangest of all, in the whirligig of time I have never seen this fierce and formidable man bowl a short ball aimed at a batsman's head, now dignified by the euphemism of bumper. His mentality was organised around the wicket, not the player.

One afternoon at a scratch match Joe Small lifted his 2 lb. 10 oz. bat and drove a half-volley so hard at John's feet that he had to skip out of the way. John bowled a faster one and Small made him skip out of the way again. It was near the end of play and what did we do?

As soon as play was over we hurried over to walk in with the players just to see John's face. It was a spectacle. He wasn't saying nothing to nobody; and his face was his own. Long after Joe told me that he hit those balls purposely back at John's feet to make him skip: he knew it would get him mad.

Yet he had his inner discipline, and it had been hard-earned. He described to me how he had beaten a great batsman all over the place only to see an easy catch dropped in the slips.

'I suppose you were mad as hell, John.'

'Me!' he said solemnly: 'Not me! When that happen' to you, you have to say, "Don't mind that, old chap," and go on bowling as if nothing happened.'

It was as if he had quoted a line of Virgil to me. He must have sensed my surprise.

'No,' he continued, 'you have to forget it at once, for if you don't it will stay inside and upset your bowling for the rest of the day.'

He had arrived at it by a road different from mine, but he had learned it well. This discipline, however, he reserved strictly for great occasions. In club games he did not disguise his always tempestuous feelings.

For some reason or other he hated Cyl St. Hill, the tall left-hander, and, in any case, he was always panting to dismiss the whole Shannon crew for nothing. I do him an injustice. John was always ready to bowl out any side for nought, preferably taking all ten wickets himself. This day he was bowling like the avenging angel, and had routed the powerful Shannon side, nine for about 38 (all nine to John), when Cyl, last man in, walked to the wicket. Cyl was no batsman. He was, as I have said, a very tall and very strong man. He was also a very determined one, and in all cricket, big as well as small, a little determination goes a long way. Cyl too was the type to say exactly what he thought of John, preferably in John's hearing.

First ball Cyl lashed out, the ball spooned up forty feet over the wicket and John had had all ten Shannon wickets, except that the wicket-keeper dropped the catch. Then came twenty glorious minutes. Cyl drove John through the covers to the boundary, a low humming hit. It was breast-high, but if you can hit hard enough there is a lot of room between gully and cover. He drove high and he drove low. He drove John straight back. When John shortened he cut him over the slips, but so hard that third man didn't bother to move. He hit him for a towering six to long-on, not too wide either. One or two went where they were not intended, but Cyl made as many as all the rest put together and Shannon, the invincible Shannon, finally reached seventy or eighty. Worst of all, I don't think John got the last wicket. When it fell he unrolled his sleeve and walked away as if he would never stop walking until he walked into the sea. Don't think he was defeated. Not he. He would put that away in his mind, and if you knew him well, and were wise enough to go to see him playing Shannon the following year, you would probably see Cyl bowled first ball for a duck, or his wicket shaved with a ball that only the skill of his famous brother could deal with so early in an innings.

One afternoon in a cup match I batted for two hours against him for twenty-five runs, and when he finally got me out I was as exhausted as if I had made 225. When he finished me off he gave me a wide-eyed look and a brief 'Well played'. I don't believe he thought much of me as a player. One day, however, I really surprised him. He was umpiring at my end. I bowled two inswingers which the batsmen tried to glance and missed, and then an outswinger from just off the leg-stump which he tried to glance again. It bowled him middle-stump. John looked at me rather startled, and I saw for the first and only time a genuine respect in his eyes.

'You move them both ways?' he said, almost as if he couldn't believe what he had seen.

'Yes,' I replied, and continued to demonstrate it.

Of all the fine cricketers of the day, John more than any made me acutely aware that I was outside the pale of big cricket. He said nothing about it, and he was never nasty or sarcastic. Simply he had high standards and knew who was good and who was not. I just was not good and he saw me accordingly. St. Hill talked to me as one man to another. He was always sympathetic and often gracious. John was quite unsentimental and whenever I pulled a boner about some technical detail, or played a stupid stroke, his face registered a resigned look which I found quite depressing. However, I wrote admiringly about John, I knew a lot. So wherever and whenever we saw each other, even in town far away from the cricket field, he and I stood or crossed the street to talk.

John was a formidable fast bowler. He was more than that. He was a formidable man. He was said to be jealous of Francis, and indeed of all other fast bowlers, and he could be furious about articles in the papers. Yet he had an absolutely independent judgment of cricketers and I always found him reasonable in his opinions. 'Francis can bowl,' he would say, shaking his head slowly. 'That feller can bowl.' He would say it a little slowly and a little sadly: he regretted that when he and Francis were bowling together he was not the man he had been ten years earlier. If at times he was contemptuous about laudatory articles on Constantine, at other times he would tell me that if Learie settled down to it he could be one of the greatest of fast bowlers. I believe I was one of his few friends. People did not love John as they loved Victor Pascall. He was not a national hero as was Constantine and his father before him. He did not evoke the enthusiasm and excitement that surrounded Wilton St. Hill. He was respected as a cricketer of tremendous force, a cricketer and nothing else. He in turn seemed to have respect for no one except in so far as that person could bat or bowl or field. All the heart-burning about who should be or should not be selected never affected John. No selection committee in the world would have dared to leave him out of anything, and he didn't worry about anyone else. If I sounded him out on some flagrant case like Piggott's he didn't hesitate to say, 'Mr Dewhurst, he can never keep like Piggie.' Having said it, he dropped the matter. He had cleared for himself a good space and he was quite satisfied with it so long as no one threatened to trespass. He was not Shannon. A sense of injustice, the desire to prove, was not evident in John at all. He was above that or below it. Yet in his utter rejection of all standards and interests except his own I see his fast bowling as stoked by more dynamite than there was in all the Shannon eleven put together.

C. L. R. JAMES, *Beyond a Boundary*, 1963

174

The year in which James published Beyond a Boundary, *West Indies, Frank Worrell at the helm, met England at Lords. This West Indies team was the strongest yet: playing under Worrell were the two hostile fast bowlers, Wes Hall and Charlie Griffith, the batsmen Conrad Hunte, Butcher and a young Rohan Kanhai, the spin duo of Gibbs and Valentine and of course, Gary Sobers. It's no surprise that the Trinidadian author V. S. Naipaul went down to St John's Wood to watch his team play.*

England *v.* West Indies

The First Day

At Waterloo and Trafalgar Square the Underground train begins to fill. Young men in tweed jackets, carrying mackintoshes and holdalls. Older men in City black, carrying umbrellas. At every station the crowd grows. Whole families now, equipped as for a rainy camping weekend. And more than a sprinkling of West Indians. At Baker Street we are like a rush-hour train. It is eleven o'clock on a Thursday morning and we are travelling north. The train empties at St John's Wood. Buy your return ticket now, the boards say. We will regret that we didn't. Later. Now we are in too much of a hurry. We pass the souvenir sellers, the man selling the West Indian newspaper, the white-coated newspaper vendors. The newspaper posters. What billing these cricket writers get!

Then inside. It is wet. Play has not begun. A Barbadian in a blue suit, a tall man standing behind the sightscreen, has lost his brother in the crowd, and is worried. He has been in London for four years and a half. He has the bearing of a student. But: 'I works. In transport.' The groundsmen in vivid green lounge against the wicket-covers. Someone rushes out to them with a plate of what looks like cakes. There is applause. Few people have eaten before such a large appreciative audience. Presently, though, there is action. The covers are removed, the groundsmen retreat into obscurity, and the rites begin.

Trueman bowling to Conrad Hunte. Four, through the slips. Four, to mid-wicket. Four, past gully. Never has a Test opened like this. A Jamaican whispers: 'I think Worrell made the right decision.' A little later: 'It's all right now. I feel we getting on top.' The bowling tightens. The batsmen are on the defensive, often in trouble.

'I think Conrad Hunte taking this Moral Rearmament a little too seriously. He don't want to hit the ball because the leather come from an animal.'

A chance.

The Jamaican says: 'If England have to win, they can't win now.'

I puzzle over this. Then he leans back and whispers again: 'England can't win now. If they have to win.'

Lunch. In front of the Tavern the middle-class West Indians. For them too this is a reunion.

'. . . and, boy, I had to leave Grenada because politics were making it too hot for me.'

'What, they have politics in Grenada?'

Laughter.

'You are lucky to be seeing me here today, let me tell you. The only thing in which I remain West Indian is cricket. Only thing.'

'. . . and when they come here, they don't even change.'

'Change? Them?'

Elsewhere:

'I hear the economic situation not too good in Trinidad these days.'

'All those damn strikes. You know our West Indian labour. Money, money. And if you say "work", they strike.'

But the cricket ever returns.

'I don't know why they pick McMorris in place of Carew. You can't have two sheet-anchors as opening batsmen. Carew would have made 16. Sixteen and out. But he wouldn't have let the bowling get on top as it is now. I feel it have a lil politics in McMorris pick, you know.'

After lunch, McMorris leg before to Trueman.

'Man, I can't say I sorry. Poke, poke.'

Hunte goes. And, 65 runs later, Sobers.

'It isn't a healthy score, is it?'

'My dear girl, I didn't know you followed cricket.'

'Man, how you could help it at home? In Barbados. And with all my brothers. It didn't look like this, though, this morning. Thirteen in the first over.'

'But that's cricket.'

A cracking drive, picked up almost on the boundary.

'Two runs only for that. So near and so far.'

'But that's life.'

'Man, you're a philosopher. It must be that advanced age of yours you've been telling me about.'

'Come, come, my dear. It isn't polite to agree with me. But seriously, what you doing up here?'

'Studying, as they say. Interior decorating. It's a hard country, boy. I came here to make money.' Chuckle.

'You should have gone somewhere else.'

In a doorway of the Tavern:

'If Collie Smith didn't dead, that boy Solomon wouldn'ta get pick, you know.'

'If Collie Smith didn't dead.'

'He used to jump out and hit Statham for six and thing, you know.'

'I not so sure that Worrell make the right decision.'

'Boy, I don't know. I had a look through binoculars. It breaking up already, you know. You didn't see the umpire stop Dexter running across the pitch?'

'Which one is Solomon? They look like twins.'

'Solomon have the cap. And Kanhai a lil fatter.'

'But how a man could get fat, eh, playing all this cricket?'

'Not getting *fat*. Just putting on a lil *weight*.'

'O Christ! He out! Kanhai.'

Afterwards, Mrs Worrell in a party at the back of the pavilion:

'Did you enjoy the cricket, Mrs Worrell?'

'All except Frank's duck.'

'A captain's privilege.'

The Second Day

McMorris, the West Indian opening batsman whose failure yesterday was so widely discussed by his compatriots around the ground, was this morning practising at the nets. To him, bowling, Sobers and Valentine. Beyond the stands, the match proper continues, Solomon and Murray batting, according to the transistors. But around the nets there is this group that prefers nearness to cricketers. McMorris is struck on the pads. 'How's that?' Sobers calls. 'Out! Out!' the West Indians behind the nets shout, and raise their fingers. McMorris turns. 'You don't out down the line in England.' Two Jamaicans, wearing the brimless porkpie hats recently come into fashion among West Indian workers in England, lean on each other's shoulders and stand, swaying, directly behind the stumps.

'Mac, boy,' one says, 'I can't tell you how I feel it yesterday when they out you. I feel it, man. Tell me, you sleep well last night? I couldn't sleep, boy.'

McMorris snicks one into the slips from Valentine. Then he hooks one from Sobers. It is his favourite shot.

'I wait for those,' he tells us.

A Jamaican sucks his teeth. 'Tcha! Him didn't bat like that yesterday.' And walks away.

The West Indian wickets in the meantime fall. Enter Wesley Hall. Trueman and he are old antagonists, and the West Indians buzz good-humouredly. During this encounter the larger interest of the match recedes. Hall drives Trueman straight back for four, the final humiliation of the fast bowler. Trueman gets his own back by hitting Hall on the ankle, and Hall clowningly exaggerates his distress. The middle-class West Indians in the Tavern are not so impressed.

'It's too un-hostile, man, to coin a word. You don't win Test matches with that attitude.'

West Indies all out for 301.

And England immediately in trouble. At ten past one Dexter comes in to face a score of 2 for 1. Twenty for one, lunch nearly due, and Griffith gets another wicket. A Jamaican, drunk on more than the bitter he is holding, talks of divine justice: Griffith's previous ball had been no-balled.

'You know, we going to see the West Indies bat again today.' But I want them to make some runs, though, I don't want it be a walk-over.'

'Yes, man. I want to see some cricket on Monday.'

But then Dexter. Tall, commanding, incapable of error or gracelessness. Every shot, whatever its result, finished, decisive. Dexter hooking: the ball seeming momentarily *arrested* by the bat before being redirected. Dexter simplifying: an illusion of time, even against these very fast bowlers.

'If they going to make runs, I want to see Dexter make them.'

'It would be nice. But I don't want him to stay too long. Barrington could stay there till kingdom come. But Dexter does score too damn fast. He could demoralise any side in half an hour. Look, they scoring now at the rate of six runs an over.'

'How you would captain the side? Take off Griffith?'

Sobers comes on. And Dexter, unbelievably, goes. West Indian interest subsides.

'I trying to sell a lil insurance these days, boy. You could sell to Barbadians. Once they over here and they start putting aside the couple of pounds every week, you could sell to them. But don't talk to the Jamaicans.'

'I know. They pay three weeks' premiums, and they want to borrow three hundred pounds.'

In the Tavern:

'You know what's wrong with our West Indians? No damn discipline. Look at this business this morning. That Hall and Trueman nonsense. Kya-kya, very funny. But that is not the way the Aussies win Tests. I tell you, what we need is *conscription*. Put every one of the idlers in the army. Give them discipline.'

The score mounts. Worrell puts himself on. He wants to destroy this partnership between Parks and Titmus before the end of play. There is determination in his run, his delivery. It transmits itself to the West Indian crowd, the West Indian team. And, sad for Parks, who had shown some strokes, Worrell gets his wicket. Trueman enters. But Hall is damaged. There can be no revenge for the morning's humiliation. And matters are now too serious for clowning anyway.

West Indies 301. England 244 for 7.

Afterwards, Mrs Worrell in her party.

'You can still bowl, then, Mrs Worrell. You can still bowl.'

'Frank willed that, didn't he, Mrs Worrell?'

'Both of us willed it.'

'So, Mrs Worrell, the old man can still bowl.'

'Old man? You are referring to my father or my husband?'

The Third Day

Lord's Ground Full, the boards said at St John's Wood station, and there was two-way traffic on Wellington Road. No one practising at the nets today. And Trueman and Titmus still batting. Hall, recovered this morning, wins his duel with Trueman by clean bowling him. But England is by no means finished. Shackleton is correct and unnervous against Hall and Griffith, Titmus regularly steals a run at the end of the over.

Titmus won't get 50; England won't make 300, won't make 301.

These are the bets being made in the free seats, West Indian against West Indian. Lord's has restrained them: in the West Indies they will gamble on who will field the next ball, how many runs will be scored in the over. For them a cricket match is an unceasing drama.

Titmus gets his 50. All over the free stands money changes hands. Then England are all out for 297. More money changes hands. It has worked out fairly. Those who backed Titmus for 50 backed England for 300.

Anxiety now, as the West Indians come out for the second innings. With the scores so even, the match is beginning all over again. 'I feel we losing a wicket before lunch. And I feel that it not going to be McMorris, but Hunte. I don't know, I just have this feeling.' Hunte hits a six off a bad ball from Trueman, and alarms the West Indians. 'Trueman vex too bad now.' What opens so brightly can't end well. So it turns out. Hunte is caught by Cowdrey off Shackleton. And in comes Kanhai, at twenty past one, with ten minutes to lunch, and the score 15 for 1. How does a batsman feel at such a time?

I inquire. And, as there are few self-respecting West Indians who are not in touch with someone who is in touch with the cricketers, I am rewarded. I hear that Kanhai, before he goes in to bat, sits silent and moody, 'tensing himself up'. As soon as the first West Indian wicket falls he puts on his gloves and, without a word, goes out.

Now, however, as he appears running down the pavilion steps, bat in one hand, the other hand lifted and slightly crooked, all his tenseness, if tenseness there ever was, has disappeared. There is nothing in that elegant figure to suggest nervousness. And when he does bat he gives an impression of instant confidence.

The crowd stirs just before the luncheon break. There is movement in the stands. Trueman is bowling his last over. McMorris is out! Caught Cowdrey again. McMorris has made his last effective appearance in this match. He goes in, they all go in. Lunch. For West Indians it is an anxious interval. Will Worrell send in Sobers after lunch? Or Butcher? or Solomon, the steady? It is Butcher; the batting order remains unchanged. Butcher and Kanhai take the score to 50. Thereafter there is a slowing up. Kanhai is subdued, unnatural, over-cautious. It isn't the West Indians' day. Kanhai is caught in the slips, by Cowdrey again. Just as no one runs down the pavilion steps more jauntily, no one walks back more sadly. His bat is a useless implement; he peels off his gloves as though stripping himself of an undeserved badge. Gloves flapping, he walks back, head bowed. This is not the manner of Sobers. Sobers never walks so fast as when he is dismissed. It is part of his personality, almost part of the grace of his play. And this walk back is something we will soon see.

84 for 4.

'You hear the latest from British Guiana?'

'What, the strike still on?'

'Things really bad out there.'

'Man, go away, eh. We facing defeat, and you want to talk politics.'

It looks like defeat. Some West Indians in the free seats withdraw from the game altogether and sit on the grass near the nets talking over private problems, pints of bitter between their feet. No need to ask, from the shouts immediately after tea, what has happened. Applause; no hands thrown up in the air; the West Indians standing still. Silence. Fresh applause, polite, English. This has only one meaning: another wicket.

The English turn slightly partisan. A green-coated Lord's employee, a cushion-seller, says to a West Indian: 'Things not going well now?' The West Indian shrugs, and concentrates on Solomon, small, red-capped, brisk, walking back to the pavilion.

'I can sell you a good seat,' the man says, 'I am quite comfortable, thank you,' the West Indian says. He isn't. Soon he moves and joins a group of other West Indians standing just behind the sightscreen.

Enter Worrell.

'If only we make 150 we back in the game. Only 150.'

And, incredibly, in the slow hour after tea, this happens. Butcher and Worrell remain, and, remaining, grow more aggressive.

The latest of the Worrell late cuts.

'The old man still sweet to watch, you know.'

The old man is Worrell, nearly thirty-nine.

The 50 partnership.

'How much more for the old lady?' The old lady is Butcher's century, due soon. And it comes, with two fours. A West Indian jumps on some eminence behind the sightscreen and dances, holding aloft a pint of bitter. Mackintoshes are thrown up in the air; arms are raised and held in massive V-signs. Two men do an impromptu jive.

'Wait until they get 200. Then you going to hear noise.'

The noise comes. It comes again, to mark the 100 partnership. Butcher, elegant, watchful, becomes attacking, even wild.

'That is Mr Butcher! That is Mr Basil Fitzpatrick Butcher!'

And in the end the score is 214 for 5.

'Boy, things was bad. Real bad. 104 for 5.'

'I didn't say nothing, but, boy, I nearly faint when Solomon out.'

In the Tavern:

'This is historic. This is the first time a West Indian team has fought back. The first time.'

'But, man, where did you get to, man? I was looking for a shoulder to lean on, and when I look for you, you gone.'

Many had in fact sought comfort in privacy. Many had joined the plebeian West Indians, to draw comfort from their shouting. But now assurance returns.

'I know that Frank has got everything staked on winning this match, let me tell you. And you know what's going to happen afterwards? At Edgbaston they are going to beat Trueman into the ground. Finish him off for the season.'

Behind the pavilion, the autograph hunters, and some West Indians.

'That girl only want to see Butcher. She would die for Butcher tonight.'

'I just want to see the great Gary and the great Rohan.'

Gary is Sobers, Rohan is Kanhai. These batsmen failed today. But they remain great. West Indies 301 and 214 for 5. England 297.

The Fourth Day

After the weekend tension, farce. We are scarcely settled when the five remaining West Indian wickets fall, for 15 runs. England, as if infected, quickly lose their two opening batsmen. Hall is bowling from the pavilion end, and his long run is accompanied by a sighing cheer which reaches its climax at the moment of delivery. Pity the English batsmen. Even at Lord's, where they might have thought they were safest, they now have to face an audience which is hostile.

And Dexter is out! Dexter, of the mighty strokes, out before lunch! Three for 31.

Outside the Tavern:

'I just meet Harold. Lance Gibbs send a message.'

How often, in the West Indian matches, conspiratorial word is sent straight from the players to their friends!

'Lance say', the messenger whispers, 'the wicket taking spin. He say it going to be all over by teatime.'

Odd, too, how the West Indians have influenced the English spectators. There, on one of the Tavern benches, something like a shouting match has gone on all morning between an English supporter and a West Indian.

'The only man who could save all-you is Graveney. And all-you ain't even pick him. You didn't see him there Thursday, standing up just next to the tea-stand in jacket and with a mackintosh thrown over his arm? Why they don't pick the man? You know what? They must think Graveney is black man.'

Simultaneously: 'Well, if Macmillan resigns I vote Socialist next election. And – I am a Tory.' The speaker is English (such distinctions are now necessary), thin, very young, with spectacles and tweed jacket. 'And,' he repeats, as though with self-awe, 'I am a Tory.'

In spite of that message from Lance Gibbs, Barrington and Cowdrey appear to be in no trouble.

'This is just what I was afraid of. You saw how Cowdrey played that ball? If they let him get set, the match is lost.'

When Cowdrey is struck on the arm by a fast rising ball from Hall, the ground is stilled. Cowdrey retires. Hall is chastened. So too are the West Indian spectators. Close comes in. And almost immediately Barrington carts Lance Gibbs for two sixes.

'Who was the man who brought that message from Lance Gibbs?'

'Rohan Kanhai did send a message, too, remember? He was going to get a century on Saturday.'

Where has Barrington got these strokes from? This aggression? And Close, why is he so stubborn? The minutes pass, the score climbs. 'These West Indian cricketers have some mighty names, eh: *Wesley* Hall. *Garfield* Sobers. *Rohan* Kanhai.'

'What about McMorris? What is his name?' A chuckle, choking speech. 'Easton.'

Nothing about McMorris, while this match lasts, can be taken seriously.

Now there are appeals for light, and the cricket stops. The Queen arrives. She is in light pink. The players reappear in blazers, the English in dark blue, the West Indians in maroon. They line up outside the pavilion gate, and hands are shaken, to a polite clapping which is as removed from the tension of the match as these courtly, bowing figures are removed from the cricketers we have been watching for four days.

With Barrington and Close settled in, and the score at the end of play 116 for 3, the match has once more swung in England's favour. Rain. The crowd waits for further play, but despairingly, and it seems that the game has been destroyed by the weather.

The Fifth Day

And so it continued to seem today. Rain held up play for more than three hours, and the crowd was small. But what a day for the 7,000 who went! Barrington, the hero of England's first innings, out at 130, when England needed 104 to win. Parks out at 138. Then Titmus, the stayer, came in, and after tea it seemed that England, needing only 31 runs with five wickets in hand, was safely home. The match was ending in anti-climax. But one shot – May's cover drive off Ramadhin at Edgbaston in 1957 – can change a match. And one ball. That ball now comes. Titmus is caught off Hall by – McMorris. And, next ball, Trueman goes. Only Close now remains for England, with 31 runs to get, and the clock advancing to six. Every ball holds drama. Every run narrows the gap. Hall bowls untiringly from the pavilion end. Will his strength never give out? Will Worrell have to bring on the slower bowlers – Sobers, himself or even Gibbs, whose message had reached us yesterday? Miraculously to some, shatteringly to others, it is Close who cracks. Seventy his personal score, an English victory only 15 runs away. Close pays for the adventuring which until then had brought him such reward. He is out, caught behind the wicket. However, the runs trickle in. And when, two balls before the end, Shackleton is run out any finish is still possible. Two fours will do the trick. Or a four and a two. Or a mighty swipe for six. Or a wicket. Cowdrey comes in, his injured left arm bandaged. And this is the ridiculous public-school heroism of cricket: a man with a bandaged arm saving his side, yet without having to face a ball. It is the peculiar *style* of cricket, and its improbable appreciation links these dissimilar people – English and West Indian.

Day after day I have left Lord's emotionally drained. What other game could have stretched hope and anxiety over six days? A slow game, but there were moments when it was torment to watch, when I joined those others, equally exhausted, sitting on the grass behind the stands. And what other game can leave so little sense of triumph or defeat? The anguish and joy of a cricket match last only while the match lasts. Close was marvellous. But it didn't seem so to me while he was in. Frustration denied generosity. But now admiration is pure. This has been a match of heroes, and there have been heroes on both sides. Close, Barrington, Titmus, Shackleton, Trueman, Dexter. Butcher, Worrell, Hall, Griffith, Kanhai, Solomon. Cricket a team game? Teams play, and one team is to be willed to victory. But it is the individual who remains in the memory, he who has purged the emotions by delight and fear.

V. S. NAIPAUL, *Queen Magazine*, 1963

Cricket inspires equal passion in the East as in the West, although even Columbus would be able to differentiate between the two schools of speed and spin that have taken root in the two Indias. Up against George John, Constantine, Holding and Roberts, India can name a veritable constellation of spinning stars, as Ramachandra Guha outlines in his excellent book, Spin and Other Turns.

India's Holy Trinity

IT is surprising that no commentator, Indian or Western, ever sought to compare the great spin trio to the 'Holy Trinity' of Hinduism. Let us think of Bedi as Brahma the Creator, the deity who is everywhere but nowhere; of Prasanna as Vishnu the Preserver, the god who has numerous incarnations and variations in form; and of Chandrasekhar as Siva the Destroyer, who with the wink of an eye, or turn of the wrists, would destroy any or all of his opponents.

But think again, and the comparison could disappear as quickly as it came to mind. It is impossible to think of the colourful and effervescent Sardar in the abstract, as formless (Brahma is not represented in iconic form, and there is only one temple in all of India dedicated to him); there can be no greater contrast of character than between the tempestuous Siva of legend and the docile Chandra; and a bhakti poet would most certainly not be moved to break into song at the mere sight of Prasanna.

Crude though it is, I am unwilling to entirely abandon the analogy. For Bishen Bedi was in a very real sense the creator of the

185

spin revolution of the Nineteen Seventies, the fulcrum around which everything else revolved. Once Eknath Solkar had bowled his mandatory opening over he would make way for Bedi, and the game would be immediately transformed – the nervously flailing bats of the opponents being met, when India played at home, at every unavailing heave by the 'ooohs' and 'ahs' of forty thousand voices. Bedi was on the spot from his first ball, pushing batsmen on the defensive before they could judge the pace of the pitch or think of the state of the game. To his captain, Bedi was completely dependable, for he never (or so it appeared) bowled a bad ball. A few overs later he would be joined by Prasanna, who maintained and indeed perpetuated this relentless pressure. Like Vishnu he came in many incarnations and had infinite variation. He used the crease even more skilfully than his confreres, and unlike Bedi and Chandra was equally adept at bowling from either side of the wicket. His glory was his control of flight: as John Woodcock once pointed out, in a peculiarly apt simile, he had the mastery in the air of a great kite-flyer.

Finally, when one or other of the finger-spinners was taken off, on came Chandrasekhar the Destroyer. Unlike Siva nothing caught fire at the mere blink of an eyelid, but the right wrist could wreak destruction with almost equal rapidity. In his report on that historic fourth day of the 1971 Oval Test, K. N. Prabhu imagined 'listeners back home glued to their radios as the [Indian] spinners set to work'. Alas, I was not one of them – then a lowly ninth grader in boarding school, and not allowed access to the common room and its magic radio after seven o'clock in the evening. The Indian first innings had just ended (at 280 in reply to the home side's 355) when we dressed for dinner, and on our return from the meal I turned reluctantly for the mandatory one and a half hours of study. My cricket mad House Captain, Vivek Bammi, went as per privilege to listen to the BBC, disregarding my pleas to let me accompany him. For a while I thumbed distractedly through my books till, minutes before we had to turn into bed, Bammi rushed into the study room to announce: 'England 101 all out, Chandra 6 for 38!'

That was an act of annihilation Siva might have wanted to claim his own. I also recall a more amusing occasion when again through no fault of mine I missed a radio description of Chandra's extraordinarily destructive powers. The Madras Test is usually played in the week of Pongal, the great harvest festival of the Tamil country. When England played a Test in Madras in January 1973, the visitors batted first and at lunch were 70 for 4. After the interval Keith Fletcher and Tony Greig defended doggedly, and the Indian spinners were desperate for a wicket. Listening to the radio in faraway Dehra Dun, so was I. But then domestic listeners were joined by the General Overseas Service of All India Radio. The commentator, a proud Tamil patriot wishing to interest New Zealand sheep farmers in his ancient culture, began a lengthy peroration on the origins and symbolic significance of the Pongal festival, its colourful rituals and its culinary delights. As he talked we heard, at quick intervals, bursts of prolonged cheering from the Chepauk crowd. At last the broadcaster finished his disquisition, and remarked: 'Meanwhile as I was telling you about Pongal, Chandrasekhar has claimed three wickets, and England are now 112 for 7.'

Looking back on those years, a score of Test matches are imprinted in my memory: Tests won by the spinners singly, in pairs or all together. Somehow, the match I remember best of all was played between India and Australia at New Delhi, from 28th November to 3rd December 1969. After Australia had comfortably won the first match of the series, played at Bombay, India were saved in the second Test at Kanpur only by a battling 137 not out from G. R. Viswanath, made on his Test debut. The visitors arrived at the Firozshah Kotla chockful of confidence, and at a press conference before the match their captain, Bill Lawry, claimed they would finish the Test in four days, leaving a day free to go fishing in the River Jamuna.

Australia batted first and scored 296, the innings dominated by a fine century by Ian Chappell. Despite a dogged 97 from Ashok Mankad, India conceded a lead of 73, a substantial deficit on a wicket already much the worse for wear. The Australian openers, with that prospect of a free day in mind, began with a swagger: Lawry cover-driving Bedi and Stackpole cutting Prasanna for boundaries. But immediately afterwards, Stackpole lost his off stump to a ball from Prasanna that went straight on, and thereafter the wickets tumbled. Although the captain himself carried his bat through the innings, in one afternoon a batting side of high quality was dismissed for a total of 107 (Lawry 49 not out), with Prasanna and Bedi each claiming five wickets. India were set 181 to win, but the match was not over for the Holy Trinity. Sent in as nightwatch-man, Bedi played the most valuable innings of his career. He kept

Wadekar, who finished with 91 not out, company for almost two hours as India won by seven wickets shortly after lunch on the fourth day. Lawry had his day off as predicted, but he was too distraught to take his rod to the river.

Perhaps I single out this Test, over all the others, because it was the nearest I got – one hundred and fifty miles away in the town of Dehra Dun – to a match won by Indian spin. (In fact, a quarter of a century was to pass before India again won a Test at the Kotla.) Through the Nineteen Seventies, as the Holy Trinity spun India to victories in Calcutta, Madras and other cities, I was always more than five hundred miles from the action.

But as it happens, my most cherished memories of the Holy Trinity have nothing to do with Test cricket. Coming of age in the Seventies, I was privileged to see three remarkable Ranji Trophy matches in which all three performed: three rich and close-fought encounters between Karnataka, for whom Prasanna and Chandrasekhar played, and Delhi, whom Bedi skippered.

The Holy Trinity notwithstanding, for me these matches were made memorable as much for the quality of the batsmanship. With the precipitous decline of spin bowling, the art of batting has also suffered a body blow. Thus where others of my generation might live to tell their grandchildren, 'You should have seen Bedi and Prasanna bowl,' I shall tell mine, 'You should have seen Bedi bowl to Brijesh Patel, and Prasanna bowl to Mohinder Amarnath.' Brijesh and Mohinder were only two of the most gifted players of spin bowling on display here: others included Surinder Amarnath and Madan Lal, for Delhi, and Sudhakar Rao and, of course, G. R. Viswanath for Karnataka.

Sometime or somewhere else I might wish to record or replay those three encounters in full. I might only note here that these matches collectively constituted the twelve most enthralling days of cricket I am ever likely to watch, not one of which I would sacrifice for all five days of a Test match, even a Test match against the West Indies won by India. Karnataka won on all three occasions (although never with ease) – results which pleased me, a lifelong Karnataka supporter, but which would perhaps not have surprised a devout Hindu, who knows that two gods are always better, and more powerful, than one.

For an Indian who grew up in the Seventies, it is impossible to think that there could ever have been a slow left-armer more classical than

Bishen Bedi, an off-break bowler as cunning as Erapalli Prasanna, or a wrist-spinner with destructive powers matching Bhagwat Chandrasekhar's. But how great were the Holy Trinity when judged 'objectively', that is, against the long sweep of cricket history? Here I believe that Prasanna ranks as one of the best half-dozen off-spinners in the history of Test cricket, alongside the Australian Hugh Trumble, the Englishman Jim Laker, the South African Hugh Tayfield, and the West Indians Sonny Ramadhin and Lance Gibbs (treating Ramadhin primarily as an off-spinner who bowled a surprise leg break). In an art more difficult to master, only the great Australian duo of Bill O'Reilly and Clarrie Grimmett were, among all googly bowlers since B. J. T. Bosanquet, as good as (or even marginally superior to) Chandrasekhar. Turning finally to Bedi, the Yorkshireman Wilfred Rhodes is a possible rival for the title of 'the greatest ever slow left-arm bowler'. I will not allow anyone else to be mentioned in the same breath.

I never watched Rhodes or O'Reilly or Laker, nor have I met anyone who did. There are, however, three contemporaries of the Holy Trinity with whom they might more readily be compared. One, Lance Gibbs, even held (briefly) the world record for the most number of Test wickets. With his high-stepping run, sharp turn, and bounding agility while fielding on the follow through, Gibbs was one of the most exciting of slow bowlers. I shall always hold him in the deepest respect, having watched him, at the age of forty, destroy an Indian side on a drying wicket in Delhi. The previous summer, I had listened in to the school radio (having by now graduated to the senior form) when his classic caught-and-bowled dismissal of the obdurate Geoffrey Boycott paved the way for a West Indies victory in the 1973 Lord's Test.

As one who relied principally on flight and turn, Lance Gibbs was every bit as orthodox as Erapalli Prasanna. But the bowler with whom Bishen Bedi is most frequently compared, England's Derek Underwood, was very dissimilar in method. He was truly unplayable on a wet wicket, prompting the joke that while other Englishmen had their umbrellas, the English cricketers needed only to carry Underwood with them in case it rained (this was in the days before wickets were covered overnight). But Underwood was much more than a wet wicket bowler. At his pace – a brisk slow-medium – his variations were perhaps not so apparent to the spectator, but the batsman was continually subject to changes in pace, flight and turn. I saw Brijesh Patel, that outstanding player of spin bowling, being

189

deceived by a late dip in flight to hit a catch back to Underwood at a crucial stage of the 1976 Delhi Test, and no less a batsman than Sunil Gavaskar is on record as saying that, only with the exception of Andy Roberts, the English spinner was the most difficult of all the bowlers he faced in a twenty-year career. Rain or shine, Underwood fully earned the appellation 'Deadly', although on the last occasion I saw him, when the television camera caught him sitting in the stands in the Melbourne Cricket Ground during the final of the 1992 World Cup, his left hand carried nothing deadlier than a cigarette.

Where the careers of Bedi and Underwood almost exactly over-lapped, Abdul Qadir's rise to greatness followed Chandrasekhar's departure from the international scene. As the premier googly bowler of his time, the mercurial Pakistani sent the same buzz of anticipation through the crowd. His action was equally dramatic – starting at an absurdly sideways angle with a lick of the fingers, then two elaborate strides, and a quick jump in delivery in culmination. Qadir was exceptionally accurate for a wrist-spinner, and bowled beautifully under pressure, especially in the one-day game. But he lacked Chandra's deceptive flight, and was harder on umpires and on his own captain than the Indian ever could be. Qadir also had the inestimable advantage of playing in an era when the best of Test batsmen – including, it must be said, some Indians – could not read wrist-spinners from the hand.

Gibbs, Underwood and Qadir all bowled in the wake, not to say shadow, of the fast men who dominated their own Test sides. Thus Gibbs provided accompaniment to pace bowlers of the calibre of Wesley Hall, Charlie Griffith and Garfield Sobers; Qadir to Imran Khan, Sarfraz Nawaz and Wasim Akram; and Underwood to John Snow, Bob Willis and Ian Botham. Only Gibbs, on the rare occasions when Sobers chose to bowl in either of his two slower styles, had a spinner of quality operating in tandem. Here their situation was far from exceptional, for the history of international cricket has been depressingly dominated by fast bowlers. Perhaps only Ramadhin and Alf Valentine, bowling for the West Indies in the Nineteen Fifties, and O'Reilly and Grimmett, doing duty for Australia two decades earlier, qualify as authentically great *pairs* of spin bowlers, winning Test matches and series all on their own.

It was their simultaneous emergence, as a trinity, that made the Indian spinners of the Seventies so distinctive. For the first, and almost certainly the last time in cricket history, Test matches were won with some regularity by a side almost completely bereft of seam bowling, and relying instead on a trio of spinners, all great in their own right and with skills that so beautifully complemented each other's. One might of course (like a good Hindu) have sectarian preferences, but in the consciousness of cricket they shall always be joined together. They were a Holy Trinity – Bedi, Prasanna, Chandrasekhar: Brahma, Vishnu, Maheshwara.

RAMACHANDRA GUHA, *Spin and Other Turns*, 1994

The temple at which these gods are worshipped is Eden Gardens in Calcutta, by reputation the most intimidating of Test match arenas. Though not so, apparently, on the day Vikram Seth's characters took a leisurely stroll through the Gardens at the New Year Test, the struggle on the cricket pitch taking a back seat rôle to the struggle for love.

A Suitable Game

AMIT and Dipankar arrived in the Humber at nine, and Arun, Varun and Pran went off with them to Eden Gardens to watch the third day of the Third Test. Just outside the stadium they met Haresh, as previously arranged, and the six of them made their way to the tier where their seats were located.

It was a wonderful morning. There was a clear blue sky, a dew still glistened on the outfield. Eden Gardens, with its emerald grass and surrounding trees, its huge scoreboard and new Ranji Stadium block, was a magnificent sight. It was packed solid, but luckily one of Arun's English colleagues at Bentsen Pryce, who had bought a bunch of season tickets for his family, was out sightseeing, and had offered his seats to Arun for the day. They were placed just next to the pavilion section, where VIPs and members of the Cricket Association of Bengal sat, and they had a fine view of the field.

India's opening batsmen were still at the crease. Since India had scored 418 and 485 in two previous innings in the series, and since England were all out for 342 in their first innings, there was a good chance that the hosts would be able to make something of the match. The Calcutta crowd – more knowledgeable and appreciative than any other in India – was looking forward to it with eager anticipation.

The chatter, which increased between overs, was reduced, but not quite to silence, every time the bowler came in to bowl. Leadbeater opened the bowling to Roy with a maiden, and Ridgway supported the attack from the other end, bowling to Mankad. Then, for the next over, instead of continuing with Leadbeater, the English skipper Howard brought Statham on.

This provoked a good deal of discussion among the group of six. Everyone started speculating as to why Leadbeater had been brought on for a single over. Amit alone said that it meant nothing at all. Perhaps, because Indian time was several hours ahead of England, Leadbeater had wanted to bowl the first English ball of 1952 and Howard had let him.

'Really, Amit,' said Pran with a laugh. 'Cricket isn't governed by poetical whims of that kind.'

'A pity,' said Amit. 'Reading old reports by Cardus always makes me think that it's just a variant of poetry – in six line stanzas.'

'I wonder where Billy is,' said Arun in rather a hangover-ish voice. 'Can't see him anywhere.'

'Oh, he's bound to be here,' said Amit. 'I can't imagine him missing a day of a Test.'

'We're off to a rather slow start,' said Dipankar. 'I hope this isn't going to be another awful draw like the last two Tests.'

'I think we're going to teach them a lesson.' This was Haresh's optimistic assessment.

'We might,' said Pran. 'But we should be careful on this wicket. It's a bowler's delight.'

And so it proved to be.

The quick loss of three of the best Indian wickets – including that of the captain – cast a chill on the stadium. When Amarnath – who had hardly had time to pad up – came onto the field to face Tattersall, there was complete silence. Even the women spectators stopped their winter knitting for a second.

He was bowled for a duck in that same fatal over.

The Indian side was collapsing like skittles. If the mayhem continued, India might be all out before lunch. High visions of a victory turned to the dread of an ignominious follow-on.

'Just like us,' said Varun morosely. 'We are a failure as a country. We can always snatch defeat out of the jaws of victory. I'm going to watch the racing in the afternoon,' he added disgustedly. He would have to watch his horses through the palings around the course rather than sit in these forty-rupee season-ticket seats, but at least there was a chance that his horse might win.

'I'm getting up to stretch my legs,' said Amit.

'I'll come with you,' said Haresh, who was annoyed by the poor show that India was putting on. 'Oh – who's that man there – the one in the navy-blue blazer with the maroon scarf – do any of you know? I seem to recognise him from somewhere.'

Pran looked across at the pavilion section and was completely taken aback.

'Oh, Malvolio!' he said, as if he had seen Banquo instead.

'What was that?' said Haresh.

'Nothing. I suddenly remembered something I had to teach next term. Cricket balls, my liege. Something just struck me. No, I – I can't say for sure that I recognise him – I think you'd better ask the Calcutta people.' Pran was not good at deception, but the last thing he wanted to encourage was a meeting berween Haresh and Kabir. Any number of complications might ensue, including a visit by Kabir to Sunny Park.

Luckily, no one else recognised him.

'I'm sure I've seen him somewhere,' Haresh persisted. 'I'm bound to remember some time. Good-looking fellow. You know, the same thing happened to me with Lata. I felt I'd seen her before – and – I'm sure I'm not mistaken. I'll go and say hello.'

Pran could do nothing further. Amit and Haresh wandered over between overs, and Haresh said to Kabir: 'Good morning. Haven't we met somewhere before?'

Kabir looked at them and smiled. He stood up. 'I don't think we have,' he said.

'Perhaps at work – or in Cawnpore?' said Haresh. 'I have the feeling – well, anyway, I'm Haresh Khanna, from Praha.'

'Glad to meet you, Sir.' Kabir shook his hand and smiled. 'Perhaps we've met in Brahmpur, that is if you come to Brahmpur on work.'

Haresh shook his head. 'I don't think so,' he said. 'Are you from Brahmpur?'

'Yes,' said Kabir. 'I'm a student at Brahmpur University. I'm keen on cricket, so I've come down for a while to watch what I can of the Test. A pretty miserable show.'

'Well, it's a dewy wicket,' said Amit in mitigation.

'Dewy wicket my foot,' said Kabir with good-natured combative-ness. 'We are always making excuses for ourselves. Roy had no business to cut that ball. And Umrigar did the same. And for Hazare and Amarnah to be bowled neck and crop in the same over: it's really too bad. They send over a team that doesn't include Hutton or Bedser or Compton or Laker or May — and we manage to disgrace ourselves anyway. We've never had a Test victory against the MCC, and if we lose this one, we don't ever deserve to win. I'm beginning to think it's a good thing I'm leaving Calcutta tomorrow morning. Anyway, tomorrow's a rest day.'

'Why, where are you going?' laughed Haresh, who liked the young man's spirit. 'Back to Brahmpur?'

'No – I've got to go to Allahabad for the Inter-'Varsity.'

'Are you on the university team?'

'Yes,' Kabir frowned. 'But I'm sorry, I haven't introduced myself. My name's Kabir. Kabir Durrani.'

'Ah,' said Haresh, his eyes disappearing. 'You're the son of Professor Durrani.'

Kabir looked at Haresh in amazement.

'We met for just a minute,' said Haresh. 'I brought young Bhaskar Tandon over to your house one day to meet your father. In fact, now I come to think of it, you were wearing cricket clothes.'

Kabir said: 'Good heavens. I think I do remember now. I'm terribly sorry. But won't you sit down? These two chairs are free — my friends have gone off to get some coffee.'

Haresh introduced Amit, and they all sat down.

After the next over Kabir turned to Haresh and said: 'I suppose you know what happened to Bhaskar at the Pul Mela?'

'Yes, indeed. I'm glad to hear he's all right now.'

'If he had been here, we wouldn't have needed that fancy Australian-style scoreboard.'

'No,' said Haresh with a smile. 'Pran's nephew,' he said to Amit by way of incomplete explanation.

'I do wish women wouldn't bring their knitting to the match,'said Kabir intolerantly. 'Hazare out. Plain. Umrigar out. Purl. It's like *A Tale of Two Cities.*'

Amit laughed at this pleasant young fellow's analogy, but was forced to come to the defence of his own city. 'Well, apart from our sections of the stadium, where people come to be seen as much as to see, Calcutta's a good place for cricket,' he said. 'In the four-rupee

194

seats the crowd knows its stuff all right. And they start queueing up for day tickets from nine o'clock the previous night.'

Kabir nodded. 'Well, you're right. And it's a lovely stadium. The greenness of the field almost hurts the eyes.'

Haresh thought back for a moment to his mistake about colours, and wondered whether it had done him any harm.

The bowling changed over once again from the Maidan end to the High Court end.

'Whenever I think of the High Court end I feel guilty,' said Amit to Haresh. Making conversation with his rival was one way of sizing him up.

Haresh, who had no sense at all that he had any rival anywhere, answered innocently: 'Why? Have you done anything against the law? Oh, I'm forgetting, your father's a judge.'

'And I'm a lawyer, that's my problem. I should be working, according to him — writing opinions, not poems.'

Kabir half turned towards Amit in astonishment.

'You're not the Amit Chatterji?'

Amit had discovered that coyness made things worse once he was recognised. 'Yes, indeed,' he said. 'The.'

'Why – I'm – how amazing – I like your stuff – a lot of it – I can't say I understand it all.'

'No, nor do I.'

A sudden thought struck Kabir. 'Why don't you come to Brahmpur to read? You have a lot of fans there in the Brahmpur Literary Society. But I hear you never give readings.'

'Well, not never,' said Amit thoughfully. 'I don't normally – but if I'm asked to come to Brahmpur, and can get leave of absence from my Muse, I might well come. I've often wondered what the town was like: the Barsaat Mahal, you know, and, of course, the Fort – and, well, other objects of beauty and interest. I've never been there before.' He paused. 'Well, would you care to join us there among the season-ticket holders? But I suppose these are better seats.'

'It's not that,' said Kabir. 'It's just that I'm with friends – they've invited me – and it's my last day in town. I'd better not. But I'm very honoured to meet you. And – well – you're sure you wouldn't take it amiss if you were invited to Brahmpur? It wouldn't interfere too much with your writing?'

'No,' said Amit mildly. 'Not Brahmpur. Just write to my pub-lishers. It'll be forwarded to me.'

The game was continuing, a little more steadily than before. It would soon be lunchtime. No more wickets had fallen, which was a blessing, but India was still in perilous straits.

'It's a real pity about Hazare. His form seems to have deserted him after that knock on the head in Bombay,' said Amit.

'Well,' said Kabir, 'you can't blame him entirely. Ridgway's bouncers can be vicious – and he'd scored a century, after all. He was pretty badly stunned. I don't think he should have been forced back out from the pavilion by the Chairman of Selectors. It's demeaning for a skipper to be ordered back – and bad for morale all around.' He went on, almost in a dream: 'I suppose Hazare is indecisive – it took him fifteen minutes to decide whether to bat or to field in the last Test. But, well, I'm discovering that I'm quite indecisive myself, so I sympathise. I've been thinking of visiting someone ever since I arrived in Calcutta, but I can't. I find I just can't. I don't know what kind of bowling I'd have to face,' he added with a rather bitter laugh. 'They say he's lost his nerve, and I think I've lost mine!' Kabir's remarks were not addressed to anyone in particular, but Amit felt – for no very good reason – a strong sense of sympathy for him.

VIKRAM SETH, *A Suitable Boy*, 1993

It is at grass roots that cricket truly flourishes in India, or where it would do if the tens of thousands of maidans *had grass. As far south as the parched, mythical Malgudi of R. K. Narayan, the game has its followers.*

The 'M.C.C.'

S WAMINATHAN had not thought of cricket as something that he himself could play. He was, of course, familiar with Hobbs, Bradman, and Duleep, and vainly tried to carry their scores in his head, as Rajam did. He filched pictures of cricket players, as Rajam did, and pasted them in an album, though he secretly did not very much care for those pictures – there was something monotonous about them. He sometimes thought that the same picture was pasted in every page of the album.

'No, Rajam, I don't think I can play. I don't know how to play.'

'That is what everybody thinks,' said Rajam. 'I don't know myself, though I collect pictures and scores.'

This was very pleasing to hear. Probably Hobbs too was shy and sceptical before he took the bat and swung it.

'We can challenge a lot of teams, including our school eleven. They think they can't be beaten,' said Swaminathan.

'What! The Board School mugs think that! We shall thrash them. Oh, yes.'

'What shall we call it?'

'Don't you know? It is the M.C.C.,' said Rajam.

'That is Hobbs's team, isn't it? They may drag us before a court if we take their name.'

'Who says that? If we get into any trouble, I shall declare before the judge that M.C.C. stands for Malgudi Cricket Club.'

Swaminathan was a little disappointed. Though as M.C.C. it sounded imposing, the name was really a bit tame. 'I think we had better try some other name, Rajam.'

'What would you suggest?'

'Well – I am for "Friends Eleven"'

'Friends Eleven?'

'Or, say, "Jumping Stars"?' said Swaminathan.

'Oh, that is not bad, not bad, you know.'

'I do think it would be glorious to call ourselves "Jumping Stars"!'

Rajam instantly had a vision of a newspaper report: 'The Jumping Stars soundly thrashed the Board High School Eleven.' 'It is a beauty, I think,' he cried, moved by the vision. He pulled out a

197

piece of paper and a pencil, and said, 'Come on, Swami, repeat the names that come to your head. It would be better to have a long list to select from. We shall underline "Jumping Stars" and "M.C.C." and give them special consideration. Come on.'

Swaminathan remained thoughtful and started, '"Friends Eleven". . ."Jumping Stars". . ."Friends Union". . .'

'I have "Friends Union" already here,' Rajam said pointing to the list.

Swaminathan went on: '"Excelsiors". . .'

'I have got it.'

'"Excelsior Union". . ."Champion Eleven". . .' A long pause.

'Are you dried up?' Rajam asked.

'No, if Mani were here, he would have suggested a few more names. . ."Champion Eleven".'

'You have just said it.'

'"Victory Union Eleven". . .'

'That is very good. I think it is very very good. People would be afraid of us.' He held the list before him and read the names with great satisfaction. He had struggled hard on the previous night to get a few names. But only 'Friends Union' and 'Excelsiors' kept coming till he felt fatigued. But what a lot of names Swaminathan was able to reel off. 'Can you meet me tomorrow evening, Swami? I shall get Mani down. Let us select a name.'

After a while Swaminathan asked, 'Look here, do you think we shall have to pay tax or something to the Government when we start the team?'

'The Government seems to tax everything in this world. My father's pay is about five hundred. But nearly two hundred and over is demanded by the Government. Anyway, what makes you think that we shall have to pay tax?'

'I mean – if we don't pay tax, the Government may not recognise our team or its name and a hundred other teams may take the same name. It might lead to all sorts of complications.'

'Suppose we have two names?' asked Rajam.

'It is not done.'

'I know a lot of teams that have two names. When I was in Bishop Waller's, we had a cricket team that we called – I don't remember the name now. I think we called it "Cricket Eleven" and "Waller's Cricket Eleven". You see, one name is for ordinary use and the other is for matches.'

'It is all very well for a rich team like your Waller's. But suppose

198

the Government demands two taxes from us?'

Rajam realised at this point that the starting of a cricket team was the most complicated problem on earth. He had simply expected to gather a dozen fellows on the *maidan* next to his compound and play, and challenge the world. But here were endless troubles, starting with the name that must be unique, Government taxes, and so on. The Government did not seem to know where it ought to interfere and where not. He had a momentary sympathy for Gandhi; no wonder he was dead against the Government.

Swaminathan seemed to be an expert in thinking out difficulties. He said, 'Even if we want to pay, whom are we to pay the taxes to?' Certainly not to His Majesty or the Viceroy. Who was the Government? What if somebody should take the money and defraud them, somebody pretending to be the Government? Probably they would have to send the taxes by Money Order to the Governor! Well, that might be treason. And then what was the amount to be paid?

They sat round Rajam's table in his room. Mani held before him a catalogue of Messrs Binns, the Shop for Sports Goods. He read, "Junior Willard Bats, Seven Eight, made of finest seasoned wood, used by Cambridge Junior Boys' Eleven".'

'Let me have a look at it . . .' said Rajam. He bent over the table and said, 'Seems to be a fine bat. Have a look at it, Swami.'

Swaminathan craned his neck and agreed that it was a fine bat, but he was indiscreet enough to say, 'It looks like any other bat in the catalogue.'

Mani's left hand shot out and held his neck and pressed his face close to the picture of the bat: 'Why do you pretend to be a cricket player if you cannot see the difference between Junior Willard and other bats? You are not fit to be even a sweeper in our team.' After this admonition the hold was relaxed.

Rajam asked, 'Swami, do you know what the catalogue man calls the Junior Willard? It seems it is the Rolls-Royce among the junior bats. Don't you know the difference between the Rolls-Royce and other cars?'

Swaminathan replied haughtily, 'I never said I saw no difference between the Rolls-Royce and other cars.'

'What is the difference?' urged Rajam.

Mani laughed and teased, 'Come on. If you really know the difference, why don't you say it?'

Swaminathan said, 'The Rolls costs a lakh of rupees, while other cars cost about ten thousand; a Rolls has engines made of silver, while other cars have iron engines.'

'Oh, oh!' jeered Rajam.

'A Rolls never gives trouble, while other cars always give trouble; a Rolls engine never stops; a Rolls-Royce never makes a noise, while other cars always make a noise.'

'Why not deliver a lecture on the Rolls-Royce?' asked Mani.

'Swami, I am glad you know so much about the Rolls-Royce. I am at the same time ashamed to find you knowing so little about Willard Junior. We had about a dozen Willard Juniors when I was in Bishop Waller's. Oh! what bats! There are actual springs inside the bat, so that when you touch the ball it flies. There is fine silk cord wound round the handle. You don't know anything, and yet you talk! Show me another bat which has silk cord and springs like the Willard.'

There was a pause, and after that Rajam said, 'Note it down, Swami.' Swaminathan noted down on a paper, 'Vilord june-ear bat.' And looking up asked, 'How many?'

'Say three. Will that do, Mani?'

'Why waste money on three bats? Two will do . . .'

But suppose one breaks in the middle of a match?' Rajam asked.

'Do you suppose we are going to supply bats to our opponents? They will have to come provided with bats. We must make it clear.'

'Even then, if our bat breaks we may have to stop playing.'

'Two will do, Rajam, unless you want to waste money.'

Rajam's enthusiasm was great. He left his chair and sat on the arm of Mani's chair, gloating over the pictures of cricket goods in the catalogue. Swaminathan, though he was considered to be a bit of a heretic, caught the enthusiasm and perched on the other arm of the chair. All the three devoured with their eyes the glossy pictures of cricket balls, bats, and wickets.

In about an hour they selected from the catalogue their team's requirements. And then came the most difficult part of the whole affair – a letter to Messrs Binns, ordering goods. Bare courtesy made Rajam offer the authorship of the letter to Mani, who declined it. Swaminathan was forced to accept it in spite of his protests, and he sat for a long time chewing his pencil without producing a word; he had infinite trouble with spelling, and the more he tried to be correct the more muddled he was becoming; in the end he sat so long thinking of spelling that even such words as 'the' and 'and' became doubtful. Rajam took on the task himself. Half an hour later he placed on the table a letter:

From
    M.C.C. (And Victory Union Eleven),
    Malgudi.

To
    Messrs Binns,
    Sportsmen,
    Mount Road,
    Madras.
DEAR SIR,
    Please send to our team two junior willard bats, six balls, wickets and other things quick. It is very urgent. We shall send you money afterwards. Don't fear. Please be urgent.
                           Yours obediently,
                           CAPTAIN RAJAM (Captain).

This letter received Swaminathan's benedictions. But Mani expressed certain doubts. He wanted to know whether 'Dear' could stand at the beginning of a letter to a perfect stranger. 'How can you call Binns "Dear Sir"? You must say "Sir".'

Rajam's explanation was: 'I won't say "Sir". It is said only by clerks. I am not Binns's clerk. I don't care to address him as "Sir".'

So this letter went as it was.

The M.C.C. and its organisers had solid proof that they were persons of count when a letter from Binns came addressed to the Captain, M.C.C., Malgudi. It was a joy, touching that beautiful envelope and turning it over in the hand. Binns were the first to recognise the M.C.C., and Rajam took a vow that he would buy every bit that his team needed from that great firm. There were three implications in this letter that filled Rajam and his friends with rapture: (1) that His Majesty's Post Office recognised their team was proved by the fact that the letter addressed to the captain was promptly delivered to him; (2) that they were really recognised by such a magnificent firm as Binns of Madras was proved by the fact that Binns cared to reply in a full letter and not on a card, and actually typed the letter! (3) Binns sent under another cover carrying four annas postage a huge catalogue. What a tribute!

The letter informed the captain that Messrs Binns thanked him for his letter and would be much obliged to him if he would kindly remit 25 per cent with the order and the balance could be paid against the V.P.P. of the railway receipt.

Three heads buzzed over the meaning of this letter. The trouble was that they could not understand whether Binns were going to send the goods or not. Mani promised to unravel the letter if somebody would tell him what 'obliged' meant. When they turned the pages of a dictionary and offered him the meaning, he was none the wiser. He felt that it was a meaningless word in that place.

'One thing is clear,' said Rajam, 'Binns thanks us for our letter. So I don't think this letter could mean a refusal to supply us goods.'

Swaminathan agreed with him, 'That is right. If he did not wish to supply you with things, would he thank you? He would have abused you.' He scrutinised the letter again to make sure that there was no mistake about the thanks.

'Why has the fool used this word?' Mani asked, referring to 'obliged' which he could not pronounce. 'It has no meaning. Is he trying to make fun of us?'

'He says something about twenty-five per cent. I wish I knew what it was,' said Rajam.

Swaminathan could hardly contain himself, 'I say, Rajam, I am surprised that you cannot understand this letter; you got sixty per cent in the last examination.'

'Have you any sense in you? What has that to do with this? Even a B.A. cannot understand this letter.'

In the end they came to the conclusion that the letter was sent to them by mistake. As far as they could see, the M.C.C. had written nothing in their previous letter to warrant such expressions as 'obliged', 'remit', and '25 per cent'. It could not be that the great firm of Binns were trying to make fun of them. Swaminathan pointed out 'To the Captain, M.C.C.' at the beginning of the letter. But he was told that it was also a part of the mistake.

This letter was put in a cover with a covering letter and dispatched. The covering letter said:

We are very sorry that you sent me somebody's letter. We are returning this somebody's letter. Please send our things immediately.

The M.C.C. were an optimistic lot. Though they were still unhonoured with a reply to their second letter, they expected the goods to arrive with every post. After ten days they thought they would start playing with whatever was available till they got the real bats, et cetera. The bottom of a dealwood case provided them with three good bats, and Rajam managed to get three used tennis balls from father's club. The Pea was there, offering four stumps that he believed he had somewhere in his house. A neat slip of ground adjoining Rajam's bungalow was to be the pitch. Everything was ready. Even if Binns took a month more to manufacture goods specially for the M.C.C. (as they faintly thought probable), there need be no delay in starting practice. By the time the real bats and the balls arrived, they would be in form to play matches.

Rajam had chosen from his class a few who, he thought, deserved to become members of the M.C.C.

At five o'clock on the opening day, the M.C.C. had assembled, all except the Pea, for whom Rajam was waiting anxiously. He had promised to bring the real stumps. It was half an hour past time and yet he was not to be seen anywhere.

At last his puny figure was discovered in the distance. There was a catch in Rajam's heart when he saw him. He strained his eyes to find out if the Pea had the things about him. But since the latter was coming from the west, he was seen in the blaze of the evening sun. All the twelve assembled in the field shaded their eyes and looked. Some said that he was carrying a bundle, while some thought that he was swinging his hands freely.

When he arrived, Rajam asked, 'Why didn't you tell us that you hadn't the stumps?'

'I have still got them,' protested the Pea, 'I shall bring them tomorrow. I am sure my father knows where they are kept.'

'You kept us waiting till now. Why did you not come earlier and tell us that you could not find them?'

'I tell you, I have been spending hours looking for them everywhere. How could I come here and tell and at the same time search?'

A cloud descended upon the gathering. For over twenty hours every one among them had been dreaming of swinging a bat and throwing a ball. And they would have realised the dream but for the Pea's wickedness. Everybody looked at him sourly. He was hated. Rajam felt like crying when he saw the deal-wood planks and the tennis balls lying useless on the ground. What a glorious evening they could have had if only the stumps had been brought!

Amidst all this gloom somebody cast a ray of light by suggesting that they might use the compound wall of Rajam's bungalow as a temporary wicket.

A portion of the wall was marked off with a piece of charcoal, and the captain arranged the field and opened the batting himself. Swaminathan took up the bowling. He held a tennis ball in his hand, took a few paces, and threw it over. Rajam swung the bat but missed it. The ball hit the wall right under the charcoal mark. Rajam was bowled out with the very first ball! There was a great shout of joy. The players pressed round Swaminathan to shake him and pat him on the back, and he was given on the very spot the title, 'Tate'.

R. K. NARAYAN, *Swami and Friends*, 1935

Cricket is equally popular across the border in Pakistan. The contribution to the game made by the likes of Imran Khan, Wasim and Waqar, with their lethal reverse swing, are included in The Greats earlier in this book. Then there is the Mohammed family, which has a long history in Pakistani cricket: Hanif Mohammed's record of 499, run out, has only recently been surpassed by Brian Lara. One record which Pakistan should claim for all time is that of the biggest margin of defeat in a first-class match, that suffered by Dera Ismail Khan.

An Innings and 851 Runs

I T happened thirteen years ago this week, and that is the appropriate time after which to commemorate it. Dera Ismail Khan – or 'Dik' to old colonial hands – is on the west bank of the Indus, itself the westernmost of the Punjab's rivers. The muddy Indus flows softly in winter, little bigger than the Thames. But in summer, when the Karakoram snows melt, the Indus trebles its volume, filling the canals and irrigating the fields of cotton and sugar-cane.

The town of Dera Ismail Khan – or Dikhan to its inhabitants – consists of a long, dusty main street and a bazaar. It is mud-bricked, one-storeyed and poor, its pride a Plaza cinema, and baking hot so that its people are swarthier than most other Pakistanis.

But for want of anywhere else in those parts, the British made the town an administrative centre, and so it remains. The Raj lingers on in the bungalows and clubs (now Army property) of the suburb: in the two mud-brick churches, each with but a weekly service, and in the one-room municipal library stocked with biographies of Palmerston and the Earl of Derby, unread since 1947, and the complete works of Scott.

Little different therefore from any other Pakistani town in which the Raj set up shop. But Dikhan once played a first-class cricket match, exactly thirteen years ago: and they had the misfortune to lose it by the margin of an innings and 851 runs.

In the sub-continent weirder sides have slipped through the net of first-class status: the Hindustan Breweries XI and the Maharastra Small Savings Minister's XI (the savings were small, presumably, not the Savings Minister himself).

In 1964 it was reasonable by such standards for the new Ayub Zonal Tournament to be accorded first-class status. In the first round Dikhan, instead of playing another small fish like Baluchistan, were drawn against the mighty Railways, the match to be played at the Railways Stadium in Lahore.

A Dikhan team was assembled, but they had no wicket-keeper until someone visiting his brother in the town volunteered. Eight of them travelled to Lahore by train, two by bus, and Inayet, their best bowler, set off on the 250-mile journey by motorbike.

Railways won the toss, batted, overcame the loss of an early wicket, and finished the first day at 415 for 2. Ijaz Husain made 124 and Javed Baber, out early next day, chipped in with 200. But when Javed was out, the rot set in as Railways collapsed to 662 for 6. Pervez Akhtar and Muhammad Sharif, however, revived Railways and took the score to 825 for 6 at the close. They slaughtered the enemy with a mighty slaughtering, and the morning and the evening were the second day.

It had occurred to the Dikhan team that a declaration was about due. They were exhausted, and it was only on the assumption that they would be batting that they went to the ground on the third day. But, risking nothing, Railways batted on to 910 for 6 before declaring, with Pervez Akhtar, who had never made a century before, 337 not out. The declaration did not please Pervez because he had Hanif's world record 499 in sight.

The bowling figures testify to a carnage. Whereas Anwar Husain represented penetration (46 overs, 3 for 295), Inayet was accuracy (59 overs, 1 for 279). They both bowled fast-medium. At one point, while walking back to his mark, Anwar, now an Army major, was moved to continue past it and to hide behind the sightscreen.

Dikhan's reply was brief. They were all out for 32. Railways then gambled on a lead of 878 and enforced the follow-on. This time Dikhan were less successful, being all out for 27. Ahad Khan took 9 for 7 with mixed spin. Whereas Railways had batted for two and a quarter days, Dikhan were dismissed twice in two hours.

The cricketers of Dikhan were too tired and dejected to go home. They stayed in Lahore for several days recuperating, and then, on their return, by the waters of the Indus, they lay down and wept.

Two of the side gave up playing cricket after that match (or even during it – but that is unfair for they used no substitute fielders: they had none). And most of them left Dikhan in the course of time to find work, so that only three members still remain there.

Inayet lives in a back street of Dikhan. His full name is Inayet Ullah, but everyone knows him as Inayet Bowler. He is about six feet tall, with long strong fingers. His wife was ill. Whether it was that, or hashish, or his job in a bank, an intense sadness shrouded him. He spoke in the local tongue, save for the odd word in English and the one sentence: 'The fielding was very poor.' He estimated that eleven or twelve catches were dropped, one of them Pervez Akhtar (337) before he had made 10, off his own bowling. When he said that, he seemed near the heart of his sadness.

No one who has experienced a hard day in the field would mock these men of Dera Ismail Khan. Their endurance was more admirable than the easy records set up against them. It would not have been unusual in such cricket if they had conceded the match, or resorted to the common expedient of walking out in protest at an umpire's decision. With their performance indelible in cricket's history and records, they and their successors live under an eternal stigma. They talk of the match, and smile about it, but with an obvious sense of shame. Ever since, they have been almost ostracised by the Pakistani authorities, for suffering the most humiliating defeat in first-class cricket, in the only first-class match they ever played.

SCYLD BERRY, *The Observer*, 27 November 1977

The oldest test-playing nation outside of England and Australia is South Africa. To the High Veldt, as to the islands and maidans, *the British colonists took their armies and their sports. One soldier to travel south across the Atlantic was Laurie Lee's uncle Sid.*

Uncle Sid

MOODY, majestic Uncle Sid was the fourth, but not least, of the brothers. This small powerful man, at first a champion cricketer, had a history blighted by rheumatism. He was a bus-driver too, after he left the Army, put in charge of our first double-deckers. Those solid-tyred, open-topped, passenger chariots were the leviathans of the roads at that time – staggering siege-towers which often ran wild and got their top-decks caught under bridges. Our Uncle Sid, one of the elite of the drivers, became a famous sight in the district. It was a thing of pride and some alarm to watch him go thundering by, perched up high in his reeking cabin, his face sweating beer and effort, while he wrenched and wrestled at the steering wheel to hold the great bus on its course. Each trip through the town destroyed roof-tiles and gutters and shook the gas mantles out of the lamps, but he always took pains to avoid women and children and scarcely ever mounted the pavements. Runaway roarer, freighted with human souls, stampeder of policemen and horses – it was Uncle Sid with his mighty hands who mastered its mad career.

Uncle Sid's story, like Uncle Charlie's, began in the South African War. As a private soldier he had earned a reputation for silence, cunning, and strength. His talent for cricket, learned on the molehills of Sheepscombe, also endowed him with special privileges. Quite soon he was chosen to play for the army and was being fed on the choicest rations. The hell-bent technique of his village game worked havoc among the officers. On a flat pitch at last, with a scorched dry wicket, after the hillocks and cow-dung of home, he was projected straightway into regions of greatness and broke records and nerves galore. His murderous bowling reduced heroes to panic: they just waved him good-bye and ran: and when he came in to bat men covered their heads and retired piecemeal to the boundaries. I can picture that squat little whizzing man knocking the cricket ball out of the ground, his face congested with brick-red fury, his shoulders bursting out of his braces. I can see him crouch for the next delivery, then spin on his short bowed legs, and clout it again half-way to Johannesburg while he heard far-off Sheepscombe cheer. In an old Transvaal newspaper, hoarded by my Mother, I once found a score-card which went something like this;

Army v. Transvaal. Pretoria 1899

ARMY

Col. 'Tigger' ffoukes-Wyte	1
Brig.-Gen. Fletcher	0
Maj. T. W. G. Staggerton-Hake	12
Capt. V. O. Spillingham	0
Major Lyle (not)	31
Pte S. Light (not)	126
Extras	7
Total (for 4 dec.)	177

TRANSVAAL 21 all out (Pte S. Light, 7 for 5)

LAURIE LEE, *Cider with Rosie*, 1959

Later, the political troubles that blighted South Africa spilled on to the cricket field. In 1969, South Africa was ostracised from the league of Test-playing nations because of its refusal to countenance black cricketers. The affair was as tawdry as the politics. Basil D'Oliveira, a coloured South African who had made England his home so that he might play and live a free man, was the pawn. Ted Corbett gives the account.

The D'Oliveira Affair

BY the end of summer D'Oliveira was still England's established all-rounder, and on that basis he was chosen for the tour of West Indies. England won the series in the Caribbean largely owing to a generous – many critics thought much too generous – declaration by Gary Sobers in the fourth Test in Trinidad, but for D'Oliveira it was a miserable trip.

There was his cricket. Eight Test innings brought just 137 runs, and he took only three wickets at a cost of 97.66 each. It sounds like a nightmare, but in fact his skipper, Colin Cowdrey, had few complaints and D'Oliveira did everything that could be expected. But the special circumstances of team and tactics meant he was reduced to a bits-and-pieces role.

It had been decided before a ball was bowled that, although the two main West Indies strike bowlers, Wes Hall and Charlie Griffith, no longer had that fine edge of speed that threatened the batsman in mind and body, they were so dangerous in combination with Gary Sobers' left-arm swerve that England ought to pack their side with batsmen. And what batsmen they were!

Geoff Boycott and John Edrich opened; Cowdrey, one of the all-time great batsmen was No. 3; with Ken Barrington, a massive accumulator of runs, and Tom Graveney, an elegant stroke player, to follow. Jim Parks, the supreme batsman–wicket-keeper was at No. 6, which left D'Oliveira to come in at No. 7 when all the hard work had been done.

As a result, he arrived at the crease in the first Test when England already had 471 runs on the scoreboard. In the second the total was

318 for 5, and it was 319 for 5 in the third. Hardly the crisis situation on which he thrived! He thought he might get to the wicket earlier in the fourth Test when Alan Knott was preferred to Parks and Dolly could slip in at No. 6. But it was the old story . . . England 260 for 4 when D'Oliveira picked up his bat.

In theory his bowling was poor too, but once again Cowdrey and the rest of the team had no grouse. Three wickets at nearly 100 runs each hides the important tactical job that D'Oliveira undertook. England's attack was largely down to John Snow, David Brown and Jeff Jones, so whenever D'Oliveira got the ball it was to 'keep it tight at that end, Bas', and he did that so effectively against Sobers and Co. that only two and a half runs an over resulted.

But none of that was immediately obvious to selectors on the other side of the Atlantic, and D'Oliveira returned to England well aware that his place in the side for the series against the Australians that season must be in danger and that if he missed out in the summer he might not get to South Africa that following winter. It was a trip he desperately wanted to make, but it was one that he already knew would result in unprecedented pressure. He had had a taste of that in the West Indies.

For most of that tour he was constantly reminded that he was a coloured man in a white team in a black man's country. The reminders came in the middle of the night, down the phone from the Caribbean islands and from people back home in England and South Africa. They were delivered when he needed sleep if he were to play a part in the next day's cricket and, an emotional man, D'Oliveira found them deeply disturbing.

Over the past few years he had got used to the good-natured banter of the dressing-room. He could take it and, when the mood was right, he could hand it back. If another player handed him black pepper and said the rest of the lads had specially asked for white, if he was told there was a separate bus for him to go to the ground and that in future he would be dining at a different table from the rest of the team, D'Oliveira could laugh with the rest. After all, it might be heavy-handed humour – young cricketers lack finesse all over the world – but it was usually a dig at apartheid and Dolly found it refreshing to joke about the system. At least in the England dressing-room he could laugh *at* it!

But these phone calls were in an altogether different tone. There were militant coloured groups who believed he was wrong to accept the comforts of the white world while they had to suffer the misery of apartheid. They were suspicious, often angry, and they did not mince words. The Caribbean voices were not impressed with his place in the England team either: 'Hey, man', these midnight voices said, 'you're one of us. Why are you playing for them?'

White voices brought another, ridiculous accusation. They suggested D'Oliveira was deliberately failing so that he would not be chosen for the South African tour because he was frightened of the consequences. There was even a hint that he had been bought off.

By now D'Oliveira had a glimpse of the future. Both pro- and anti-apartheid forces saw him as a worthwhile political figure to be used and abused for their ends; while all he wanted was to play cricket. If he had doubts, it is not surprising. The England players made him welcome in their dressing-room, but should he really be taking this road at all?

Worst of all, he had no one to help him with the doubts. Not only was there no other Cape coloured in the side; he was the first of his sort. When he got home to England there were friends and advisers who could help him search out the right answer so that when he received a phone call offering 'a good reward' if he declared he was not available for the South Africa tour, he turned it down. In the West Indies he was on his own, with his poor performances and the constant barrage of questions about a political situation that was well beyond his control.

Later D'Oliveira was to blame his failures in the West Indies on a hectic social life, and anyone who sampled Caribbean hospitality will understand that it is easy to fall into the trap of accepting every invitation and suffering loss of form as a result. D'Oliveira is not the only cricketer who has failed for that reason. When this was combined with the political pressure, it is no surprise he returned to England worried about his Test future.

Perhaps this combination of abuse and the background of his bad results in West Indies also got to him the the summer of 1968, when he rarely looked the powerful batsman and intelligent bowler who had turned into a Test regular. He played in the first Test at Old Trafford but even though he had top score in the second innings, Australia won by 159 runs and D'Oliveira was left out of the Lord's Test on the morning of the match. And he did not look likely to regain his place for his form with Worcestershire also suffered, and until the final Test at the Oval he did not come into the selectors' calculations.

There then happened one of those strange sequences that change the course of history. The Northants skipper, Roger Prideaux, dropped out of the fifth Test with a heavy cold and that gave Cowdrey, once again the captain, a new chance to put right the side which he had always believed was unbalanced.

England were one down in the series, and if they were to go level, Cowdrey reckoned that he would need two spinners on an Oval pitch that promised to encourage his slow bowlers in the last two days. So a medium-pacer who was also an all-rounder was needed to support his new ball attack. D'Oliveira was the only serious contender, and although he was not in the best of nick, he had the experience and he was a fighter. Cowdrey put his case to the rest of the selectors and they gave him his way. The plan worked too, in a way that would do credit to the fiction-writers of schoolboy comics.

The recall was a shock for D'Oliveira for two reasons. In the previous week he had received a number of calls from a South African businessman, Tiene Oosthuizen, who was offering £4,000 a year, a car, a house and generous expenses for the next ten years (£3,000 a year was a high wage in those days) if D'Oliveira would return to South Africa to organise cricket facilities for coloured schoolchildren. There were two conditions: D'Oliveira had to declare he was not available for the tour of South Africa, and he had to do so before the tour party was picked.

D'Oliveira stalled. He said he would give an answer after the tour party was chosen, and drove home to Worcester so concerned about the offer that he thought of nothing else until he drew up at the traffic lights in the centre of town and saw Fred Trueman in the car alongside.

'What the heck do you think you're doing here?' growled the blunt Trueman. 'You should be in London. Prideaux has dropped out and you're in the Test side.' Dolly realised immediately that his hopes of making the tour party had been revived because he fancied his chances of making runs against an Australian attack he thought of as 'ordinary'.

His judgement proved right. On the morning of the second day he told his wife on the phone: 'Just turn on the television and sit down to watch. I'm going to be there all day.' By the end of that momentous day, D'Oliveira had made 158, John Edrich had made 164 and England totalled 494. When D'Oliveira reached his century the umpire, Charlie Elliott, whispered: 'Lord, you're going to cause some problems now.' Even the witty Elliott cannot have imagined how many!

Thanks to a century from Bill Lawry, Australia saved the follow-on and then lost the match with six minutes to spare, after Cowdrey had recruited hundreds of spectators to dry out the pitch, which had been under water for three-quarters of its area at lunch. The pitch then gave Derek Underwood just enough help to skittle out the tail and finish with 7 for 50. D'Oliveira also took a vital wicket.

That seemed to seal the D'Oliveira fate, but he confessed later that the rest of the match passed him by. 'I could not wait for Wednesday when the tour party was announced', he said years later. No one doubted that he would tour South Africa now, and before he left the Oval, Cowdrey and the chairman of selectors, Doug Insole, asked him if he wanted a tour place and whether he understood the pressure that would result. Dolly said he could cope and set off home for Worcester, a match against Sussex at New Road the following day and the team announcement in the afternoon. He was taking nothing for granted, but he believed that his dream of a return trip to South Africa was about to come true.

With him on that two-hour journey home was Peter Smith, at that time chief cricket-writer for Reg Hayter's agency, and later to be cricket correspondent at the *News of the World* and the *Daily Mail* and media relations manager at the TCCB. Hayter's had D'Oliveira under contract, and Smith was detailed to look after him during the difficult days that were bound to follow whether he were picked for the South Africa tour or not. Either way, every newspaper in the country would be after D'Oliveira and Hayter's wanted to be sure they would be first.

Smith immediately began to tape D'Oliveira's thoughts on the forthcoming tour, and it is a sign of Dolly's confidence that he was willing to answer the questions. What, Smith asked for a ghosted column to appear later that week, did D'Oliveira feel about going home as an England player, taking part in matches at famous grounds like Newlands in Cape Town, Wanderers in Johannesburg or Kingsmead in Durban and batting before hundreds of his own kind? A dream come true, D'Oliveira said, and at that moment neither man had the slightest doubt that a hope born in Signal Hill all those years ago was about to turn into a wonderful reality.

I shall let Peter Smith tell the story from now on. No one else was so close to the action, either as a guest in the D'Oliveira house in Worcester, or at his side in the Worcestershire dressing-room when the news came through, or as his agent.

Peter recalls: 'The squad was not to be released until the

Wednesday afternoon, because the selectors' choice had first to be approved by the full MCC committee. That happened with every tour party but this time the outcome of the selectors' deliberations was awaited, not just by the cricket fans, but by politicians, propagandists and every section of the Press.

'It was a dramatic, human story about a man denied all his rights in his own country who was about to step ashore there again after going abroad to find the freedom to play cricket.

'It was a story with something for everyone and for that reason I had been detailed to spend the next few days at D'Oliveira's side – at his request – to help him cope with all the attention. He was anxious not to say even one word that could be misconstrued and embarrass South Africa, the selectors or MCC.

'He wanted to be left alone to concentrate on his cricket for Worcestershire and to build on the form he had rediscovered at the Oval.

'I cannot imagine that Basil will ever forget the next couple of days, although the whole of the next six weeks was a traumatic experience for both of us, but for him especially. There was pain and there was passion and it was a distressing period.

'Outwardly on the Wednesday morning Bas showed little emotion – and he is an emotional man – but I could not help noticing at breakfast that every time he touched his teacup the saucer rattled. He spent a lot of that day at the crease, because his good form continued and he made 128 off the Sussex attack.

'It was a remarkable performance, but I have wondered since if he was really happier out in the middle getting on with his job than he would have been back in the dressing-room. Doing his normal job gave him something to think about and made him forget all the pressure.

'After he was out, there was a lot of strain, because late in the afternoon a whole series of rumours swept the Worcester ground. You can imagine. Bas was in the squad. Bas was out of the squad. It all got too much, and in the end he was glad to be back in the dressing-room to shut the door on the outside world.

'Towards six o'clock, when the announcement was expected, groups of spectators began to gather round transistor radios. It was a big moment for any Worcestershire fan but nowhere was the atmosphere so tense as it was in the dressing-room, where the players were all round a portable radio. The BBC announcer began to read the names and you could almost slice the silence with a knife, and then came the gasp when Bas's name should have been read in the alphabetical order and he was missing.

'Of course everyone kept listening because they could not believe he was not in the party and that there had been a mistake and his name would come up at the end. Bas waited until all the fifteen names had been read – they were going to name another fast bowler later – and then he was led away by the skipper Tom Graveney into a small room behind the dressing-room.

'I have rarely seen a dressing-room so shocked. All the players muttered things like "Bad luck, Bas", and Tom Graveney muttered: 'I never thought they would do that to you, Bas"; you could tell that they were almost as shattered as Bas.

'Almost as soon as he got into the physio's room, Bas totally lost control under the realisation that his dream had been shattered, and that as the years caught up with him there would not be another chance. Seeing him crying, Graveney and the secretary, Joe Lister, who was later secretary at Yorkshire, agreed that he should go home straight away. Within ten minutes of the team announcement he was being driven home.

'There was another emotional moment at home when he literally fell into the arms of Naomi as she opened the front door. There were hugs from Damian, his eldest son (later Damian played for Worcestershire too), but I remember the youngest boy Shaun just standing there looking very bewildered and obviously far too young to understand.

'Then Bas simply took off into the bedroom to shut himself away from the world. At that moment the phone began to ring. That night it rang and rang and rang, apart from three hours in the middle of the night. So that the family could get some sleep, I made up a bed at the bottom of the stairs and took the phone off its hook every time it rang.

'By next morning of course Bas was more himself, and to his credit he recovered from the initial disappointment very quickly and began to immerse himself in cricket once again as he helped Worcestershire beat Sussex.'

Long before Peter Smith ended his vigil at the bottom of the D'Oliveira staircase, the newspapers, TV and radio were holding furious debate about the rights and wrongs of leaving Dolly out of the squad for South Africa.

The cricket specialists were quick to point out that his omission meant England had no genuine all-rounder in the side and that made it ill-balanced. Doug Insole, as chairman of the selectors, announced that they had ignored D'Oliveira's claims as a bowler because he had failed to take wickets in West Indies and considered himself solely as a batsman. Both he and Colin Milburn, a far better run-scorer than D'Oliveira, failed to make the seven regarded as serious batsmen.

The selectors' choice as an all-rounder, of sorts, was Tom Cartwright, a legendary medium-pace bowler even during his playing career, but no more than an occasional batsman, although he had made a century or two. He had been on the previous tour of South Africa four years earlier, but he had not been an England regular since and was the surprise choice in this party.

So once again, as Cowdrey had underlined when he urged the call-up of D'Oliveira at the Oval, the side lacked balance. That led to charges that the selectors had picked their party on political grounds rather than in pure cricket terms so that the tour could go ahead without any embarrassment to South Africa. The more the charge was denied, the more the accusation was made until finally Insole was forced to defend himself and the rest of the selectors in a statement.

He said: 'Of course, it's a convenient conclusion but if everyone believes that we did not want D'Oliveira to go to South Africa, they might ask themselves why we picked him for the Oval and so put him in the minds of the public as a contender. If we had decided against choosing him for South Africa, it would have been ridiculous to pick him for the Oval.'

That statement did not stop the rumours or the sensational stories. There were tales of secret talks with South African officials, from government level downwards. Protests were made in both Houses of Parliament, resignation letters poured into Lord's, and there were demands for a special meeting of MCC. The *News of the World* wanted D'Oliveira to write on the tour for them, but Mr Vorster soon hinted that he might not be welcome: 'Guests who have ulterior motives usually find they are not invited', he commented.

Only in South Africa was D'Oliveira's omission a cause for joy. It was announced by the Interior Minister at a meeting of the National Party and brought cheers. That should have been a warning about what to expect when D'Oliveira was picked, just a fortnight later.

Right from the moment he was chosen, Cartwright announced that he had a painful condition of the right shoulder, his bowling arm, and he was ordered by the selectors to have a fitness test during a one-day match at Edgbaston on 14 September. It was discovered that the shoulder was not responding to treatment, Cartwright was forced to drop out of the tour, and D'Oliveira was named as his replacement.

Once more Peter Smith takes up the story: 'I phoned Bas with the news in Plymouth where he was at a cricket dinner and I heard later that the whole night was transformed from a formal dinner into a big, big celebration. Once again I suggested that he would be better off out of the way and drove him deeper into Cornwall. He had just 24 hours to savour the idea of returning to South Africa as he wandered among the late holiday-makers in Looe harbour, and then his dream was smashed once again. This time there was no second chance.'

There was no hope of that in Prime Minister Vorster's speech in Bloemfontein, a part of Orange Free State that contains Boers who make the rest of South Africa look like namby-pamby liberals. He could not have picked an audience more likely to cheer him to the echo if he had searched the length and breadth of his country as he thundered: 'It is not an MCC team. It is the team of the anti-apartheid movement. We are not prepared to accept a team thrust upon us. It is the team of the political opponents of South Africa.'

Vorster then turned cricket commentator by pointing out that Cartwright was a bowler yet was being replaced by D'Oliveira, even after the England selectors had admitted that his bowling was of little consequence in overseas conditions and had considered him purely as a batsman.

That statement was echoed throughout South Africa to justify the decision to reject the tour party. MCC wasted no time in coming back with an equally clear statement of their intentions. The secretary, Billy Griffith, replied: 'Our position is clear. If the chosen team is not acceptable to South Africa, the MCC will call the tour off.'

It was also clear that they were not about to ditch D'Oliveira in order to save the tour. Nor would they allow D'Oliveira to drop out. He did consider making himself unavailable, but Colin Cowdrey would not hear of it.

That statement – indeed all their actions throughout what had already been called the D'Oliveira Affair – reflects well on MCC, who are often written off as a 200-year-old organisation, head buried in the sand, and remote from the real world. Their refusal to be bullied by South Africa, a country with whom they had a long friendship, and the fact that they stood by D'Oliveira, their last choice, a coloured player and a professional, marks them down as men of principle.

TED CORBETT, Cricket on the Run, 1990

From the ridiculous looking-glass world of apartheid to the plainly ridiculous world of Willie Rushton. The earliest reference to cricket came from the Odyssey *and the islands of the Aegean, so it is comforting to learn that the game is still being played out there, or on one island at least, Corfu, not a hundred miles from Odysseus's Ithaca.*

Cricket in Corfu

ALTHOUGH I've always known cricket existed on Corfu, I'd always imagined that it was played by British expatriates. In fact, the Corfiots have played cricket since the Napoleonic Wars, learning it from watching the British army and navy at play.

The ground is magnificent. It's in Corfu Town's Spionada Square. One side of the ground is a Rue de Rivoli-like parade of bars and cafés, one of which serves as a pavilion. Opposite stands the old Fort and the former Royal Palace dominates the Harbour End. The pitch is rough grass, except where a gravel path crosses it and the wicket is matting. It serves also as the local park so before play can begin, sweet papers, ice cream wrappers and canine offerings have to be removed.

A local rule is that only one ball is allowed per game. The reason is soon clear. The new ball, after a few trips over the gravel path, loses all sense of shine and respectability. Thus, if the Corfiots win the toss, they field enjoying the best of the ball and leaving only a battered relic for the opposition's bowlers. If they lose the toss they announce that a new ball will not be available until their turn to bowl. These tactics are extremely successful and the only solution is to take your own bag of new balls.

The games begin after the siesta and consist of 33 overs a side.

The tactics of the 33-over game they also have down to a nicety. The crowds are extremely knowledgeable and voluble and volatile.

The Philanderers go for a fortnight, with their women folk, who for once have no cause to complain about being dragged about like a cricket-bag, and they play the Britannia Club, local British residents as the name suggests and Corfu's two sides. Byron (named after another cricketing poet) and Gymnasticos.

Some Useful Greek Cricketing Terms

Fermadoros	*Wicket–keeper*
Bombada	*a full toss*
Pintz	*A yorker*
Primo slaco	*Long hop*
Apo psila	*Caught*
Apo xyla	*Bowled'*
Psili tis gris	*A bumper*
Sotto	*Out*
Blotto	*Been in the pavilion too long under the influence of ouzo*
Owdat?	*Howzat?*

There appears to be no word for 'not out' as the cry of 'Owdat?' automatically causes a Corfiot umpire to up the finger.

WILLIE RUSHTON, *Pigsticking*, 1977

'Mackay has played
back defensively'

THE BEAUTY
OF THE GAME

'RIME O' BAT OF O' MY SKY-EM'

Wake! for the Ruddy Ball has taken flight
That scatters the slow Wicket of the Night;
   And the swift Batsman of the Dawn has driven
Against the Star-spiked Rails a fiery Smite.

Wake, my Beloved! take the Bat that clears
The sluggish Liver, and Dyspeptics cheers:
   Tomorrow? Why, tomorrow I may be
Myself with Hambledon and all its Peers.

Today a Score of Batsmen brings, you say?
Yes, but where leaves the Bats of yesterday?
   And this same summer day that brings a Knight
May take the Grace and Ranjitsinhji away.

Willsher the famed is gone with all his 'throws'.
And Alfred's Six-foot Reach where no man knows;
   And Hornby – the great hitter – his own Son
Plays in his place, yet recks not the Red Rose.

And Silver Billy, Fuller Pilch and Small,
Alike the pigmy Briggs and Ulyett tall,
   Have swung their Bats an hour or two before,
But none played out the last and silent Ball.

Well, let them Perish! What have we do to
With Gilbert Grace the Great, or that Hindu?
   Let Hirst and Spooner slog them as they list,
Or Warren bowl his 'snorter'; care not you!

With me along the Strip of Herbage strown,
That is not laid or watered, rolled or sown,
   Where name of Lord's and Oval is forgot,
And peace to Nicholas on his bomb-girt Throne.

A level Wicket, as the Ground allow,
A driving Bat, a lively Ball, and thou
   Before me bowling on the Cricket-pitch –
O Cricket-pitch were Paradise enow!

2

I listened where the Grass was shaven small,
And heard the Bat that groaned against the Ball:
   Thou pitchest Here and There, and Left and Right,
Nor deem I where the Spot thou next may'st Fall.

Forward I play, and Back, and Left and Right,
And overthrown at once, or stay till Night:
   But this I know, where nothing else I know,
The last is Thine, how so the Bat shall smite.

This thing is sure, where nothing else is sure,
The boldest Bat may but a Space endure;
   And he who One or who a Hundred hits
Falleth at ending to thy Force or Lure.

Wherefore am I allotted but a Day
To taste Delight, and make so brief a stay;
   For meed of all my labour laid aside,
Endeth alike the Player and the Play.

Behold, there is an Arm behind the Ball,
Nor the Bat's Stroke of its own Striking all;
   And who the Gamesters, to what end the Game,
I think thereof our witting is but small.

Against the Attack and Twist of Circumstance
Though I oppose Defence and Shifty Glance,
   What Power gives Nerve to me, and what Assaults,–
This is the Riddle. Let dull bats cry 'Chance'.

Is there a Foe that domineers the Ball?
And one that Shapes and wields us Willows all?
   Be patient if Thy Creature in Thy Hand
Break, and the so-long-guarded Wicket fall!

Thus spoke the Bat. Perchance a foolish Speech
And wooden, for a Bat has straitened Reach:
   Yet thought I, I had heard Philosophers
Prate much on this wise, and aspire to Teach.

Ah, let us take our Stand, and play the Game,
But rather for the cause than for the Fame;
   Albeit right evil is the Ground, and we
Know our Defence thereon will be but lame.

O Love, if thou and I could but Conspire
Against this Pitch of Life, so false with Mire,
   Would we not Doctor it afresh, and then
Roll it out smoother to the Bat's Desire?

FRANCIS THOMPSON

Again, we pay homage to cricket's purported (by Homer, Altham and myself, at least) Middle Eastern roots. Though Thompson kept his tongue firmly in his cheek as he aped Omar Khayyam, few sports have matched the literature and reportage of cricket. Even those who hate the game have been inspired by it.

A Necessary Evil

···

> . . . We look
> Across shrill meadows – but to find
> The cricket-bat defeats the book,
> Matter triumphant over mind.

THERE is much of truth contained in the cynical saying, attributed to the Duke of Wellington, that the Battle of Waterloo was won upon the playing-fields of Eton. The very same quality of heroism which intelligent boys prove in the course of learning to endure the spectacle of school-matches, in the process of becoming accustomed to ennui, does one day undoubtedly help them in the battlefield, does teach them to undergo unflinchingly the greater boredom of watching and participating in a larger, more evil, and quite as unnecessary stupidity. A boy who learns to like cricket will learn to like anything: while, if forced when very young to play it against his better judgement, he will mind nothing so much in adult life. Indeed, after being at an English private and public school, the remainder of life, however hard, seems a holiday: and even the War came to many a boy leaving school as a relief rather than a catastrophe.

Other games, it may be, have their advantages over cricket. Football, for example, has one which is inestimable – that, at the worst, it can only last for an hour and a half as against the ennui of the full three days which a cricket match may entail: while, too, an expert though unwilling player, can, with the aid of the leather strips and lumps thoughtfully provided on the soles and heels of boots sacred for this waste of time, mete out severe punishment to those chiefly responsible for the game, probably without being detected, or, if discovered, without being held guilty of anything more heinous than an exaggerated enthusiasm. Golf, again, acts in the same way as does a grouse-moor – interns all those addicted to it. A golf course outside a big town serves an excellent purpose in that it segregates, as though in a concentration camp, all the idle and idiot well-to-do, while the over-exertion of the game itself causes them to die some ten or fifteen years earlier than they would by nature, thus acting as a sort of fifteen per cent life-tax on stupidity. While alive, it not only removes them for the whole day from the sight of those who have work to do, or leisure which they know how to spend profitably, but causes them to don voluntarily a baggy and chequered uniform, which proclaims them for what they are, at half a mile or so off, and thus enables the sane man to escape them. Similarly, a grouse-moor, like a magic carpet, whisks away its devotees to one of the bleakest, most misty and appropriate places in the northern hemisphere, and there imprisons them, to the sound of bagpipes, throughout their most dangerous months.

But cricket has its own peculiar merits as a training school for manhood. It is the very cumulative strain of boredom which this game imposes that constitutes its superiority. Any game, too, which, by laying down fixed rules, teaches boys not to think for themselves, will be of help to them in their mature years; while, should these years coincide with a period of war, the lesson will be of inestimable value. Curiously enough, though schoolmasters inculcate the doctrine that an inter-school match is a thing of vital importance to the schools taking part in it, that defeat to a team is equivalent to the loss of a battle by an army, yet certain rules are laid down; and the boy, who, believing these protestations of his teachers, sought genuinely to help his side by the invention and use of some ingenious mechanism, by the breaking of some old rule, or establishment of some new one, would quickly be disillusioned, called to order by the umpire, lowered in the esteem of his comrades, and perhaps afterwards disgraced publicly. Had Nelson, for example, won a cricket match instead of the Battle of Copenhagen, by regarding the umpire through a telescope applied to his blind eye, how much would his fame have suffered. But, fortunately for the English, Nelson was never at school – or if, as some say, he was, quickly ran away from it – for there can be no doubt, we fear, that his action was hardly 'playing the game'. Things have progressed since then, for no General (we do not speak of Admirals, for they have a tradition of eccentricity: and it may be here worthwhile to enquire to what extent the superiority of the officers of the English fleet over the officers of the English army is due to the fact that they do not go to public schools) on any side during either the Boer, or Late Great Bore, Wars even thought of winning a battle. No, the behaviour of all parties was correct and decorous in the extreme. In the end, the European War was won by *never* winning a battle, by vast mutual slaughter, and intolerable ennui. The only relief is that, owing to their inefficiency and slowness, it is unnecessary and almost impossible to remember the names of the 'leaders', except as a warning.

It is at cricket, then, that the schoolboy first learns the oft-repeated, dreary lesson that all men must march in time with the pace of the slowest among them. Thus the intelligent boy is made father to the stupid man.

OSBERT SITWELL, *Before the Bombardment*, 1926

Osbert Sitwell would have enjoyed the company of Lord Manning, who considered cricket 'a game which the English, not being a spiritual people, have invented in order to give themselves some conception of eternity'. The pair could have been joined at the bar by William Temple who 'looked on cricket as organised loafing'. Even those who have adored the game, like 'Robinson Crusoe', can accept that some people take it a touch too seriously.

A Branch of Religion

I HAVE never regarded cricket as a branch of religion. I have met, and somehow survived, many of its blindest worshippers. I have staggered, pale and woozly, from the company of those who reject the two-eyed stance as Plymouth Brethren reject all forms of pleasure except money-making. I have never believed that cricket can hold Empires together, or that cricketers chosen to represent their country in distant parts should be told, year after year, that they are Ambassadors. If they are, I can think of some damned odd ones.

The air of holy pomp started from the main temple at Lord's, and it breathed over the Press like a miasma. '*Procul, O Procul Este, Profani!*' We are not as other men. Sometimes I look back at reports of games in which I took part, and I have thought: 'And are these arid periphrases, these formal droolings, these desiccated shibboleths really supposed to represent what was done and how it

was done? What has become of that earthy striving, that comic, tragic thing which was our match of cricket?'
R. C. ROBERTSON-GLASGOW, *46 Not Out*, 1948

Taking it too seriously can start at a very early age.

The Game of Cricket

I wish you'd speak to Mary, Nurse,
She's really getting worse and worse.
Just now when Tommy gave her out
She cried and then began to pout
And then she tried to take the ball
Although she cannot bowl at all.
And now she's standing on the pitch,
The miserable little Bitch!

ANON

But in the ridiculous lies the sublime, when, unshaped, waiting for the touch of a master to reveal beauty in the most unlikely of pursuits.

Cook of Lancashire

COOK has toiled for Lancashire longer than any of us care to remember. A portly man he is, blown up like a bladder, as Falstaff said of himself, with sighing and grief – Cook's sighs and grief having been provoked by the spectacle of catches dropped from his bowling and stumps missed by inches. How he hangs his head on one side and looks the picture of hot frustration as the umpire pretends not to have heard that frantic 'H'at!' of his, which every-body but an umpire is bound to hear a mile away. The crowd, with its usual instinct for the characteristic point about a man, says Cook is unlucky. There must be some truth in this; at any rate one seldom sees a wicket falling like a gift from heaven into Cook's hands – he has to work and perspire for most of his summer's successes. If a batsman should give a chance that some fieldsman all thumbs puts to the grass, you can be certain Cook is the bowler. It is the way of the world – the honest toiler is not wooed by Fortune; she prefers to wait on coxcomb genius with its pride and peacock feathers. Cook, of course, is clever, but somehow the man's capacity for hard work strikes you even before his skill. Besides, Cook has a likeable ampli-tude of flesh – and cleverness owns a stark leanness, hardly making for fellow-feeling. A Rhodes, a Trumble, stirs you to admiration by calculated art; Cook wins your affection because there is about him nothing that is not Nature's own making – Cook was surely fashioned on the green grass by wind, sun, and rain. He is not subtle – hard labour never is. His bowling is as old in its way as the hills, being quite without the tricks of the moment. Years and years ago bowlers were getting batsmen out exactly as Cook today gets them out – by length and accurate aim. You may even say of Cook's art that it is as ancient as your grandfather; you could not make a finer compliment to it. If Alfred Shaw came back to our cricket fields this summer he would discover a few matters startling to him. Parkin would not please him always, for Shaw was a stickler for perfect pitch. 'Many things there are in your modern bowling that strike me as flat blasphemy,' we can easily conceive Shaw saying. 'But Cook belongs to the faith we old 'uns were born in.'

That ancient faith insisted on length, direction, and natural and not excessive spin. The greatest of these was length. There was no 'mystery' bowling in Shaw's time; the batsman knew well enough the sort of ball he had to counter. The old bowlers trusted their simple arts absolutely; with honest technique they challenged honest technique in the light of open day. There is not always this technical self-sufficiency in modern bowling: a Parkin, for example, will come by a lot of wickets by balls frankly indifferent – considered in the strictly technical sense. Parkin, as I have said before some-where, is the Artful Dodger of cricket; his success depends largely on your not knowing exactly what is up his sleeve. How different is it with Cook. His bowling is as open-hearted as the man himself; every time he moves into action he might well say, like the old lady in Dickens: 'I will not deceive you.' When Cook is at work with Parkin you have in captivating contrast two extreme types of man's mind and character – Parkin, the artist, playing cricket mainly for self-expression; Cook, the craftsman, intent on his duty, on making himself worthy of his hire: Parkin, the Romantic, a lover of strangeness, the adventurer ever; Cook, content, with old and safe ways of doing things – no speculation in his eyes: Parkin as wayward as Fancy; Cook as consistent as prosaic fact.

To speak of Cook as a sort of Falstaff of cricket – as some writers have done - is to see no more of him than his flesh. Cook may be called Falstaffian only in so far as he would most certainly confess to an alacrity in sinking; but he has nothing of Falstaffian wit. Wit implies some sort of masterfulness, and Cook's great attributes are perseverance and fortitude, for which attributes masterfulness has no use. Cook is the honourable old servitor all over, performing his work skilfully, but modestly, and even humbly. We have seen how sturdy is his faith in the old-fashioned bowling; he is old-fashioned, too, in his belief in sweaty toil. The greatest lover of honest nature that ever lived was Chaucer, and he would have taken a 'heavenish' delight in the sight of Cook's noble capacity for perspiration:

I joye for to see him sweat,
His forehead dropped as a stillatorie.

It would be easy to give here impressive statistics in evidence of Cook's valuable cricket for Lancashire. But no lover of the game in Lancashire can be in need of such evidence – besides, statistics will never reveal the truth about Cook. They go by results, and Cook is the last man in the world to be judged by results. How could cold figures, percentages – 'Damned dots,' as Randolph Churchill called them – tell of that tireless endeavour which is Cook's great virtue, whether he is getting wickets or not? Why, one of the biggest-hearted performances of his career was at Lord's against Middlesex, but statistics have only this unedifying way of making a record of it: 'Cook, 54 overs, 12 maidens, 150 runs, 1 wicket.' Yet Cook's bowling in that match was beautiful enough to remind Mr Sydney Pardon of Attewell and Shaw. Hour after hour in scorching heat Cook pitched the ball a rare length and stuck to the weary task of waiting for Hearne to waver in vigilance. It was a typical Cook performance; one in which the man's patience in travail was as admirable as his rare skill. That skill of Cook's must not be underrated, of course; the fact that his sterling industry stirs in us almost a moral approbation must not make us forget that in his own school Cook has been one of the best bowlers of his time. He has, as we have on occasion seen, made one of the soundest judges of cricket think of the classical masters of length. At his finest, Cook is two bowlers in one – a man for sticky grounds and a man for perfect grounds. With rain and sun about he is not far removed from a Schofield Haigh; he can serve out a nasty break-back from round the wicket. On a fast turf he can make excellent pace from the pitch, and he has the ability to swing away from the bat, and that without using the over-tossed length which so many bowlers require before they can give some slight swerve to the ball. He has probably bowled fewer bad ones than any other cricketer of his time – not even excepting Rhodes, whose acquaintance with the half-volley is not small.

Cook, of course, like all honest Englishmen, loves his grievances. Do not allow his rubicund face to get you thinking he is ineffectually genial – a soft-mannered man suffering misfortune daily without a kick! No; Cook has been given by nature a grand capacity for a lusty 'grouch,' as protection against the slings and arrows. 'Tha's got a fine edge on thi' bat,' he will tell the cricketer who has led a charmed life in the slips against his bowling. I know no story about this superb Cook of ours more characteristic than this. One summer Lancashire played Derbyshire at Chesterfield. I was unable to watch the match, but the papers said that the wicket was bumpy and most unfavourable to batsmen. Anyhow, Parkin and Cook bowled unchanged through the first Derbyshire innings, and Parkin took 7 for 15 and Cook 3 for 15. In the second innings Parkin had 7 for 58 and Cook 1 for 56. At Sheffield, the day after this match, I picked up the Lancashire XI and saw Cook straightway. 'Good match at Chesterfield,' said I; 'it must have been a brute of a wicket.' 'Oh, I don't know so much about that,' Cook replied, in a tone suggesting he was geting tired of a world which is always misunderstanding things; 'it were only bad at one end.' Good old Cook! some day you will enter your heaven, a place where the pitch is after your own heart at both ends; a place where you will bowl with the wind at your back eternally; a place with plenty of varnish on the stumps; a place of infallible fieldsmen and of umpires that are not a little bit hard of hearing.

NEVILLE CARDUS, *Days in the Sun*, 1924

It's the characters like Cook who put poetry into the game, adding the certain something which lifts the game out of the humdrum of the sports pages to create a pageantry of success and failure. Another such player was Roy Marshall, who would make few lists of all-time greats but whose arrival at the wicket would set tongues a-wagging. What ferocious deeds would the opener pull off today? And if he failed, he failed magnificently. A like-mind was Derek Randall, all fidgets and fuss, awkward grace and irrationality. 'Rags' was beautifully sketched by Simon Hughes.

Randall the Happy Hooker

LATER I endeared myself even less to the Notts followers. I took the first Notts wicket, which brought in their hero Derek Randall at number 3. He was cheered all the way to the wicket as he practised his forward defensive, mumbling, 'Coom on Rags, coom on.'

'He's a nervous starter and a compulsive hooker,' Brearley whispered. 'Give him a bouncer second ball.'

Randall hoiked it wildly into the hands of Edmonds at deep square leg and departed for a duck, head bowed. There was a dense hush around the ground. I was engulfed by elated colleagues, but I couldn't help feeling a bit of a spoilsport. W. G. Grace's voice echoed in my ears: 'They've come to see me bat, son, not you bowl.'

I bowled 23 overs that afternoon and took five wickets, though it must be emphasised that the pitch was a cabbage patch. It emerged later that one of my wickets the umpire thought was a snick to the keeper was actually the sound of Clive Rice's gold chain clanking against his perspex visor. Fashion triumphing over common sense in his case, I suppose. Still, I led the team off the field at close of play to comments like, 'Top drawer!' and 'You'll do for me.' It gave me the nerve to ask Edmonds if I could borrow his car to pop out for the evening. I didn't tell him I was going to a posh party a hundred miles away.

Having cavorted around half the night with a girl I'd got off with in the back seat of a DAF, I was rather bleary-eyed when I returned to pick Edmonds up at the hotel next morning for the Sunday League match. I was made twelfth man, and the team had gone out on to the field, I subsided into a deep sleep. Throughout the Notts innings I was completely oblivious to the Middlesex fielders' frantic signals for sunhats and drinks and got some dark looks when they returned. 'That was a pisshole effort,' said Barlow, self-appointed youth-bollocking officer. 'We were waving all afternoon and Eddie Hemmings had to bring us our gear in the end. And now you haven't even poured the tea out or got the bowlers a drink.' No wonder he was on his third marriage.

The atmosphere had become a shade frosty and I realised that returning to a team after a long break was like going home to your parents for Christmas. Initially they make quite a fuss of you, cooking your favourite meals, giving you the best chair, but it isn't long before they start ticking you off for being a messy eater and getting mud on the carpet.

If negligence is bad, clumsiness is worse. When the championship match resumed the next morning, I dropped a dolly, which deprived us of an extra bonus point – a precious teapot shattered on the kitchen floor. At lunchtime the players' irritation had turned to despair, and they sat in the dressing room glumly munching egg and cress baps and idly flicking through disintegrating copies of *Men Only*.

But on county cricket's restless rollercoaster, you can soon get back on track. When Randall came whistling into bat for the second time, I was in the middle of an over. 'Try a bouncer second ball again,' advised Brearley. 'He's a nutter – he's bound to have another go at it.' The trap ostentatiously set, I bounced, Randall hooked, and the ball looped down deep square leg's throat. He had fallen twice, second ball, for the most transparent ploy in the game, each time without troubling the scorers. It had to go down as the most foolhardy pair in history, made even more absurd by Brearley's later admission that he had actually outlined the ploy to Randall himself when they'd had dinner together the previous night. It is this self-inflicted vulnerability that makes players like Randall, forever walking the tightrope between triumph and calamity, so deeply treasured.

SIMON HUGHES, *A Lot of Hard Yakka*, 1997

Even cricket's bit players are fascinating.

SPARROW AT LORDS MUSEUM

Dead sparrow at Lords
Stuffed under glass with the ball
That killed you in mid flight
(Bowled by Jehanger Khan, Cambridge, 1935),
How impressive you are
Encased for ever with your murderer.

More impressive than the photographs
Of Hobbs or Compton or W.G.
Or the show of cricket bats throughout the ages.

Reverently we peer at you in your open tomb:
M.C.C. members and their wives in tow,
Open shirted boozers from the Cricketers Bar.
Sentimental children and West Indians
Having a day off from their London bus;
Heartened we return to clap the batsmen in.

Dead sparrow encased for ever with your ball
You signify the sacrifice of Life to Art,
The sacrifice that we are glad you made:
And Doctor Grace himself has noted your small fall.

MICHAEL IVENS

The sparrow was slain by a Mr Pearce off Khan's bowling. The dead bird plummeted from the sky and hit the wicket without dislodging the bails, saving the umpire from a tricky decision. Only in cricket would such dilemmas be raised. Cricket's folklore includes the most unlikely characters, like Dicky Barlow of Lancashire, the county's first great professional, and hymned as such by Francis Thompson in his most famous poem, At Lord's. A rum character, Mr Barlow. He was the original stonewaller who boasted he had batted through the innings fifty times. His finest moment came against Nottinghamshire when he spent two-and-half hours at the crease in making five runs. A. N. Hornby, his captain, was the opposite, a dashing strokemaker. Their combination could cajole any proser to verse, at least through the reveries of memory. That is the problem. The players who strut the modern stage are never as fine as the sepia memories of our childhood. Sachin Tendulkar and Brian Lara can but struggle to gain the approval of a generation raised on Sobers and Dexter, or even Richards and Gavaskar. Robertson-Glasgow again.

THE ONE WAY CRITIC

Upon the groaning bench he took his seat –
   Sunlight and shadow on the dew-blessed grass –
He spread the *Daily Moan* beneath his feet,
   Hitched to his eye an astigmatic glass,
Then, like a corn crake calling to an owl
   That knows no answer, he began to curse,
Remarking, with an unnattractive scowl,
   'The state of cricket goes from bad to worse;
Where are the bowlers of my boyhood's prime?
   Where are the batsmen of the pristine years?
Where are the fieldsmen of the former time?'
   And, as he spoke, my eyelids filled with tears;
For I perhaps alone, knew they were dead,
   Mynn an old myth, and Hambledon a name,
And it occurred to me that I had read
   (In classroom) 'All things always are the same';
So, comfort drawing from this maxim, turned
   To the myopic moaner on the seat;
A flame of rage, not pity, in me burned,
   Yet I replied in accents clear and sweet –
'There *were* no bowlers in your boyhood's prime,
   There *were* no batsmen in the pristine years,
There *were* no fieldsmen in that former time' –
   My voice grew firm, my eyes were dry of tears –
'*Your* fathers cursed the bowlers you adored,
   Your fathers damned the batsmen of your choice,

233

Your fine, ecstatic rapture they deplored,
    Theirs was the *One-Way Critic's* ageless voice,
And their immortal curse is yours today,
    The croak which kills all airy Cricket Dryads,
Withers the light on tree and grass and spray,
    The strangling fugue of senile jeremiads.'

*   *   *

I ceas'd; and turn'd to Larwood's bounding run,
And Woolley's rapier flashing in the sun.
                    R. C. ROBERTSON-GLASGOW

Seemingly as quickly as it came, the season's close draws on. Another year has passed from April to autumn, and the summer's accoutrements have to be packed away.

VALEDICTION: TO THE CRICKET SEASON

As a boy who has lost a girl so sadly
tears up a photograph or her early letters,
knowing that what has gone is gone for ever,
    a lustful bustful,

the exhange of confidences, the hours of cuddling,
the paraphernalia of what some call sharing,
so we mourn you; televisually prepare for
    their filthy football,

professional fouls and the late late tackle
breakaway forwards held back by a jersey,
the winning or losing almost equally nasty.
    The English summer

is never perfect, but you are a feature
as pleasing to us as a day of sunshine,
to spectators at least a calm, straw–hatted
   Edwardian dandy.

Not really a game of physical contact,
the batsman pardons the ungentlemanly bouncer,
the only foul would be leg theory,
   bodyline bowling;

as nostalgic as those old school stories
the plock of bat on ball penetrates outfields,
calming to the mind. Warm pints of bitter
   and county cricket

are long married in our friendly folklore
of white marquees, the spires of cathedrals,
pitch-wandering dogs, boys on the boundary,
   mystified girlfriends,
all of it as much a myth and a ritual
as the fairy stories written by learned
elf-haunted dons who invent a cosmos
   neat but escapist,

where the rules are forever, can never be broken,
and a dragon, as it were, can be l.b.w.
if he puts a foot the wrong side of the mountain.
   You are the bright one

that shines in the memory; as old-fashioned writers
say 'she was a maid of some seventeen summers',
we don't reckon age by the passing of winters,
   by happier seasons

we count up that final inescapable total,
remember huge sixes by maverick sloggers –
compensating, like love, for the field that's deserted,
   the padlocked pavilion.

                                   GAVIN EWART

With autumn's arrival, the stumps are drawn, bat and pads put away and a season's play worked into snapshots of memory: the glorious drives of July, the late swing of late August. But the art of reminiscence is best left to 'Cricketer' who, fittingly, shall have the last word.

The Best-Laid Plans

AH, but now came the most exquisite of the game's delights – the arduous cultivation of strategem, the patient preparation of a bowler's snare against a good batsman on a flawless pitch, the preliminary investigation of his tricks and the sizing-up of his temperament; then the choosing of the likely bait and the subsequent angling, based on a 'feeding' of his pet stroke; it might all be spread over many overs and all the time you are terrified lest your captain should lose patience and take you off. At last the moment is here; you drop the ball on the spot of your heart's desire; sight, judgment and supple right arm and fingers are your sure ally; the ideal length and spin are vouchsafed unto you – and the batsman 'bites' and up she goes, a mis-hit to cover. If the catch is held, God's in his heaven; fieldsmen stand round you in a circle, while you explain the trick; the umpire (an old soldier) confidentially tells you he could see it all coming. The westering sun falls on your face, and while you are now resting awhile, you are aware that a breeze is running deliciously over your body. Many such times might a cricketer chant Nunc Dimittis; he may subsequently go through many varied days and experiences and nevermore will satisfaction, so deep and full, suffuse the whole of his being, and give him better reason to say 'This is a good life!'

On the other hand, after the cunning unhurried laying of the decoy, cover-point might easily miss the catch, in which case all is ashes and unspeakable injustice and mortification. The poor fool of a fieldsman approaches you with a 'Frightfully sorry, old chap – but she was spinning like –' and you are supposed to laugh it off with a 'Well tried,' or some such lie.

As I say, I did not bat seriously. But to be the official number eleven in the order of going in is not always irresponsibility and easy nerves and conscience. There are times when this batsman has to support an unreasonable burden, times when the weakest link in the chain is expected to withstand the severest strain. He may have to go to the wicket with a crucial question at stake of saving a 'follow on'; worse still, he may have to face that most searching of mortal ordeals – eight to win and the last man in. Such a situation was my portion once on a calm day in Worcestershire, aeons ago, during the golden age of country cricket reported every week in *The Field*; columns of scores and lovely names, 'Somerset Stragglers,' 'Sussex Martlets,' 'Devonshire Dumplings,' 'Derbyshire Friars,' or 'Shropshire Gentlemen, with Thompson' – Thompson being the paid professional. On this calm day in June, I had bowled tolerably, and our eleven had been given not too many runs to score for victory. The wicket was good and we began well, so that when the tinkle of teacups sounded on the drowsy afternoon air, a tranquil end to the encounter was only a matter of time. After refreshment we all settled in our deck-chairs once more: I mean those of us occupying a place low down in the batting order. Pipes were lighted, and some dalliance with lady spectators was feasible, when suddenly a collapse began in the field before us, only a moment ago a field of formal procedure and rural decoration. A man of immense physical substance – I think he was Burrows the Worcestershire fast bowler – had returned to the attack with a new ferocity; stumps flew about like splinters. I was obliged to haul myself from a deck-chair, go into the dark dressing-room, and put on pads with my fingers fumbling, making a mess of straps and holes and buckles. All the time I secretly prayed that the batsmen now facing the music would endure and conquer. But no; I heard another sickening noise of a dismantled wicket in the failing light.

I walked down the wooden steps when we wanted exactly eight runs. Everything depended on me; the other batsman was our 'crack'; he was seventy not out and well in charge of the bowling, even the bowling of the resurrected Burrows. A ripple of handclaps supposedly to encourage me came to my ear, but it was as noise from a far removed and very eternal universe; the world was now nothing but mine own fears and prayers. The long, lonely walk to the scene of crisis was ageing, and oh! the unfriendliness of everybody when I got there – most cricketers know of this sensation of bereft isolation. I began to take guard by force of habit, only to be told that the next ball would begin a new over from this end. Confusion and humiliation, and a public revelation of one's so far hidden poltroonery.

I must be ready to run, to collaborate with my masterful partner, to see that he obtained the bowling, and if possible always a single from the sixth ball. I might run him out. But these dread apprehensions were as naught to the actual happening; the master could not score a run at all in this first over, bowled to him as I backed up with my every nerve a pin-point of suspense. I was delivered unto Burrows, at the other end. I saw the ghostly fieldsmen changing position. I heard the remote umpire say 'Two leg, sir.' I felt somebody patting my block-hole; I felt a hand tightening the grip on my trousers above the left hip. A ventriloquial voice said, 'A little closer, Harry.' Then I saw Burrows looming and growing as he charged at me, larger and larger, a figure on the cinema that comes at you, widening and widening circles until the screen is overwhelmed and your vision is ready to burst into explosions of blinding nearness.

What to do? Play back or forward or not move an inch from the block-hole, or take courage and go for glory and swing the bat and to hell with it? Thought quicker than light shot through the brain. What in God's name to do? – but here is the ball, hot from muscle and temper, a ball of fire, a ball of – Merciful heaven, it is nothing of the kind; it is a straight half-volley to the off. But dare I? If I mis-hit I shall be outcast, mocked at, the vainest of earthworms; but if I hit truly – I did indeed hit truly. From the middle of the good blade, running up my arms, came sensations of joy beyond compare, music and tympani of nerves, vibrant to the brain and the heart; a four smack from the middle of the bat. A ball was thrown back from the distance, then I had a terrible momentary feeling of having looked over the rim of error into the void. Applause and shouts hailed me hero; and I experienced the illusion of a growth in actual stature.

Next, anti-climax; for there were more balls to face alone from Burrows, now outraged and silent. Four to win, remember. Again he strides and again the mighty arm swings. Gloria in Excelsis, if it isn't a long-hop this time, to leg! I couldn't believe my eyes. And nobody placed deep on that side of the field. I must not falter; Burrows already is cursing his folly, vowing revenge next ball, if I miss this chance worth a soul's ransom. I do not understand why I did not excitedly cleave the air 'too soon,' but I didn't. I waited until the ball was 'leaving me'; then I struck it almost from behind. No more certain boundary hit has been executed; the ball went there quicker than from the bat. I had 'won the match' in two blows myself. And I did not wake up; it was not a dream. Thirty-five years ago, and true and real this present minute. I can see it all, the formal chase of a fieldsman after my decisive stroke; he ran only a few yards. The cheering and the intense relief to mind and nerve. Then at once the feeling that it is over, and will never come back, the actual ecstatic doing of it, never . . .

Other games, they tell me, have their like felicities and their crowns of thorns. No cricketer believes it; no cricketer, if he is honest, will admit that of all the pleasures he may dwell upon in the evening of his days, any one will return with the poignancy of those vanished hours on the summer field; for we can, to the very end, partake of other delights, of reading and music and wine and conversation and candlelight and even of love. But sure as sure, the day will come too soon when (happily he never knows it) the cricketer hits a ball for the last time, bowls a ball for the last time, fields a ball for the last time, and for the last time walks home with his companions to the pavilion in the evening glow, his sweater flung across his shoulders.

NEVILLE CARDUS, *Second Innings*, 1950

'I seem to have lost a pebble. One short'

239

ACKNOWLEDGEMENTS

For permission to reprint copyright material the publishers gratefully acknowledge the following sources:

Text:
H.S. ALTHAM, from *History of Cricket*, HarperCollins Publishers Ltd (Allen & Unwin 1926). JOHN ARLOTT, *Wisden's Cricketer's Almanack 1975* for the essay on Sir Garfield Sobers; and HarperCollins Publishers Ltd for the extract from *Basingstoke Boy* by J. Arlott and R. Robinson (Willow Books 1990). TREVOR BAILEY, from *Sir Gary*, HarperCollins (Collins 1976). JULIAN BARNES, from *Cross Channel*, (Jonathan Cape 1992). SCYLD BERRY, The Observer for the article *An Inninngs and 851 Runs*. JOHN BETJEMAN, for the lines from *Summoned by Bells*, (John Murray 1960). NEVILLE CARDUS, for extracts from *Days in the Sun*, and *Second Innings*, reproduced by kind permission of the copyright holder, Margaret Hughes; for Test match article from Manchester Guardian, 1930, by permission of The Guardian as owner of the copyright. G.K. CHESTERTON, for 'Lines on a Cricket Match' by permission of A.P. Watt on behalf of The Royal Literary Fund. TED CORBETT, for *Cricket on the Run* (Stanley Paul 1990). GAVIN EWART, for 'Valediction: to the Cricket Season' from *Collected Ewart 1933–1980* (Hutchinson 1980) by kind permission of Margo Ewart. HERBERT FARJEON, for the extract from *Herbert Farjeon's Cricket Bag* (Macdonald & Co 1946) copyright Gervase Farjeon. PAUL FITZPATRICK, The Guardian as owner of the copyright of the article on a Test match 1981. DAVID FOOT, from *Tortured Genius* (William Heinemann 1982). DAVID FRITH, from *The Fast Men*, HarperCollins Publishers Ltd (Allen & Unwin 1982). BENNY GREEN, from *A History of Cricket* (Barrie and Jenkins 1988) reproduced by kind permission of the estate of Benny Green). RAMACHANDRA GUHA, the extract on pp 185–191 from *Spin and Other Turns* is reproduced courtesy the publishers (Penguin Books India Pvt Ltd 1994) and the author. JAMES HERRIOT, from *A Vet in Harness* (Michael Joseph 1976). SIMON HUGHES, from *A Lot of Hard Yakka* (Headline 1997, William Hill Sports Book of the Year). C.L.R. JAMES, from *Beyond a Boundary* (Hutchinson 1963). FRANK KEATING, 'Batting On' from Punch Magazine February 1990, reproduced by permission of Punch Ltd. LAURIE LEE, from *Cider With Rosie* (Hogarth Press 1960). ROBERT LOW, from *WG* (Richard Cohen Books 1997), reproduced with permission of Curtis Brown Ltd, London on behalf of Robert Low, copyright Robert Low. ARTHUR MAILEY, from *10 for 66 and All That* (Phoenix House, 1955). MIKE MARQUSEE, from *Anyone But England*, permission given by Mike Marqusee and Two Heads Publishing. G.D. MARTINEAU for *The Field is Full of Shades* (Sporting Hand 1946). J.C. MASTERMAN, from *Fincham v. Besterton* (Gollanz 1935) reprinted by permission of the Literary Estate of the late Sir John Masterman. V.S. NAIPAUL, © 1963 V.S. Naipaul, reprinted with the permission of Gillon Aitken Associates Ltd. RAY ROBINSON, from *Between the Wickets*, HarperCollins (Collins 1946). ALAN ROSS, for his poem 'Watching Benaud Bowl' from *Australia 63* (Eyre & Spottiswoode 1963). WILLIE RUSHTON, from

ACKNOWLEDGEMENTS

Pigsticking (Macdonald and Janes 1977). VIKRAM SETH, from *A Suitable Boy* (Phoenix House 1993). OSBERT SITWELL, from *Before the Bombardment* (Duckworth 1996). E.W. SWANTON, for 'Old Trafford Fourth Test, Last Day' 1956 and 'Frank Worrel, Honoured at the Abbey, 1967' © E.W. Swanton. G.M. TREVELYAN, from *English Social History*, reprinted by kind permission of Addison Wesley Longman (Longman Green 1944). SIR PELHAM WARNER, from *Lords, 1789-1945* and Eric Dobby Publishers (Harrap 1946). SIMON WILDE, from *Letting Rip* (H.F. & G Witherby 1994). JOHN WOODCOCK, for the article 'W. Indies could go on to make 1,000' © Times Newspapers Limited, 1976.

Every effort has been made to contact authors and copyright holders. It was not possible in all cases to do so.

Illustrations:
The drawings of the two batsmen on pages 1, 27, 68, 119, 159, 220 and the fielders on various pages throughtout the book are by Fougasse. They are reproduced by kind permission of the executors of the estate of the late Cyril Kenneth Bird.
The drawings on pages 26, 67, 118, 158, 219, 239 are by Bernard Hollowood and are reproduced by kind permission of Mrs Marjorie Duncan Hollowood on behalf of the estate of the late Bernard Hollowood. All rights reserved. They first appeared in *Cricket on the Brain* by Bernard Hollowood (Eyre & Spottiswoode 1972).

INDEX OF AUTHORS